MUNDA TRAIL

Books by Eric Hammel

76 Hours: The Invasion of Tarawa (with John E. Lane)
Chosin: Heroic Ordeal of the Korean War
The Root: The Marines in Beirut
Ace! A Marinine Night-Fighter Pilot in World War II
(with R. Bruce Porter)
Duel for the Golan: The 100-Hour Battle That Saved Israel
(with Jerry Asher)
Guadalcanal: Starvation Island
Guadalcanal: The Carrier Battles
Guadalcanal: Decision at Sea

MUNDA TRAIL

THE
NEW
GEORGIA
CAMPAIGN

ERIC HAMMEL

Orion Books • New York

D
767.99
N44
H35
1989

Published by Orion Books, a division of
Crown Publishers, Inc.,
225 Park Avenue South,
New York, New York 10003

ORION and colophon are trademarks of Crown Publishers, Inc.

Manufactured in the United States of America

Library of Congress Cataloging-in-Publication Data

Hammel, Eric M.
Munda trail: turning the tide against Japan
in the South Pacific/Eric M. Hammel.
p.   cm.
1. World War, 1939–1945—Campaigns—Solomon Islands—New Georgia.
2. New Georgia (Solomon Islands)—History.   I. Title.
D767.99.N44H35   1989   940.54′26—dc19   88-12684

ISBN 0-517-56972-8

Design by Jake Victor Thomas

10 9 8 7 6 5 4 3 2 1

First Edition

In Memory of

WILLIAM NAYLOR
JAMES RANKIN
JOSEPH ZIMMER

Contents

Guide to Abbreviations
and Terms

AirSols	Aircraft, Solomons
Arisaka	Japanese .25-caliber infantry rifle
Avenger	U.S. Douglas TBF torpedo bomber
B-25	U.S. North American Mitchell medium bomber
BAR	U.S. Browning Automatic Rifle
Betty	Japanese Mitsubishi G4M medium bomber
BGen	Brigadier General
Butai	Japanese unit or detachment
Capt	Captain
Catalina	U.S. Consolidated PBY amphibian patrol bomber
Cdr	Commander
Col	Colonel
ComAir	Commander, Aircraft
ComAirSols	Commander, Aircraft, Solomon Islands
Corsair	U.S. Vought F4U fighter
CP	Command Post
D+4	Four days after D-Day
D-5	Five days before D-Day
D-Day	Day of invasion or major attack
Dauntless	U.S. Douglas SBD dive-bomber
DUKW	U.S. amphibian truck
Exec	Executive Officer
F4F	U.S. Grumman Wildcat fighter
F4U	U.S. Vought Corsair fighter
GI	Government Issue; i.e. U.S. soldier

HIJMS	His Imperial Japanese Majesty's Ship
IJN	Imperial Japanese Navy
KIA	Killed in Action
LCI	U.S. Landing Craft, Infantry
LCT	U.S. Landing Craft, Tank
LCVP	U.S. Landing Craft, Vehicle, Personnel
LST	U.S. Landing Ship, Tank
LtCol	Lieutenant Colonel
M1	U.S. .30-caliber infantry rifle
M2	U.S. .30-caliber infantry carbine
M3	U.S. light tank
Maj	Major
MGen	Major General
mm	Millimeter
Nambu	Japanese 7.7mm light machine gun
NGOF	New Georgia Occupation Force
PBY	U.S. Consolidated Catalina amphibian patrol bomber
PT	U.S. Patrol Torpedo boat
RAdm	Rear Admiral
Rikusentai	Japanese naval infantry
SBD	U.S. Douglas Dauntless dive-bomber
Seabee	U.S. Navy Construction Battalion (Engineer)
SNLF	Japanese Special Naval Landing Force
TBF	U.S. Grumman Avenger torpedo bomber
USA	U.S. Army
USMC	U.S. Marine Corps
USN	U.S. Navy
USS	United States Ship

VAdm   Vice Admiral
Val   Japanese Aichi D3A dive-bomber

WIA   Wounded in Action
Wildcat   U.S. Grumman F4F fighter

Zero   Japanese Mitsubishi A6M fighter

Preface

Among America's many "forgotten" battles is the New Georgia Campaign, which ultimately occupied three valuable and scarce U.S. Army infantry divisions for two months in mid-1943, the watershed year of the Pacific War, when events were still largely undecided.

The importance of the New Georgia Campaign's central event—the land drive to capture the Munda air base from its Japanese builders and defenders—resides not so much in a feat of American arms at a trying time but rather in the age-old and enduring lessons encountered in turning merely trained soldiers into veteran warriors.

These lessons are evident at the start of every new war, indeed whenever military units are blooded. It had happened a year earlier, at the outset of the Guadalcanal Campaign, but the lessons were somewhat obscured when that so-called offensive quickly degenerated within days into a do-or-die defensive effort. By mid-1943, these lessons had also been driven home to the U.S. Army, which invaded North Africa in late 1942. However, the German enemy encountered by green American soldiers in Tunisia was on the run, already defeated by the veteran British 8th Army. (This fact did not prevent a resounding German victory over green U.S. regiments at Kasserine Pass.) In any event, the U.S. Army that was fighting in North Africa, and would fight in Europe, was not then cross-pollinating with the U.S. Army—largely a National Guard Army—that was approaching combat in the South Pacific. The U.S. infantry divisions that would find themselves locked in first combat on New Georgia earned their baptisms without recourse to blooded commanders and blooded peers fresh from victorious combat in their own theater of the war. The terrible lessons they faced had to be learned as if no one had every learned them before.

So, because of the fractious nature of the initial effort at New Georgia, and because relatively small infantry formations faced those unavoidable ancient lessons in which amateurs die and from which veterans emerge, the drive up the Munda Trail provides in isolated microcosm a graphic study of the universal military truths attending the feeding of innocents to the ravenous, insatiable dogs of war.

There is yet another level at which the drive up the Munda Trail should hold the interest of the modern reader or military philosopher. It was at New Georgia that the terror of war neurosis—combat fatigue—was first defined and widely diagnosed. As any first-year medical student knows, the mere definition of a new disease often triggers a new epidemic. Once the genie has been let out of the bottle, chaos might reign. It did at New Georgia.

The combination of innocent would-be warriors facing the first test of battle and the definition—the legitimization—of a new mental disorder make the drive up the strange and alien terrain of the Munda Trail a one-of-a-kind military episode.

Prologue

If ever a military event has condemned a nation to defeat, the Guadalcanal Campaign so condemned Japan. In addition to meting out the first defeat on land Japan ever suffered at the hands of a foreign enemy, the six-month ordeal of Guadalcanal stopped that nation in its path of conquest, and turned it forever from its serious economic and military objectives.

The military prowess of a Japan at the peak of her strength was pitted there against the uncertain might of a reawakening America. Japan was beaten. More than a land battle, Guadalcanal was a *total* battle in three dimensions—land, sea, and air.

The warring nations suffered equally in shipping losses, but America was able to replace her naval forces while Japan was not. Japan suffered the irrecoverable loss of 600 combat aircraft and, horribly, the irrecoverable loss of about 600 experienced pilots and combat aircrewmen; she lost superbly trained naval aviators who had been painstakingly taught their craft during the whole of the previous decade. Japan would build new and better aircraft, but she would never be able to train her sons so well as she had trained the superb airmen who died in unremitting combat over and for Guadalcanal.

The area was enormous, stretching 600 miles from Rabaul, in the Bismarck Archipelago, southeastward along the double chain of the Solomons to the northern shore of the deathtrap U.S. Marines had called The Canal.

Neither side intended to stake so much on Guadalcanal. It just happened that way. Japan found herself ahead of her schedule of conquest, and decided to advance before her gains could be amply consolidated; she struck, as it were, while the iron was still hot. Her objective had been the New Hebrides, New Caledonia, the Fijis, and the Samoas, from where she would cut the lifeline from America to New Zealand and Australia. A weak United States had no business launching a counterthrust, but she sent an augmented division of raw Marines to meet the professionals of Nippon.

The Imperial Army did not initially believe that the fighting on Guadalcanal could be of any significance, so it proceeded with its New Guinea invasion while committing small units to piecemeal

action against the static defensive perimeter the American Marines
established around their crude airfield. When these small units were
destroyed, the Imperial Army sent in larger units. And, when
these suffered serious defeats, yet larger units were sent against the
Marine perimeter. The showdown came in the form of a vast,
protracted land, sea, and air assault over more than a hundred
thousand square miles of ocean and land. Japan lost. Within a
month, two fresh U.S. Army divisions and one fresh U.S. Marine
division took to the offensive. Exactly six months after the initial
American landings, Japan conceded the first of her major defeats
and pulled the remnants of two beaten infantry divisions to relative safety.

A permanent Allied base was established at Lunga, site of the
original Marine perimeter on Guadalcanal's northern coast. Within
months, a U.S. Army infantry division composed mainly of green
New England National Guardsmen arrived to help pry the pa-
thetic remnants of Japan's defeat from their lonely jungle warrens.
The weeks in the rain forest at Guadalcanal proved to be little more
than a live-fire training exercise for the 43rd Infantry Division, but
the growing war and burgeoning U.S. naval and air power promised the New Englanders that bigger and better adventures were
in the offing.

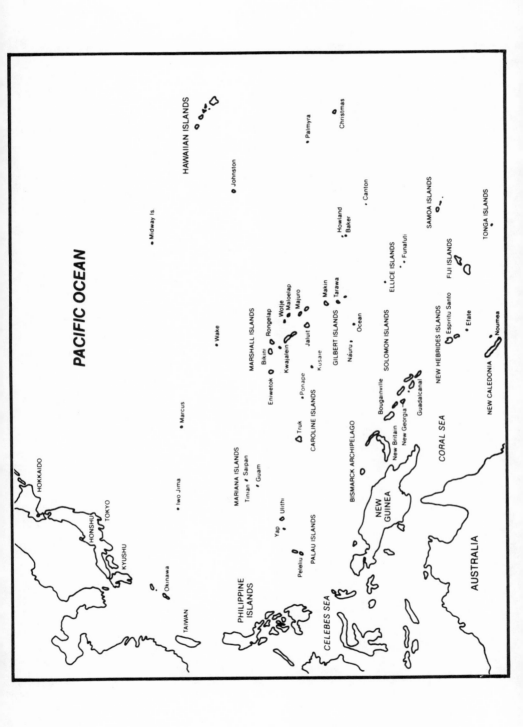

THE SOLOMON ISLANDS

THE SOLOMON ISLANDS

MALAITA

SANTA YSABEL

Rekata Bay

Russell Islands

GUADALCANAL

Cape Esperance

Henderson Field

NEW GEORGIA

THE

SLOT

CHOISEUL

BOUGAINVILLE

Shortland
Islands

BUKA

Kavieng

NEW IRELAND

Rabaul

NEW BRITAIN

Lae

NEW GUINEA

PART I

———— ✳ ————

Before

1

M unda Field was a product of defeat.
    The defeat had not yet been meted out by late October
1942, but it was clearly in the offing, a defeat as much a result of
overconfidence as of losses in battle. Six months earlier, in May
1942, the victorious Imperial Navy had marched with impunity
over the densely forested Solomon Islands. Each step forward had
renewed and reinvigorated the heady sense of destiny the warriors
of Nippon carried with them as a birthright. Each step forward
demanded that one more follow. So rapid the advance, so powerful the lure of yet newer conquests and greater glory, that the decisive blunder of the first year of the war occurred.

    Rather than adhere to their carefully conceived play, which in-
corporated specific plans for building and staffing air bases down
the length of the Solomons stepping stones, the exuberant leaders
of the victorious advance simply ignored the time-consuming and
restraining misery of a careful consolidation of gains. The advance
easily outpaced the building capacity of the rear echelons. Indeed,
even when faced in August and September by the first confrontations with a hitherto defeated enemy, the overextended and over-
confident Japanese admirals and generals continued to ignore the
vital requirement that intermediate Solomons bases be built and
staffed. By October, their entire effort and capacity was being
funneled into the breech at Guadalcanal. The badly needed air
bases that were to have dotted the Solomons were left for better
times.

    Those better times never came.

    In great measure, Japan avoided victory because she lacked more
than a few intermediate auxiliary airstrips along all of the 600 air
miles between her main bases at Rabaul and the battle front at
Guadalcanal. Forced to operate at maximum range, even moderately damaged Japanese aircraft stood an excellent chance of going
down in that vast expanse of rain forest and sea.

    No firm, final decision regarding the intermediate strips was
reached until October 1942. Late that month, Imperial Army
forces on Guadalcanal suffered what was clearly the decisive land
defeat of the campaign. In recognizing the defeat, 8th Area Army,

the newly commissioned administrative headquarters responsible
for all land forces in New Guinea and the Solomons, took firm
control and ordered a major air base built at Munda Point, on New
Georgia Island, about 150 miles northwest of Henderson Field, the
contested American air base that was the object of the Guadalcanal Campaign.

Japanese engineering teams sent from Rabaul began surveying
the runways on November 21, 1942, a week after the Imperial
Navy suffered its decisive defeat of the Guadalcanal Campaign. By
that time American fighters based at the Henderson Field complex
virtually controlled the air over the Eastern and Central Solomons. It was necessary that detection of the new airfield be avoided
as long as possible. The greater portion of the construction operation was to take place under the most stringent security possible.

Airfield construction techniques were cleverly rewritten to allow for most of the task to be completed while sight-impeding
stands of coconut palms and jungle growth still grew on what
would be the main runway. Trees and scrub would be removed
only when no other work could be carried out, thus preventing firm
aerial detection for as long as possible, hopefully as long as would
be necessary.

Strong security units were shipped in, for a small group of British Commonwealth–officered native constabulary was operating
throughout New Georgia, and had been since remaining behind
during the British retreat in early 1942. The group's leader was
Major Donald Kennedy, a New Zealander. Part of an organization that called itself the Coastwatchers, these men were a constant source of irritation to the Japanese. Major Kennedy was about
the most troublesome of the Coastwatchers. Certainly, he was the
most combative of a group that frequently eschewed outward hos-
tilities against superior forces. Kennedy routinely conducted raid-
ing forays and other general nuisances. The Japanese were
extremely wary of the Coastwatchers throughout the Solomons,
and of Donald Kennedy in particular. Disproportionately large
combat forces were drawn away from important tasks to hunt them
down or, at best, keep them from becoming even more troublesome.

As it turned out, it was Kennedy's group that knocked the pin-
ions from beneath the Munda ruse, despite elaborate attempts by
the Japanese to keep Kennedy from making the discovery.

Kennedy's chief subordinates were Lieutenant Dick Horton and

Sergeant Harry Wickham. Wickham, a half-caste trader and native of the area, operated a station directly overlooking Munda
Point. Horton covered Rendova Island, largest of the many barrier islands surrounding southeastern New Georgia. Kennedy
himself was ensconced at the main base, at Segi Point.

Within a week of the groundbreaking at Munda, islanders operating under Harry Wickham had it spotted. They reported their
findings and Wickham radioed the news to the Allied base at
Guadalcanal.

Within a short time, Allied reconnaissance aircraft were over
Munda Point. They could see nothing due to the presence of the
trees and brush the Japanese had left in place. Photoreconnais-
sance missions were then launched. Commander Robert Quackenbush's South Pacific Photographic Interpretation Unit, based at
Henderson Field, was responsible for pinpointing the new airstrip. The first thing uncovered by Quackenbush's unit was that
Munda was the focal point of vastly increased Japanese activity.
The beaches adjacent to the point were suitable for around-the-
clock use by supply craft, and there were extensive natural cleared
areas in the vicinity suitable for use as dispersal points for troops,
supplies, and equipment, all under the natural cover of coconut
trees. Though ground observers continued to report progress on
construction of an all-weather runway, and though the area seemed
adequate to support the strip, no firm photographic fix could be
made for some time.

Commander Quackenbush's photo-interpretation unit watched
the slow buildup around Munda. Each returning mission brought
additional evidence. Then, after a lengthy interval, small patches
of white began to expand and consolidate; this seemed to be
crushed coral topping spread over the proposed runway areas as
they were slowly cleared. Soon, three or four distinct areas took
shape. These were of uniform width and all in a line; lateral extension of these areas coincided with the general direction of the
prevailing wind. The photo-interpretation unit had made a firm fix.

The American technicians charged with pinpointing the new
airstrip were amazed at the novel approach the Japanese had taken
to security. But, as the Japanese engineers succeeded in complet-
ing more of their effort, they could not help but give themselves
away, chiefly through the use of the coral topping, which was
lighter in color than the surface of the surrounding terrain. Still,
by the time the Allied commanders were convinced that an air-

strip was in fact taking shape, the Japanese had won enough time; Munda Field would soon be operational.

The last of the obscuring coconut palms were uprooted on December 17. The Japanese had put down 3,200 feet of all-weather coral-topped runway, enough to support fighter operations. They immediately began work on a 1,500 foot extension, enough to support bomber operations.

Shortly after Munda Field was completed, a satellite runway was started at Vila, on nearby Kolombangara Island. Strong ground security units were deployed to protect and screen the two new air bases. It soon became clear to observers that the Japanese were constructing a strong defensive position in the Central Solomons. Their main bases lay to the north, in the Bismarcks and Northern Solomons, but any Allied effort to reduce the main bases would first have to contend with—and would be delayed by—the new defenses in the Central Solomons. It was implicit in the Japanese move that Imperial Army and perhaps Imperial Navy headquarters located in Rabaul were at long last facing reality in the form of a regional defensive strategy.

Although Munda and Vila fields were successfully completed, the Japanese guarding them were in for some hard times. Lieutenant Horton, on Rendova, began directing U.S. Navy and Marine dive-bombing attacks and, likewise, reporting pending Japanese air strikes to Guadalcanal almost before the Japanese aircraft left his sight. Sergeant Wickham, from his vantage point overlooking Munda, called air strikes against gun emplacements around the new air base, thereby increasing the proficiency of the Allied bomber crews, which until then were notoriously ineffective on missions requiring pinpoint bombing in heavily forested terrain.

As the air raids against Munda and Vila warmed up, 8th Area Army, which was commanded by General Hitoshi Imamura, a newcomer to the region, set itself the task of completely reorganizing the defense of the Solomons and New Guinea.

Under Imamura's immediate command were the 17th Army and 18th Army (each comparable to an American corps). The latter was waging an on again, off again war of attrition in New Guinea, while the two infantry divisions composing 17th Army were undergoing virtual annihilation on Guadalcanal. With the loss of Guadalcanal in early February 1943, both armies were ordered to reorganize and reequip to meet the Allies wherever they might strike next. This was something more than tacit recognition that the Allies had at least temporarily achieved the strategic initiative in the region.

By the early spring of 1943, Imperial General Headquarters in Tokyo had clearly adopted a defensive posture. The Pacific War entered a new phase.

Following its resounding and unequivocal defeat at Guadalcanal, 17th Army lost over half its veteran strength. One first-line independent infantry brigade and one first-line infantry division had been so badly mauled in the protracted campaign that they were transferred to Burma and the Philippines, respectively, to recuperate. The mediocre 38th Infantry Division, a second-rate unit that had not made a glowing contribution at Guadalcanal, was retained, but it had to be completely reequipped, and it received many green replacements to fill out its battered ranks.

Sixth Infantry Division, a highly rated veteran command, which had won a degree of ignominy as the "Rape of Nanking" Division in China, had not been committed to Guadalcanal and was intact at the conclusion of the Guadalcanal Campaign. This unit was charged with the defense of Bougainville, as were elements of the recently arrived 17th Infantry Division, which were divided between bases on New Britain and northern Bougainville. It was clear that vital Japanese interests were at stake once the line at Bougainville was threatened, but it was not by any means clear—even to the Japanese—what might occur if the Allies stepped forward as far as the Central Solomons, toward Munda. Clearly, the new air base would not be abandoned without a fight, but the bulk of 17th Army had been properly committed to the strategically vital Northern Solomons, from which Allied air and amphibious incursions could certainly be launched against Rabaul itself.

The Imperial Navy, which had been brutally mauled in the six months it had taken to arrive at a decision at Guadalcanal, did its own reorganizing in February 1943. Admiral Isoroku Yamamoto, commander-in-chief of the Combined Fleet, the navy's operational arm, did most of his work safely ensconced at his Truk headquarters. His chief representative at Rabaul was Vice Admiral Jinichi Kusaka, whose Southeastern Fleet was on equal footing with General Imamura's 8th Area Army. This dual command structure in the Solomons and Bismarcks could have led to serious interservice bickering—a factor that had had considerable adverse impact upon the outcome of the Guadalcanal Campaign—had not Kusaka and Imamura enjoyed a cordial friendship of long standing.

Kusaka's primary subordinate units were 8th Fleet and 11th Air Fleet. Naval ground forces included Rear Admiral Minoru Ota's 8th Combined Special Naval Landing Force, a regiment-sized command comprising two small battalions of infantry-trained bluejackets—*rikusentai*—somewhat comparable to American Marines. Ota's unit was under Admiral Kusaka's direct control, and he placed its component battalion-size units where he thought they might do the most good, often duplicating existing Imperial Army garrisons.

The mere fact that Admiral Kusaka was placing ground units in the Central Solomons was a prime illustration of the basic policy schism that had appeared between the two services. General Imamura and his superiors at Imperial General Headquarters had decided to place the first line of their defense of Rabaul in southern Bougainville. Except for the Imperial Army security detachments guarding Munda and Vila fields, the Central Solomons was not to be extensively nor even seriously defended by 8th Area Army.

The Imperial Navy, however, hoped to do the bulk of the fighting as far from Rabaul as possible; the greater the distance, the longer it might take the Allies to get there; the more defenses along the way, the more chance of winning or bringing about a stalemate. This was the thinking behind the commitment of Admiral Ota's *rikusentai* to New Georgia and Kolombangara. In time, Admiral Kusaka talked General Imamura into placing at least small tactical infantry units within reach of the two intermediate airfields.

Air support was to be in the hands of the Imperial Navy's 25th and 26th Air Flotillas, which made up 11th Air Fleet. The Imperial Army's Rabaul-headquartered 6th Air Division, which arrived too late to have an impact upon the Guadalcanal fighting, was to be committed largely to supporting operations of 18th Army in New Guinea.

The principal problem encountered by the Japanese in assuming a defensive posture in the Solomons lay in the fact that they had absolutely no inkling of Allied intentions. It was too early in the war to have ascertained a pattern; none, in fact existed. Rabaul was the obvious long-range target, but the Allies had the unmistakable advantage of being able to decide upon the method of attack, the timing of a new offensive move, and the route of advance. These were advantages that Japan had somehow frittered away at Guadalcanal, forever as it turned out.

The one factor favoring Japan in February 1943 was that the Allies themselves did not know where the next offensive was to be launched. They had virtually no fresh infantry with which to launch it and precious few naval or logistical assets with which to support it. Unable to immediately and decisively follow up on their close-run victory at Guadalcanal, the Allies could do little more than nibble around the edges of the Japanese holdings, mainly with their ascendant air groups. And the Japanese, who had been knocked breathless by their unexpected and costly defeat, could do little more than look on and wait for the Allies to strike.

For the moment, victory and defeat alike rendered the contestants incapable of further action.

2

With the Japanese evacuation of Guadalcanal on February 9, 1943, the Pacific War was set to enter its third phase. The defensive opening had ended and the confused stopgap initial offensive had been successfully waged. Now the organized offensive could begin.

Control of the Guadalcanal fighting had been in the hands of the U.S. Navy as a direct result of some nearly disastrous interservice bickering at the outset of the offensive. Due to the impatience of General Douglas MacArthur and his planners in May 1942, Guadalcanal and the remainder of the Solomons had very nearly been bypassed despite the overwhelming necessity of capturing them as bases (and, as it turned out, to wage a battle at the extremity of the ranges of Japanese fighter aircraft). For myriad reasons, many of them personal or political, MacArthur had wanted Rabaul as a staging area for his highly publicized "return" to the Philippines. In May 1942, he had been willing to allow the Japanese to control his rear in the Solomons. The Navy, however, had argued the better case, and Guadalcanal had been chosen for the initial offensive. (It boggles the mind to consider the possible scenario of a do-or-die campaign waged at the front step of one of Japan's best-defended regional bases, particularly when considering the narrowly won decision in a campaign that Japan did not take seriously until after it had been lost. The picture of the actual ill-prepared American offensive at Guadalcanal is hard enough to swallow!)

Due to a great many pressures prior to the August 7, 1942, D-Day at Guadalcanal, General MacArthur had issued a tentative strategic brief on July 2, 1942, covering the entire Solomons–New Guinea–Bismarcks region. In substance, this brief called for a careful two-prong drive along the Solomons and northern New Guinea, ultimately leading to the capture of the main regional Japanese bases at Rabaul and Kavieng. This basic plan was to be the foundation for all planning at subsequent strategic conferences involving the capture of Rabaul. However, by December 1942, in view of the rapidly changing situation throughout the world, drastic alterations were very much in order.

*　　*　　*

A preliminary plan was adopted late in the Guadalcanal Campaign, when victory was in sight, calling for the establishment of an advance base in the Russell Islands, about sixty-five miles closer to Munda than the Henderson Field air-base complex; an excellent small-boat anchorage at Wernham Cove would serve as an advance PT-boat base for strikes against Japanese lines of supply and communication from Bougainville to Munda.

In addition, Vice Admiral William Halsey, commander of the South Pacific Area and South Pacific Force, foresaw a potential danger from the Japanese then based in the Russells. They could easily have hindered base operations once Guadalcanal was fully secured, and the islands might even have served as a staging area for mounting a major spoiling attack on Guadalcanal in the hope of winning time for bases to the rear to be strengthened against the inevitable American onslaught.

Admiral Ernest King, commander-in-chief of the U.S. Fleet, had to approve the basic Russells occupation plan, and he balked. King felt that a steady drive northward to Rabaul would be a waste of time, men, and material. He favored skipping the Central Solomons entirely for a direct assault against the Admiralty and Shortland groups, thereby cutting the lines of supply to the Japanese bases in the Central Solomons and allowing them to "rot on the vine" under an Allied naval blockade. Although King's "bypass" concept itself was sound—as evidenced by numerous examples at later stages of the Pacific War—execution was a bit beyond the means of the limited naval and ground forces then in the Pacific. Further, as Admiral Halsey pointed out, Guadalcanal was itself in acute danger of being struck by a new Japanese buildup. A buffer was needed to deny the means for a new Japanese counterinvasion. The persuasive logic of this argument finally wrenched an approval from the crusty King.

On January 23, 1943, Admiral Chester Nimitz, commander-in-chief of both the Pacific Fleet and the Pacific Ocean Area, issued verbal approval to Halsey for the commencement of planning for the occupation of the Russell Islands. The task was to be accomplished as soon after the final reduction of the Japanese 17th Army on Guadalcanal as possible. The plan was coded CLEANSLATE.

On February 7, Halsey detailed his amphibious force commander, Rear Admiral Richmond Kelly Turner, to begin formulating the tactical plans for CLEANSLATE. Turner was assisted

by Major General Millard Harmon, commanding general of all
U.S. Army forces in the South Pacific.

The first assumption was that the Japanese would wage a stubborn defense, including air and naval counterstrokes as soon as they
could be marshaled. A massive combat landing was therefore in
order. Lack of adequate transport, however, precluded speed in the
initial stages of landing and buildup. Each available transport and
cargoman would have to be loaded and off-loaded several times in
order to shuttle in additional personnel and their equipment. The
plan was in every way contrary to established doctrines and most
definitely in defiance of the lessons learned during the opening
stages of the Guadalcanal Campaign. There was, however, no
possible alternative, and the plan would simply have to suffice. The
Americans' only ace-in-the-hole was the proximity of massive aerial supports based on Guadalcanal.

Major General John Hester's 43rd Infantry Division was tabbed
for the ground assault role on February 10. The division was totally without experience; it had just been shipped into Guadalcanal and had hardly undertaken even mop-up assignments in rear
areas.

While the 43rd Infantry Division was totally green, it was the
only fully intact unit of sufficient size in the entire Pacific. The
103rd Infantry Regiment, plus supports, was to seize Banika Island while the 3rd Marine Raider Battalion, operating under General Hester's command, was to lead off at Pavuvu Island. The
169th Infantry Regiment was to follow the Raiders in to Pavuvu
by one day. One Marine defense battalion and part of another were
divided between the two islands. While planned and executed as a
major combat landing, the entire operation was rated little higher
than a practice ship-to-shore movement.

The South Pacific Amphibious Force (Task Force 62) mounted
out of Guadalcanal at 2300 hours, February 20, and with strong
naval screening forces moved on the Russells. The amphibious
force split at dawn, February 21. Then, under a strong aerial umbrella, the objectives were assaulted. There were no hitches. As
reported by a reconnaissance team on February 19, the Japanese
had vanished. Surprisingly, they had not even bothered to construct defensive emplacements anywhere in the group. The occupation of the Russells was to be one of the very few dry holes
encountered in the Pacific. The 43rd Infantry Division ended its
baptism by fire unbaptised.

Shortly after the occupation forces developed some rudimentary defenses, a radar station and a PT-boat base were activated at Wernham Cove. By the end of February, Admiral Turner controlled a fully operational advance base manned by some 9,000 combat and support personnel. The command of the Russells ground forces was soon passed to XIV Army Corps, the largest tactical ground echelon in the South Pacific.

On February 12, 1943, General Douglas MacArthur's Southwest Pacific Area staff issued the first complete draft of its operational plan for the drive on Rabaul. The plan, coded ELKTON, was based on MacArthur's presumption that control of all phases of the coming offensives was to be his, and that Halsey's separate South Pacific Amphibious Force would be under his direct control during the occupation of New Guinea, the Solomons, and the Bismarcks. This was a natural presumption since the remainder of the drive on Rabaul would take place within the geographical confines of MacArthur's own Southwest Pacific Area. (Guadalcanal and the Russells were physically within the boundaries of Halsey's South Pacific Area.) Whereas MacArthur had had little to offer Halsey until that time, Halsey's naval flotillas and air groups were vital to the ultimate strategy in the region. As a result, although MacArthur had never had to operate under another area commander, Halsey was being asked to operate, in his capacity as a naval-force commander (not as an area commander), under MacArthur's jurisdiction for the remainder of the drive on Rabaul.

One day prior to the release of the ELKTON plan, Halsey sent his deputy, Rear Admiral Theodore Wilkinson, to Brisbane, site of MacArthur's headquarters, to help coordinate the remainder of the planning for the Solomons–New Guinea offensive. Shortly after ELKTON was released, MacArthur applied to the U.S. Joint Chiefs of Staff for permission to send a delegation to Washington to explain the plan in detail. Halsey demanded equal representation, and got it.

The staff officers arrived in the capital on March 10, and began conferring with Admiral King two days later. At this series of talks, known as the Pacific Military Conference, the important groundwork for the Pacific War strategy was established. MacArthur's plan, a somewhat modified version of the original, dubbed ELKTON II and dated February 28, was presented by Major General Richard Sutherland, MacArthur's chief of staff. Again, in ELK-

TON II, MacArthur presumed that the task would be undertaken with himself in direct control. It was further stated that Admiral Halsey had already expressed his willingness to operate within such a command structure.

The intelligence estimate upon which ELKTON II was based pointed out that Japanese defenses were concentrated on the northern coast of New Guinea, northwest of Buna; on New Britain, around Rabaul; on New Ireland, around Kavieng; and southwestward through the Solomons, from Rabaul to Munda. In the main, land areas were unprotected and largely unmonitored. Characteristically, defenses consisted of perimeter-type establishments at key points, particularly around air and logistics bases.

It was thought that 79,000 to 94,000 Japanese combat and base personnel of all types, with 383 aircraft, 4 battleships, 2 aircraft carriers, 14 cruisers, 11 seaplane tenders, 40 destroyers, several auxiliaries, 50 merchantmen of at least 3,000 tons, and a large number of smaller craft were directly on hand to carry out defensive measures throughout the target area. It was further thought that immediately forthcoming reinforcements from other areas might comprise as many as 10,000 to 12,000 infantry, 250 aircraft, and large contingents of the Truk-based Combined Fleet. Strategic reinforcements over a six-month period might include up to 615 aircraft over all previous commitments, and 10 to 15 combat divisions, plus supports. This "timetable" was contingent more upon availability of transport than on the availability of the actual forces.

A breakdown of the tactical objectives of the EKLTON II strategy was presented next:

1. Seizure of airdromes on Huon Peninsula, New Guinea, to provide air support for operations against New Britain;

2. Seizure of Munda Field and other bases on New Georgia for the support of operations against targets to the north;

3. Seizure of the air bases on New Britain and Bougainville to support direct operations against Rabaul and Kavieng;

4. Capture of Kavieng and the isolation of Rabaul (or vice versa);

5. Capture of Rabaul (or Kavieng).

After the plan—which made no attempt at proposing a timetable—had been presented, the conferees heard Major General Sutherland tick off a lengthy list of required forces, including five fully equipped infantry divisions and forty-five air groups over and above the units already deployed in the Pacific.

There was a snag in these proposals, one that would put a damper on MacArthur's strategy permanently. It was a factor that no military man could hope to overcome.

The setback arose from the imperatives of international politics. The Casablanca Conference had determined that Germany was the main enemy and should be brought to her knees as quickly as possible. The United States was all but totally supplying her allies, and there was only so much to go around from the "Arsenal of Democracy." As the Casablanca Conference was proceeding, training camps in the United States were just beginning to catch up to troop-allotment schedules. New units were forming daily, and these had to be trained and equipped. Both took time. The same held for forming new air groups. Aircraft were sufficiently hard to build in quantity, and aircrews were even harder to build. A great deal of time was needed—at least a year of training was required for every technical specialty aboard a bomber of any type, and at least the same amount of time to train a fighter pilot. The little bit of everything that was being turned out in early 1943 was being allocated mainly to the war against Hitler.

There were fewer transports and cargomen going to the Pacific War effort than to the European Theater, despite the fact that shipping was of vital importance in the former's vast island-strewn distances. So it was hard to get combat units allocated to the Pacific, and harder still to get them there. Of the manpower assigned against Japan, moreover, only a very small portion was serving in combat units. And of that small number, only a much smaller number could be effectively employed at any given time; the remainder might be serving as garrison forces or refitting and recuperating between campaigns or undergoing advanced training prior to entering combat.

The Joint Chiefs realized, of course, the paramount necessity of maintaining the offensive initiative against Rabaul, but it had no more than words of solace to offer the troop-starved commanders. Reinforcements would be forthcoming, but the planners were advised against counting on them.

Halsey's and MacArthur's delegates were asked what they thought they might accomplish by the end of 1943. The answer:

an advance as far as southeastern Bougainville, seizure of eastern New Guinea as far as Madang, occupation of the Trobriand Islands, and an advance into the Cape Gloucester region of western New Britain. With that, the Pacific Military Conference ended as such.

Because of the lack of sufficient infantry forces for carrying out simultaneous operations in the Solomons and New Guinea, it was decided, after some wrangling, that either Halsey or MacArthur would strike as the opportunity dictated; that is, if the Japanese reinforced New Guinea at the expense of their Solomons bases, Halsey would strike in the Solomons, or vice versa. Meanwhile, both area commanders decided to keep jabbing away in order to keep their own troops from sitting idle while preventing the Japanese from regaining the offensive initiative they had lost at the turn of the year.

Command, as manifested through the right to have the last word in any given matter, still had to be ironed out without getting one service into worse straits with the other. It was agreed that MacArthur should command the forces of the Southwest Pacific Area, but that Halsey would hold direct operational control over South Pacific forces engaged in the Southwest Pacific's territory; Halsey would command under what came to be termed "general directives" from MacArthur.

The jealousy with which each service—not to mention the principals themselves—guarded the prerogatives of command had very nearly undone the American effort in the Pacific almost from the outset. The jealousy itself had not been diminished after nearly a year on the offensive, but the principals had at least come to the conclusion that Japan was the more dangerous enemy.

At the time of the Pacific Military Conference, Admiral King, the Navy's overall operational commander, adamantly refused to break up his Pacific Fleet into smaller area-controlled units. This, he said, would have hindered fleet mobility. King's chief deputy in the Pacific, Admiral Chester Nimitz, was to retain supreme command over all naval vessels, air units, Marine units, and naval base forces operating under either Halsey or MacArthur. The result was that Halsey, as Nimitz's chief subordinate in a naval command capacity (commander of the South Pacific Force), could command naval operations east of the 159° longitudinal Army-Navy line of demarcation (separating the South Pacific Area from the Southwest Pacific Area) and was directly responsible to Nimitz—not MacArthur—west of the line. In this instance, any shipping requested by MacArthur had to be given to him by either Halsey or Nimitz, and that shipping could be withdrawn pretty much at the whim of either of them. The net effect was that MacArthur was prevented from building a permanent force of shipping under his de facto command. This was exactly the effect desired by the suspicious senior Navy officers, and exactly contrary to MacArthur's fondest wishes.

With nearly everything of a practical nature settled, the Joint Chiefs issued the "28 March Directive" authorizing the execution of decisions and policies reached during the Pacific Military Conference.

Once the proposed ends and much of the means had been agreed to, Halsey and MacArthur met face to face to shape the agreements into a viable tactical plan, with emphasis upon timing. On March 28, 1943, MacArthur's headquarters issued ELKTON III. The landings at New Georgia and in the Trobriands were to be simultaneous. Major forces would be withheld from both ventures. CARTWHEEL was to be the codename for the operational phases of the ELKTON III strategy through the seizure of Kavieng and Rabaul.

During the first three days of March 1943, the Allies scored a decisive victory over the Japanese, one that was to have far-reaching influence upon the outcome of MacArthur's New Guinea drive. The Japanese 51st Infantry Division was obliterated in the Bismarck Sea while en route to New Guinea from Rabaul. Eight transports and four destroyers were sunk by around-the-clock Allied shuttle-bombing sorties. The Japanese were utterly demoralized in the most expensive, most complete defeat in a single action of the entire Pacific War. All Japanese troop movements for the remainder of the war would be adversely affected by the spectre of the Bismarck Sea battle, in which the Allies lost six aircraft.

3

W hile top-echelon bickering over the choice of targets and lines
of command was raging from Washington to Nou-
mea to Brisbane, Brigadier General DeWitt Peck, the Marine
heading the South Pacific War Plans Staff, quietly set about de-
vising a preliminary scheme for pushing the Allies into the Central Solomons. As soon as Peck's plan, which had been dubbed
TOENAILS, was completed in January 1943, Admiral Halsey
sent the Marine general to Washington to present the outline to the
Joint Chiefs, which accepted the plan but summarily rejected
Peck's plea for additional ground forces.

At the top-level meeting at Pearl Harbor in March, the TOE-
NAILS plan was endorsed with a recommendation that it be set
into motion by April 1, 1943. General Douglas MacArthur, who
agreed with the plan in principle, balked at the suggested date of
execution. It was too close to the opening date of his Southwest
Pacific offensive and might result in the loss of much of the valuable naval transport and support he was so desperately counting
upon. The problem was handed to the Joint Chiefs for a solution.
They, in their turn, asked MacArthur to set the date. During the
Brisbane policy talks with Halsey, the general firmly set the date
for the initial landing at May 15, to coincide with the projected
advances by his forces in New Guinea and the Trobriands.

Whereas MacArthur's Southwest Pacific Area was administered
almost solely by Army officers, and was therefore reasonably un-
confused in delineation of responsibility and lines of command, the
South Pacific worked under a haphazard command structure put
together by pure chance during the frustrating confusion of the six-
month Guadalcanal ordeal.

The South Pacific was nominally a Navy-controlled area whose
commander, Halsey, was directly responsible to Admiral Nimitz
(in his capacity as Pacific Ocean Area commander, a post he held
in addition to his responsibilities as Pacific Fleet commander-in-
chief). Under Halsey were administrative echelons for the three
branches of service: Major General Clayton Vogel commanded I
Marine Amphibious Corps; Major General Millard Harmon com-

manded all Army forces in the area; and Halsey himself commanded all naval forces in the area as South Pacific Force commander, a post subordinate to his area command in precisely the way Nimitz's command of the Pacific Fleet was technically subordinate to his command of the Pacific Ocean Area.

I Marine Amphibious Corps consisted roughly of six Marine defense battalions, four Marine Raider battalions, three Marine parachute battalions, two Marine aircraft wings, three Marine divisions, and a plethora of special, service, experimental, garrison, and administrative commands and units.

After being relieved at Guadalcanal in late 1942, 1st Marine Division had been sent to Australia, where it was technically under MacArthur's control. Second Marine Division finished out the Guadalcanal Campaign and was sent to New Zealand for rest and refitting; it was also technically under MacArthur's control. Third Marine Division, just recently activated, was strewn from San Diego to the Fijis and from Samoa to New Zealand; it was not yet considered fully operational.

The tactical elements of General Harmon's Army command were divided into two general command structures. In the instance of air units, Major General Nathan Twining commanded the newly activated 13th Air Force, comprising all Army Air Forces units in the South Pacific. The major tactical ground echelon was XIV Corps, activated during the Guadalcanal fighting under Major General Alexander Patch, but recently passed on to Major General Oscar Griswold. XIV Corps was responsible for all Army ground units in the South Pacific. Completely flexible in structure, XIV Corps at times more nearly resembled a full army than a corps. In addition to myriad and ever-changing special and service units, XIV Corps basically comprised the veteran Americal and 25th Infantry Divisions and the green 43rd and 37th Infantry Divisions.

Subordinate naval commands operating in the South Pacific were complexly arranged and infinitely more numerous than Army or Marine organizations. Rear Admiral Richmond Kelly Turner was responsible for all transport in the South Pacific, with the title Commander, South Pacific Amphibious Command (Task Force 62). Rear Admiral Aubrey Fitch commanded all aircraft and all air installations (Navy, Marine, Army, Australian, and New Zealand) as Commander, Aircraft, South Pacific (ComAirSoPac).

Heading a reasonably integrated, all-service, all-nation command, Fitch reported directly to Halsey in the latter's capacity as South Pacific Force commander.

Directly under Fitch were several area-based tactical organizations, chiefly Aircraft, Solomons (AirSols), under Rear Admiral Marc Mitscher (ComAirSols). Mitscher's command, like Fitch's, comprised units of all services and all nations directly assigned to it.

Fleet and task-force commands, including Turner's Task Force 62, were largely impermanent affairs through which rotated the squadrons and divisions that composed the U.S. Fleet. In large part, a task force, task group, or task unit designation referred more to the officer in command than to the ships that composed it; the ships often changed and, where they themselves remained, the commanders and their staffs were permanent. This utterly confusing development was a direct result of Admiral King's adamant refusal to tie ships to any given area at the expense of the strategic mobility of the U.S. Fleet.

Logistics for the Central Solomons offensive was a matter of utmost importance. Guadalcanal had been kept viable—barely —through a widely concerted hit-and/or-miss mode of action and inaction. This could not go on. Great pains were taken to administer the storage of sufficient reserves of equipment, ammunition, food, medical supplies, and fuel for the combat forces. Whereas each branch of service was responsible for the handling and storage of its own equipment and supplies, the Army Service Supply Command, South Pacific, was the most extensively organized echelon of its type and, in general, it handled the bulk of landborne supply for all the services. The Navy, of course, was responsible for shipping nearly all goods into the area, though Marine, Navy, and Army air-transport commands shared the burden.

Noumea, in New Caledonia, was the center of the bustling, rapidly expanding logistical complex. Existing facilities, though on the crude side and by no means extensive, would have to suffice. After the campaign to win her, Guadalcanal was methodically transformed into an extensive forward depot to service the Central Solomons offensive from close range. As soon as the TOENAILS plan was approved, the combined efforts of the services established the large strategic and tactical logistical reserves required to support the offensive.

The South Pacific logistical commands began assembling their stocks as early as January 1943. Operation DRYGOODS, the

stockpiling at Guadalcanal, was planned on the basis of a suggestion by Admiral Turner, and was carried through to a conclusion
in the latter half of February. Noumea was jammed full of goods,
and Guadalcanal-based supply units were severely hampered by
inadequate shore cargo-handling facilities. The little that could be
built at Guadalcanal was knocked out by a particularly severe May
storm; floating quays were ripped loose, bridges on trails to inland
dumps were washed away, and havoc was general.

The logistics staffs improvised madly. Ships were rerouted directly past Noumea to Guadalcanal, and selected high-priority
cargoes were discharged first wherever possible. The introduction
of the ugly six-wheeled 2½-ton DUKW amphibious truck saved a
good deal of grief on the beaches by providing the simple expedient of running cargoes directly from ships at anchor, over cleared
beaches, to inland dumps.

Slowly at first, then more rapidly and with greater efficiency,
the reserve supply level at Guadalcanal rose to 54,274 tons in June,
discounting organizational equipment, maintenance supplies, and
petroleum products. The Russells were stocked with 13,085 tons
of assorted reserve equipment along with 23,775 barrels of fuel and
lubricants from the Guadalcanal reserve stocks. Fuel at Guadalcanal was stored to an 80,000-barrel capacity in bulk storage tanks.
Operational units would have no bones to pick with Halsey's service squadron.

Because there were so many objectives in the Central Solomons, and because those objectives were spread over a relatively
wide and largely impenetrable area, it was decided that the offensive would be undertaken by means of a series of short, hard jabs.

Feeling somewhat rushed by the prescribed May 15 deadline for
getting under way, the South Pacific staff began to wrangle with
MacArthur, who relented a bit and firmly set the date for the
commencement of operations at June 30. This decision gave Halsey's planners a fair three months in which to work things out.
Given the time, an extensive survey of all prospective landing sites
and a number of the objectives was carried out.

To form a general basis for the survey, planners correlated information from largely outdated hydrographic and sailing charts.
This, along with information provided by Allied Coastwatchers
working at or near proposed landing sites, would form a general
picture of what would have to be accomplished.

Major Donald Kennedy, on New Georgia, was a generally reliable source of information. Although his primary duty was staying out of harm's way so that he could observe and file reports, Kennedy persisted in undertaking a long string of dangerous offensive actions against his unwilling hosts. During the course of his vigil, Major Kennedy saved a respectable number of Allied aircrews downed on or near New Georgia. By the same token, his force of islanders hunted down and dispatched a respectable number of Japanese aviators who were also downed on or near New Georgia. Kennedy's discovery and subsequent monitoring of the progress at Munda Field provided the reason for an enlarged program of reconnaissance missions in which the doughty New Zealander played host to an ever-increasing number of outsiders.

Six Marines commanded by Navy Lieutenant William Coultis, a South Pacific staff officer, landed at Roviana Lagoon, in New Georgia, for a three-week mission, during which the beaches were scouted and sounded, trails reconnoitered, and the Coastwatcher stations contacted. Coultis informed Admiral Halsey, just after the 28 March Directive from the Joint Chiefs had been issued, that landings in the Roviana area were practicable.

Next, because the then current plan envisaged a landing at Segi Point, one officer and two enlisted Marines from each of the four Marine Raider battalions were shipped to New Georgia aboard a Catalina flying boat. After contacting Major Kennedy, who provided each three-man team with a native scout, the Raiders spent three weeks on foot and canoe reconnaissance missions. In addition to scouting the Segi area, the Raiders looked for possible landing sites on Vangunu and Kolombangara Islands.

Major General Millard Harmon, who had opposed the Segi undertaking on grounds that the beaches were unfavorable for a large-scale amphibious undertaking, received concrete evidence from the Raiders that he was, in fact, correct. The Segi plan was duly scrapped, and Admiral Halsey ordered I Marine Amphibious Corps to coordinate its planning efforts with those of XIV Corps.

For what remained of the three-month planning period, a constant stream of small reconnaissance missions was undertaken at every conceivable landing site in the New Georgia Group. A three-man team led by the commander of the 4th Marine Raider Battalion, Lieutenant Colonel Mickey Currin, landed in late March and, after plodding from one proposed landing site to another, found that many of proposed beaches were suitable for the missions assigned them. Kolombangara Island was the center of a protracted flurry of attention; another Marine team scouted Zanana Beach, a few miles from Munda Field, as well as Roviana Lagoon and the overland trails between these sites and Rice Anchorage, in Kula Gulf; yet another Raider patrol landed at Grassi Lagoon to survey a possible PT-boat base. Second Lieutenant Harold Schrier, of 2nd Marine Raider Battalion, led two separate missions in early and mid-June to mark landing beaches on Vangunu Island. Rendova Island was thoroughly reconnoitered, and a Navy team actually surveyed the land around Segi Point to begin laying out a proposed fighter strip.

The information brought back was varied and complex. Often as not, it resulted in running changes of plans and orders. To be sure, one party arriving back just before the departure of the assault force handed in a report that resulted in a plan change that was carried out on the move.

A rather large group of officers, commanded by a Captain Arthur Norwood, of the 43rd Division's 152nd Field Artillery Battalion, landed at Segi Point just a few weeks prior to the scheduled assault. Its task was to check on possible artillery sites around Wickham Anchorage. After casting his critical artilleryman's eye over Segi, Norwood concluded that there were good battery positions available and recommended that Major Donald Kennedy's existing observation post be incorporated as an artillery observation post. Norwood also recommended that a road be cut through a native garden to a coconut grove that was admirably suited as a battery site. He also felt that a battery of 90mm antiaircraft guns could be emplaced on a high ridge near the sea, and that the guns could be moved farther from the precipice after the jungle growth had been removed. He even estimated that the antiaircraft guns could be placed in battery within five to six hours of landing.

Captain Norwood's report, like many others, was rather pedestrian in nature; it constituted several small pieces in an increasingly complex network of decisions and recommendations that would have to be taken into account and, in many cases, executed when the moment of truth came. In order to get at the details, men like Captain Norwood had to leave the relative safety of their unit bivouacs, travel stealthily into enemy territory, place their well-being in the hands of a rather garrulous Coastwatcher and his handful of armed islanders, and creep around the rain forest in search of minutiae destined, perhaps, for the scrap heap.

Six infantry and artillery officers who landed with Norwood's team set off on an extremely hazardous mission to Oliana Bay. This group, commanded by Captain Harold Slager, of the 152nd Field Artillery Battalion, spent twelve days moving about Rendova, Vangunu, the vicinity of Viru Harbor, and Segi—all of which were occupied by Japanese infantry detachments. During its stay, Slager's group monitored the living habits and deployment of the occupation forces, the lay of the land, and possible landing sites. They sounded the water and measured the beach at Oliana Bay, and their report mentioned, among other details, that the Japanese troops were husky and apparently well fed.

Three members of Slager's team—Lieutenants James Lamb, Frederick Burnaby, and Ellis Satterthwaite—were left behind when Slager and the others were withdrawn to Guadalcanal to file their reports. The three were to guide a landing force to the beach on D-Day by lighting a line of signal lights under the noses of the Japanese.

On the basis of on-the-ground and aerial observation, it was ultimately determined that about 3,000 Japanese were based at Munda, 7,000 were on Kolombangara, and about 300 were situated around Wickham Anchorage. These were extremely accurate estimates. Most of the shoreline was monitored by a network of twenty- or thirty-man detachments (*butai*). About 400 aircraft of all types, based in the Northern Solomons and Bismarcks, would be available to contest the landings, and additional aircraft could be committed from Truk. It was firmly and accurately determined that the invasion fleet would meet no seaborne opposition.

In order to attain local superiority as quickly as possible, and to secure as many objectives as there were troops to take, the final TOENAILS draft called for the landing of four separate landing forces: at Rendova Island, Viru Harbor, Segi Point, and Wickham Anchorage. The Segi objective would furnish ground for an advance fighter strip.

Following the initial landing phases, small craft operating out of Guadalcanal and the Russells were to stage through Viru Harbor and Wickham Anchorage to bolster the main staging base, at Rendova. Munda Point, its defenses, and the airbase complex, were to be under constant harassing fires from 155mm and 105mm guns and howitzers emplaced on Rendova and a number of the barrier islets. Munda was to be assaulted by troops entering from the four first-phase objectives after the outlying *butai* had been destroyed or dispersed—in effect, mopping up in reverse. An operation of sweeping drives would follow the fall of Munda Field. Heavy and medium artillery would be emplaced to harass Vila Field, on Kolombangara, and an offensive would be launched against that objective.

Major General John Hester, commanding 43rd Infantry Division, would command both the Munda and Vila drives under the designation Commanding General, New Georgia Occupation Force (NGOF). All units operating on New Georgia would be under Hester's tactical or operational control, depending upon deployment. The 43rd Division would provide the bulk of the operating forces, and would draw support from several Marine Raider and 37th Infantry Division infantry battalions. The latter division would itself remain on standby at Guadalcanal as the area reserve; it could be committed if needed, but only under an express order from Admiral Halsey himself.

In the final days before the Central Solomons offensive was to be mounted, all naval units under Admiral Halsey's command were redesignated components of the newly created Third Fleet, which was, in substance, the South Pacific Force. Naval units operating in the Southwest Pacific Area were redesignated Seventh Fleet. These were, as before, administrative units, and the tactical makeup of the various fleets could be altered by chance or design under Admiral King's ironclad directives regarding the mobility of the U.S. Fleet.

Four Navy task forces were assigned to the New Georgia operation: Task Force 31 (i.e., first task force of Third Fleet) comprised Rear Admiral Kelly Turner's transports and cargomen; Task Force 33 comprised Rear Admiral Aubrey Fitch's land-based aircraft; Task Force 72 comprised the Seventh Fleet's submarine force, which was based in Australia; Task Force 36 comprised the naval covering forces, which would operate under Halsey's direct control.

Task Force 33 was bolstered by a division of new light aircraft carriers to help soften up the four initial land objectives. Starting on D-5, Admiral Fitch's aircraft were to attempt the isolation of Munda, Ballale, Kahili, Kieta, and Vila airfields. A daylight combat air patrol was to be maintained by fighters; PBY Catalina flying boats armed with bombs or torpedoes would provide nighttime cover. Commencing on D-Day, eighteen Marine SBD Dauntless

dive-bombers were to remain on constant alert at the newly commissioned airfield in the Russells, Advance Base Knucklehead.
Army Air Forces medium bombers based at Henderson Field were
to be prepared for on-call air support of ground units, and transport aircraft, also based at Guadalcanal, were to have made arrangements for air-dropping supplies and equipment to ground
units that could not be supplied over ground supply lines.

A peculiar sort of chain of command was established for the
administration of support aircraft. It was put forth by Major General Alexander Vandegrift, who had commanded 1st Marine Division at Guadalcanal, and was accepted by Admiral Halsey mainly
because Vandegrift had learned a great deal about command
structures during the harder days of the Guadalcanal fighting. After
taking off from bases on Guadalcanal or Advance Base Knucklehead, all aircraft would be under the control of the Commanding
General, Aircraft, New Georgia (ComAir, New Georgia—Brigadier General Francis Mulcahy, concurrently commanding 2nd
Marine Aircraft Wing), as long as they were moving to operate in
his area. Fighters operating directly over Turner's Task Force 31
would be under the orders of a command-and-control team aboard
one of the supporting destroyers. Bombers flying to New Georgia
took their orders from a team aboard Turner's flagship. This ship-
to-air command arrangement would continue until air-command
groups could establish themselves ashore. Rear Admiral Aubrey
Fitch was in overall control of aerial operations throughout the area,
and Real Admiral Marc Mitscher controlled all aerial activity at
established bases on Guadalcanal or in the Russells under the designation of Commander, Aircraft, Solomons (ComAirSols and
Commander, Task Group 33.1).

By June 30, Admiral Fitch had 455 operational tactical aircraft
in the combat zone: 213 fighters, 170 light and medium bombers,
and 72 heavy bombers. This force outnumbered and certainly
outgunned the opposition throughout the Solomons and Bismarcks by approximately two to one. There was very little worry
about gaining local air superiority early in the offensive.

The New Georgia Occupation Force (Task Group 36.6) would
include, at the outset of the operations: 43rd Infantry Division; 9th
Marine Defense Battalion; Headquarters, 1st Marine Raider Regiment; 1st and 4th Marine Raider Battalions; 70th Coast Artillery
Battalion; 136th Field Artillery Battalion; one and one-half naval
construction battalions; elements of the 1st Commando, Fiji Guer-

rillas; radar units, a naval operating base detachment, and a small-boat pool.

The New Georgia Occupation Force (NGOF) was to be administered by members of both Major General John Hester's 43rd Division Headquarters and administrators from General Harmon's headquarters. Staff-section chiefs from 43rd Division Headquarters would run the NGOF while their assistants took over staff functions at the division level. The Force Artillery Group—43rd Division Artillery and attachments—fell under the command of Brigadier General Harold Barker, the 43rd Division artillery commander.

The command arrangements had many shortcomings and, from the very outset, Major General Millard Harmon was volubly dubious. It was therefore decided to order Major General Oscar Griswold, commanding XIV Corps at Guadalcanal, to keep himself abreast of developments on New Georgia, and to be prepared to assume control of the NGOF upon receipt of orders from Harmon or Halsey. Admiral Halsey fully concurred with Harmon's backup command program, but stopped well short of suggesting that Griswold's corps staff assume responsibility for the operation.

The Central Solomons offensive was to begin with the embarkation of Hester's heavily reinforced 43rd Infantry Division. Men and equipment were to be transported from Guadalcanal and the Russells to the four initial objectives aboard a strange mix of destroyer-transports, transports, cargomen, minelayers, and minesweepers. Segi, Viru, and Wickham Anchorage were to be assaulted by relatively small forces as their acquisition was mainly to assure open lines of communication to Rendova from rear areas. The main body of the NGOF would launch a direct assault on Rendova Island, with two subsidiary landings going in a bit behind the main assault.

Newly landed field artillery batteries were to be emplaced on Rendova and a number of the barrier islets in order to keep Munda and the NGOF route of advance under direct harassing and supporting fires. Naval gunfire would be employed as needed, when available.

For the several days following D-Day, slow-moving, flat-bottomed LSTs and LCIs, with some smaller LCTs, would carry in additional troops and supplies. These follow-on echelons would leave the Russells or Guadalcanal at night in order to arrive early enough to be well on the way back by the following evening. Shore-based antiaircraft batteries provided by 9th Marine Defense Battalion would cover the supply echelons from Wickham Anchorage all the way to Viru Harbor.

It was hoped that by D+4 there would be a large enough force and stockpile of equipment and supplies to allow the main assault force to be ferried through Roviana Lagoon to undertake a direct assault on Zanana Beach, on New Georgia proper. However, there was no absolutely firm commitment for the day of that landing.

Simultaneous with the assault on Zanana Beach, a force of Marine Raiders would land in the vicinity of Enogai Inlet from Kula Gulf to interdict a main overland route between Kolombangara and Munda. The primary purpose of this side operation was to keep the Japanese on Kolombangara from moving to the aid of a very limited New Georgia garrison.

Once Munda had fallen, a mop-up operation would sweep the Japanese from the remainder of New Georgia. Next, a large assault force would be formed and sent to seize Vila Field. Once Vila was in Allied hands, the remainder of Kolombangara would be seized. From there, Vella Lavella Island would be occupied.

To undertake the multifaceted initial operation, Rear Admiral Kelly Turner organized the assault and support forces into five major groups:

1. *Western Force* (Task Group 31.1), commanded directly by Admiral Turner, would seize Rendova Island and undertake subsequent overland attacks against Munda, finishing with the occupation of Vila.

2. *Eastern Force*, commanded by Rear Admiral George Fort, was to oversee the assault upon and occupation of bases at Segi Point, Wickham Anchorage, and Viru Harbor.

3. *New Georgia Occupation Force*, commanded by Major General Hester and incorporating the Western Landing Force (43rd Division, plus attached units) under Hester; the Eastern Landing Force, which was the tactical ground unit of Admiral Fort's command; and Force Reserve, which was, initially, the headquarters of 1st Marine Raider Regiment and the 1st Marine Raider Battalion.

4. *New Georgia Air Force*, commanded by Brigadier Francis Mulcahy, and consisting primarily of Mulcahy's own 2nd Marine Aircraft Wing, which was based at Henderson Field, Guadalcanal, and Advance Base Knucklehead, in the Russells.

5. *Assault Flotillas*, consisting entirely of the landing craft of all sizes and types to be used in ferrying the NGOF from Rendova to Zanana Beach.

Several additional assault elements would be retained temporarily under Turner's direct command during the initial assault phase. One of these was the Onaiavisi Occupation Unit, which comprised "Barracuda" Companies A and B of the 1st Battalion, 169th Infantry Regiment, which were to land from a pair of destroyer-transports and a minesweeper on Sasavelle and Baraulu Islands (on either side of Onaiavisi Entrance) to hold that ground until the NGOF had landed successfully at Zanana Beach. The second assault unit under Turner's direct command was the Rendova Advance Unit, which comprised "Barracuda" Companies C and G (less a platoon each) of the 172nd Infantry Regiment augmented by a group of British-officered native constabulary from the British Solomon Islands Protectorate Defense Force. This force was to land from a pair of destroyer-transports before dawn on June 30 at Rendova in order to cover the main assault by the Western Landing Force. The latter, comprising 6,300 troops, would begin its move on the beach at 0640 hours, June 30.

The transports were to be covered by eight destroyers. There was to be no preliminary naval gunfire, but the captains of all the warships were directed to be prepared to undertake direct support and counterbattery fire if necessary.

Admiral Turner would relinquish control of the New Georgia Occupation Force to General Hester upon direct orders from Admiral Halsey.

Due to many serious errors made by the Allies during the Guadalcanal Campaign, much of the planning for the New Georgia effort was devoted to logistical buildups, backups, and transport. A tragic awkwardness in ship-to-shore movement of supplies had itself very nearly killed off a division of inexperienced Marines in August 1942. The logistical establishment for the New Georgia Campaign was a drastic and stunning modification of early doctrine.

The presence of the DRYGOODS stocks at Guadalcanal was of paramount importance in simplifying transport. Such stocks had not existed ten months earlier. Ample munitions and a thirty-day level of goods of all types were to be landed at Rendova, with even more goods scheduled to be divided between Segi, Viru, and Wickham. In addition, a constant flow of reserve stores was to be maintained until all types of equipment, spares, and supplies reached a sixty-day level. XIV Corps, which oversaw the DRY-GOODS stocks, was ordered to make the necessary supplies available to Admiral Turner, who was to be responsible for moving them from Guadalcanal to the combat zone.

To avoid putting more supplies onto the beach than could be effectively handled initially—which was precisely what had caused the snag at Guadalcanal—Turner was to see that there was sufficient manpower for moving gear over the beaches to inland dumps. Orders and methods were clear and simple. All transports and cargomen were to be prepared for rapid unloading. Ships would be squared away before reaching the anchorages and were to work hatches from both sides where possible. Unloading details were to consist of 150 soldiers for each cargoman and transport, 150 soldiers for each LST, 50 soldiers for each LCT, and 25 soldiers for each LCI. The shore party was to be 300 strong. Supplies moving across the beaches were to be directed to appropriate inland dumps with the minimum of confusion and as much speed as possible.

It looked good on paper.

With a tactical plan that more or less pleased everyone, ground forces everyone felt were sufficient, and excellent intelligence, the personnel to be involved in TOENAILS spent the month preceding the landing making final preparations—checking gear and weapons, conducting amphibious drills in the New Hebrides, studying new orders and intelligence matter, and making pacts with God. South Pacific aircraft, and some naval forces, carried out a systematic pummeling of Munda, and medium and heavy bombers from the Southwest Pacific Area flew long-range missions against Rabaul to disrupt the various Japanese headquarters, air bases, and lines of supply.

All, said the commanders, was in readiness. They had exhaustively measured the many objectives, they had seen to the buildup of adequate supplies, they had more than enough combat aircraft on hand, adequate reserves were in place, training had been thorough and exhaustive, and everyone knew his place and his job. The senior commanders asked their subordinates, one another, and themselves what could possibly go wrong. If they discovered something that could go wrong, they corrected it or allowed for it in their plans. In the end, they could not anticipate a single possible error. They each knew that errors were inevitable, but they assured themselves and one another that they had done the best they could. And then they sent other men to test the completeness of their efforts.

Several weeks before the operation was to begin, Lieutenant Colonel Henry Shafer, the commanding officer of the 37th Infantry Division's 136th Field Artillery Battalion, received two entirely unexpected visitors at his battalion command post on Guadalcanal. The two introduced themselves as Brigadier General Harold Barker, commanding general of the 43rd Division Artillery Group, and his operations officer, Lieutenant Colonel Ed Berry. The purpose of their visit was to discuss the details of an impending operation by the 43rd Division against the Japanese on New Georgia, in which the 136th Field Artillery Battalion was to be detached from the 37th Division and attached to the 43rd Division Artillery Group for the duration of the upcoming offensive.

Everybody was surprised. Shafer was surprised because he found himself being briefed on a pending operation by strangers, which seemed fantastic. Barker and Berry were surprised that Shafer had zero information about anything to do with an invasion of New Georgia. Shafer was further surprised to learn that the attachment of his twelve-gun 155mm howitzer battalion to 43rd Division Artillery had been specifically ordered by Rear Admiral Kelly Turner, a naval officer with no apparent connection to the functioning of Army artillery units. Shafer then compounded his vistors' surprise by immediately contacting Brigadier General Leo Kreber, the commanding general of the 37th Division Artillery Group, his immediate superior. Kreber was amazed, to put it mildly, and wonder if General Barker had mistaken Shafer's command post for the division artillery command post. To round out everyone's surprise, General Kreber revealed that, like Shafer, *he* had no information about the project. Kreber told Shafer to wait while he, Kreber, contacted Major General Robert Beightler, the commanding general of the 37th Infantry Division.

General Kreber called Lieutenant Colonel Shafer back to say that

General Beightler also was surprised by General Barker's visit and was reluctant to see the piecemeal commitment of components of the division under another command. According to Kreber, Beightler was at that moment requesting full details from Noumea.

By then, General Barker's surprise was equaled by his embarrassment, but everyone settled down to await the news from South Pacific Area headquarters, which arrived before the afternoon was over. At that point, Brigadier General Barker began conducting the briefing he had arrived at Shafer's command post to conduct. No further mention of the confusion was made, but everyone involved wondered if further surprises awaited them.

PART II

---　＊　---

Invasion

4

Many of the Allied reconnaissance teams sent to the New Georgia area between March and June 1943 entered through the Segi enclave of Major Donald Kennedy. This vast increase in activity did not go unnoticed by the Japanese, who had been only too acutely aware of Kennedy's presence for too long. In time, these groups of armed Allied soldiers, sailors, and Marines marching within the perimeter of the Empire of Japan with such galling impunity were adding decided insult to a deep-seated injury. Something had to be done.

Kennedy's immediate adversary in eastern New Georgia was First Lieutenant Tagaki, of the Imperial Army, the commander of a 235-man outpost consisting primarily of his own 3rd Company, 229th Infantry, and a small detachment of *rikusentai* from the Kure 6th and Yokosuka 7th Special Naval Landing Forces. Viru Butai, as Tagaki's unit was called, also possessed several well-emplaced light and medium fieldpieces and coastal guns, and it controlled a varying number of landing barges. Despite Lieutenant Tagaki's edge in strength, coupled with a routine of vigorous patrolling, Viru Butai had been getting soundly beaten over a period of several months. Casualties were mounting under the pressure exerted by Kennedy's islanders, and Tagaki was finding that his normally stoic subordinates were just plain afraid to participate in patrols. Japanese infantry never minded big, showy assaults against tough odds, but tramping off to die in the silent rain forest at the hands of unseen, unreachable assailants was getting to them.

Major General Noburo Sasaki, commander of the Southeast Detached Force and responsible for the defense of the Munda sector, finally felt that Kennedy had gone a bit far in what had turned into a quiet little exercise in futility. Kennedy would have to be put out of operation. General Sasaki ordered Colonel Genjiro Hirata, whose 229th Infantry Regiment was responsible for the Viru area, to send a vastly superior force against the Allied base at Segi. In his turn, Hirata ordered Major Masao Hara to mount his entire 1st Battalion, 229th Infantry, against Segi. The battalion would strike out from its base at Viru Harbor on June 17 and march southeastward into Segi, destroy the base, and conduct a mop-up of outposts throughout the sector.

The Japanese telegraphed their punch. Before Hara's main body could even get going, Lieutenant Tagaki's soldiers and *rikusentai* began going about their business with a vim and vigor heretofore unnoticed by Kennedy's cohorts. The very aggressiveness with which the Japanese infantry sought out the Coastwatchers indicated a quantum leap in morale, which suggested that something big was in the offing.

Kennedy was powerful but not foolhardy. He knew he had Tagaki's Viru Butai going in circles, and he felt that he could keep it that way until the impending invasion was launched. But he had no way of holding off an aggressive battalion sweep through his sector.

The situation seemed grave. Not only might Kennedy stand beaten—itself a grave loss—but the Allies would face the calamity of losing the vital airfield site only days before it was scheduled to be claimed. Landing a small force on a safe stretch of beach was one thing; landing that same small force against serious opposition was out of the question. Kennedy calmly hit the panic button.

In safer waters, Rear Admiral Kelly Turner reacted violently. The South Pacific Amphibious Force commander scoured his landing forces for a unit that could mount out virtually on zero notice. In the original TOENAILS plan, the job of securing Segi had fallen to the 1st Battalion, 103rd Infantry Regiment, and a small detachment of Seabees. Neither the infantry battalion nor the Navy combat engineers were quite ready. The only force that was available was two companies of Lieutenant Colonel Mickey Currin's 4th Marine Raider Battalion. Two destroyer-transports, *Dent* and *Waters*, were tabbed to carry the two Raider companies and Currin's battalion headquarters to Segi, and, if need be, to provide on-call gunfire support.

Mickey Currin was not thrilled about the piecemeal deployment of his finely honed battalion, but his force was all there was. He issued what little he had in the way of directives and led his Raiders aboard the destroyer-transports on the morning of June 20.

As the Raiders were mounting out, two companies of the 1st Battalion, 103rd, were ordered to board destroyer-transports *Schley* and *Crosby* and prepare themselves to conduct a backup landing at Segi Point on the morning of June 22. Admiral Turner passed the word to Lieutenant Colonel Currin that he could request even more troops if they were required—and available.

Waters and *Dent* made excellent time to Segi, arriving hours before dawn on June 21. Major Kennedy had bonfires lighted on the beach, and canoe-borne islanders guided the flotilla through coral-studded waters. The destroyer-transports repeatedly scraped against underwater obstructions in the extremely close waters, but they managed to reach their debarkation station without untoward incident. The Raiders boarded their landing craft at 0530 and, despite preparations against heavy opposition, simply filed ashore on the quiet beach after an uneventful twenty-minute boat ride. The beach was fully secured by 1030.

The Central Solomons Campaign had begun. Quietly.

Crosby and *Schley* arrived off Segi Point at 0600, June 22, and A and C Companies, 103rd Infantry, were landed ashore without mishap. By 0730, the two Army companies had moved into their own sectors of the tight defensive cordon Lieutenant Colonel Currin had organized around the beachhead. A U.S. Navy survey team, which had accompanied the backup force, set to work laying out the fighter strip.

For the several days following the landings, Kennedy's islanders guided American Marines and soldiers on routine scouting operations against the Japanese outposts in the area. Other patrols ranged farther afield in order to find the best route to Viru Harbor, which had been the 4th Raider Battalion's original objective, and for which Lieutenant Colonel Currin remained responsible.

In order to protect Njai Passage, leading from The Slot to Segi Point, Currin deployed a strong security outpost at Patutive Point on Vangunu Island. No Japanese were actually encountered by the security force, but the area was overflowing with footprints, abandoned military gear, trail blazes, and abandoned patrol campsites—all of which indicated the presence of a considerable and active force of defenders.

About the only adverse incident arising out of the precipitous occupation of Segi by the battalion-size landing force was the displacement of Donald Kennedy. Something of a recluse, Kennedy mildly resented having so many people around. More to the point, hundreds of green Marines and soldiers were endangering the loyal islanders with their tendency to shoot first and ask questions later. So Kennedy moved to a quieter locale. That, as much as anything, attested to the success of the occupation.

5

O nce the uneventful early occupation of Segi had been completed, Lieutenant Colonel Mickey Currin felt called upon
to determine how he was to undertake the mission detailed to his
battalion in the original plans: the assault against the Japanese base
forces around Viru Harbor, which had to be accomplished more
or less in concert with the main assault against Rendova on June
30.

Although no plan for accomplishing the mission was in the offing when Currin's force left Guadalcanal on June 20, Currin had
been assured by his chief, Rear Admiral George Fort, that a re-
vised operations plan would be in his hands in plenty of time.
Getting the plan to 4th Raider Battalion headquarters required an
all-night canoe trip by Currin's adjutant, who was paddled by several islanders from Segi to Hele Island and then out into the middle of Blanche Channel. There, the staff officer was passed a copy
of the new plan from destroyer-transport *Schley*. The plan was in
Mickey Currin's hands by the morning of June 25.

Formulated on June 21 and modified on June 22, the plan detailed Captain Anthony Walker's P Company, 4th Raiders, to proceed from Segi via rubber raft and canoe on June 28 to Nono
Village, at the mouth of the Choi River, about three miles west of
Segi. From Nono, Walker was to march overland to Viru to launch
an assault against Tetemara Village at 0700 on June 30. As soon as
Walker's assault was underway, a 355-man infantry force built
around B Company, 103rd Infantry, would be landed from a pair
of destroyer-transports.

A Japanese 3-inch coast defense gun at Tetemara would have to
be neutralized before the reserve force could land. Once it did,
Captain Walker would assume command of the entire occupation
force, which would be bolstered by an antiaircraft battery, a naval
base platoon, and a half company of Seabees. Development of an
advance PT-boat base would commence as soon as the area was
secure.

As soon as it was read carefully, the plan came under the severe
criticism of Lieutenant Colonel Currin. First, the intelligence ba-

sis for the operation was badly outdated—the estimate of a reconnaissance team that, with the assistance of Kennedy's scouts, had
canoed to Nono from Segi and hiked alongside the Choi River
without encountering opposition. This patrol, and earlier missions, reported the presence of about 100 Japanese at Viru. Consequently, the plan did not account for the arrival of the main body
of the 1st Battalion, 229th Infantry. Currin could not restrain
himself from noting that it was the presence of this strong battalion that had caused Currin's makeshift force to be dispatched to
Segi on June 20 at the expense of the original plan!

In addition to the lapse of logic, Currin had several objections
to the plan based on personal observations he had made while
leading a reconnaissance patrol in early April. It was quite clear
that the aerial distances between points on New Georgia in no way
resembled actual marching distances. For example, two unforda-
ble streams between Nono and Viru Harbor would have to be
completely circumvented, thus adding many miles of miserable
hiking to an already cramped schedule. Moreover, a heavily armed
combat force—even one as trail-toughened as Currin's Raiders—
could not hope to travel as quickly as a lightly armed reconnaissance team.

Reconnaissance missions carried out after the occupation of Segi
by Currin's own patrols indicated that Regi Village, a mile east of
Nono, possessed the only suitable beach for landing an adequate
combat force. Moreover, there were no Japanese in Regi. According to reports provided by Donald Kennedy's scouts, Nono was
occupied. Paddling rubber rafts ashore into hostile fire was considered by Currin and his officers to be something less than the best
way to achieve the objective.

To top everything off, Admiral Fort's plan assigned no missions
to Headquarters or O Companies, 4th Raiders. In fact, unassisted
by any other available unit, P Company was to clear the New
Georgia side of Wickham Anchorage after finishing the job at
Tetemara.

Currin had an alternative plan. His entire force would land at
Regi Village, which was just seven air miles from the objective, and
would proceed overland to a point east of Viru Harbor. There, it
would split into two groups for simultaneous assaults down both
sides of the inlet. The eastern group would assault Tombe Village
while the larger western group would take on the defenses around
Tetemara.

Currin presented his plan in a radio transmission to Admiral Fort at 1600, June 27. He added that he required an immediate response since time was his single worst enemy. Admiral Fort recognized that the man on the spot was in the best position to formulate the most suitable plan, so he radioed his complete approval within ninety minutes.

The Raiders pulled up stakes at 2000, June 27, and began an eight-mile canoe trip to Regi. It was, in the words of one of Currin's staff officers, "a weird and moonless night." The route of the darkened formation led through the myriad rocks and pinnacles that studded Panga Bay. Just before reaching Regi, a sudden scare was thrown into the entire force. Native scouts had gone ahead to check the beach and, while the Raiders waited quietly offshore, a trick of moonlight revealed what seemed to be the wake of a Japanese destroyer. The Raiders prepared for an action they had no hope of winning, but the phantasmagoric sight receded as mysteriously as it had appeared.

The scouts reported back a short time later that the beach was clear. Currin ordered the rafts to land at about 0100, and they began slipping noiselessly ashore within the half hour. Small groups of tense Marines stealthily organized a temporary defensive position while, closer to the beach, the battalion headquarters began organizing for the march to Viru Harbor. Once all the Raiders were ashore, along with a team of local guides, a party of islanders set out for Segi with the full complement of rubber rafts in tow behind their war canoes.

At 0630, after sleeping in shifts to regain some of the strength lost in the arduous trip from Segi, the Raiders formed up and began the grueling march on Viru Harbor. O Company took the column's vanguard and Headquarters Company followed directly. P Company moved behind the command group, keeping a close watch on the column's vulnerable rear.

A five-man Japanese patrol blundered into the rear of the Raider column at 0930. The rear guard deployed in an instant and brought down four of the Japanese with the first hail of bullets. The fifth man escaped while the main body of Marines hurried on in hopes of remaining unseen.

Despite a redoubling of attention at the column's rear, a second group of Japanese overtook the rear guard at 1130. Machine guns attached to the P Company security platoon were broken out and hurriedly placed in action. The Japanese put up a determined but indecisive fight before pulling back an hour after contact. Five Raiders were cut off from the main body during the course of the maneuvering, and these men could not find their way back to the main force. In the end, they elected to march overland to Segi and, after suffering considerable privation, arrived safely at that destination some days later.

Meanwhile, Lieutenant Colonel Mickey Currin also had problems. The latest encounter with the Japanese was only an hour long, but it played havoc with the force's tight working schedule. Currin attempted to contact Admiral Turner's headquarters to say that he would be arriving at Viru a full day behind schedule. Unfortunately, Major Donald Kennedy, who received Currin's message from a pair of local scouts, could not raise the Russells by radio. Currin, of course, had no way of knowing that his message had not gotten through, so he acted within the limitations the loss of time had imposed; he had no way to make up the lost time, so he did not try.

The morning and early afternoon of June 29 passed without incident, marked only by the slow grind of plodding feet over miles of virgin, stinking, muddy jungle ridges and lowlands. At 1400, Captain Anthony Walker, of P Company, dispatched a sixty-man force under First Lieutenant Devillo Brown to push ahead down the trail and strike off on a side trail to Tombe, on the near side of Viru Harbor. The rest of the Raiders would follow the main trail to Tetemara, on the inland side of Viru Harbor.

Lieutenant Brown's augmented platoon pushed rapidly ahead toward its objective. Soon, the point fire team encountered a ridge running directly across the trail. Since the Choi River ran down one side of the ridge and a large swamp blocked the other side, Brown's force was obliged to go straight over the ridge. As the point fire team mounted the slope, at least forty-five Japanese emplaced on the crest opened fire with three Nambu light machine guns and small arms. The lead man of the point fire team was killed by the first blast of gunfire. The surviving pointmen scrambled into the brush on either side of the trail, and the remainder of the reinforced Raider platoon did the same. Before everyone was quite settled, another member of the point fire team, a close friend of the man who had been killed, stood up on the open trail and walked straight up the ridge, firing his Thompson submachine gun. He was shot dead.

As soon as Lieutenant Brown could assess the situation, he deployed his men in a skirmish line in the high grass near the base of the ridge. By then, the Raiders were quite calm, willing to mount an assault. As soon as the accompanying machine guns established a base of fire, Brown started maneuvering the platoon up the slope. As the Raiders crawled through the high grass, they fired blindly at the Japanese positions. Fortunately, the apparently inexperienced defenders tended to fire over the heads of the crawling Raiders, an error typically made by riflemen occupying the high ground. As the action developed, one Marine rifle squad fired cover over the other two as everyone advanced steadily and carefully. While the riflemen were advancing, the sergeant commanding the machine-gun section became dissatisfied with the fall of the bullets from his two .30-caliber light machine guns, so he stood up in the high grass to get a better look at the Japanese position. He was immediately bowled over by the impact of a Japanese bullet. As soon as he recovered from the impact, however, the machine-gun section leader stood up again. He was laced with bullets from a Japanese machine gun and killed.

The main body of Raiders stopped as soon as the noise of the gunfight filtered through the close rain forest. Immediately, the P Company executive officer was sent ahead with two squads to reinforce Brown's force while the balance of the Raider force deployed off the trail, ready to defend itself or advance if needed. As Mickey Currin listened to the muffled gunfire from ahead, he repeatedly tried to reach Lieutenant Brown by radio, but the command radio was not putting out a strong enough signal. If Brown had sent back runners, it was apparent that they were not getting through. Currin had no idea whether Brown's force was involved in a patrol action, or if it was embroiled in a full-scale battle for its life with an overwhelming Japanese infantry force.

Slowly, Lieutenant Brown's advancing rifle squads closed on the top of the ridge, and several Raiders hurled homemade hand grenades—plastic explosives stuffed into empty ration cans and detonated by a fuse. These concussion-type grenades were better suited to the rain forest than fragmentation grenades, which could easily maim the thrower if they got caught in branches overhead. The flurry of explosions stunned the Japanese, whose fire seemed to diminish for the moment. For some reason, one of the Raiders yelled, "Mortars! Mortars!" just as Lieutenant Brown rose to his feet to lead a spirited final assault on the Japanese base of fire. By then, the ridgeline was cleared of live Japanese, who had apparently faded into the rain forest at the last moment. Nevertheless, the Raiders counted eighteen Japanese corpses to five of their own killed and one wounded. All the Japanese left their packs on the ridge, forty-five in all.

The P Company executive officer and his two squads arrived moments after the Japanese survivors bolted. After waiting as long as he could stand the suspense, Mickey Currin walked down the trail to see for himself what was going on. He arrived as Brown's platoon and the reinforcements were burying the dead Raiders, a hard decision aimed at preventing the burden from slowing the column.

When Currin saw that all was well, he ordered the main body to bypass the scene of the action. Brown's platoon was to rejoin the main body as soon as the dead had been interred. Finally, the one wounded Raider had to be cared for without slowing the column. Reluctantly, Currin ordered a precious rifle squad to carry the man at its own pace in the trace of the main body.

The main body moved out once again, crossed the Choi River for the second time that day, skirted an impassable swamp, then recrossed the meandering Choi yet again before establishing a night defensive position a few miles west of the river. Brown's platoon arrived shortly after the main body, and the slow-moving litter squad arrived safely at about 2100.

Currin's schedule had been devastated. Any hope he had entertained in the morning of making up some time had been dashed by the ambush of Lieutenant Brown's platoon. All the force commander could do was resign himself completely to carrying out his mission a full day late—provided nothing kept him from it longer.

During the night of June 29–30, Currin's balky command radio failed completely; he was unable to report his position to his superiors, and he could only hope that the runners he had sent to report to Donald Kennedy had gotten through. As his troops would have no opportunity to knock out the 3-inch coastal gun defending Viru Harbor, it was possible that the destroyer-transports would be fired on as they entered the harbor.

As the Raiders were preparing to move out in the morning, destroyer-transports *Kilty*, *Hopkins*, and *Crosby* edged into the anchorage. The transport commander had received roundabout warning of a possible delay in the Raider assault, but he decided to remain close by in the event Currin showed up earlier than anticipated and required naval gunfire support. Shells from the Japanese 3-inch gun began splashing around the destroyers at 0730, and all three precipitously pulled out of range. At 1000, Admiral Fort authorized them to land the occupation force at Nono the following morning. Lacking any news from Currin's force, there was nothing more anyone could do.

On the Japanese side, Major Masao Hara, the commander of the 1st Battalion, 229th Infantry, reported exultantly to his superiors that he had repulsed an attempted American landing at Viru Harbor. In fact, Major General Noburo Sasaki had expressly ordered Hara to withdraw his battalion to the Munda defense sector prior to the encounter; Hara had no business even being there.

Early on the morning of June 30, the Raider main body reached the junction of the trails to Tombe and Tetemara. Currin had originally intended sending only Brown's reinforced platoon against Tombe. However, in view of the opposition encountered along the way from Regi, he had to assume that a forewarned and, perhaps, reinforced garrison was holding the small outpost. It was decided, therefore, to send two P Company platoons under Captain Anthony Walker against the eastern side of the harbor. As there was no way to support it, Walker's force would be completely on its own. One platoon under the P Company executive officer would remain with the main body for the assault on Tetemara.

Scouts accompanying the Raiders claimed they could lead the main body to Tetemara by way of a swamp trail unknown to the Japanese. Though the new route did not show up on any maps he possessed, Currin was inclined to take the gamble; he was certain the more direct trail would be blocked by a large Japanese force once the survivors of the ambush got home.

While no Japanese were encountered along the way, Currin's main body was slowed considerably by the worst terrain yet encountered. By mid-morning, the Raiders had forded the Viru River and struggled over some extremely jumbled terrain in the vicinity of the Tita River. Then the Tita itself had to be forded. The going was extremely arduous for the heavily laden Raiders. By the time they reached the banks of the Mango River, there was only an hour of daylight remaining. The Raiders and scouts joined hands in the swift, deep, fifty-yard-wide river and snaked a human chain to reasonably dry ground.

The column nearly bogged down in the fetid darkness of a particularly large mangrove swamp. The water was knee-deep, and submerged tangles of roots and vines trapped the weary hikers. Within minutes, the Raiders were totally stopped. Islanders experienced with the terrain distributed chunks of phosphorescent "tree light" from decaying logs. Every man was thus able to keep contact with the man directly in front of him by watching the dim glow ahead. The column closed up and began making headway.

The last Raider scrambled onto firm, dry ground after four hours in the swamp. Ahead lay the last half-mile to Tetemara—a steep, uphill climb. The haggard, weary men groped clumsily upward in the blackness of full night. Many finished the climactic, nearly vertical muddy climb on hands and knees.

To the east, Captain Anthony Walker's two-platoon assault force bivouacked a short distance from Tombe. At 0900, July 1, Walker opened the P Company attack with an assault by Lieutenant Brown's platoon and followed through with a swift backup assault by his remaining platoon and the company headquarters. Thirteen Japanese were killed in the surprise attack, and the remainder of the small garrison scattered into the rain forest. The objective was carried without loss.

The Japanese at Tetemara heard the gunfire from Tombe and ran into the open just as six Navy and Marine Dauntless dive-bombers opened a strafing and bombing attack on their campsite. The timing was coincidental; a ship-based air liaison party had requested the strike on its own initiative some hours before.

While Mickey Currin's force could hear the air strike, it could see nothing. However, after fifteen minutes, the troops were ordered to move on the village. Captain Ray Luckel's O Company took the downward slope of the screening hill and fanned out in the hope of confining the defenders to an area between the harbor and the sea. Supporting machine guns had been attached directly to the assault platoons, and the increased firepower permitted the various units to maintain a slow, steady advance. Only a few outguard positions were encountered, and these were overrun. In time, the advance bogged down in the face of strong, determined fire from the main Japanese defensive area.

After an hour of desperate maneuvering and solid firing, the

Raiders had gained only 100 yards against the stubborn defenders. They pressed on and by 1305 had secured a low ridge from which the ground sloped away into Tetemara.

The Japanese began withdrawing to the northeast, yelling oaths as they plunged away from the advancing Marines. Anticipating a counterattack, Currin committed his P Company reserve platoon and two machine-gun squads. Just in time! The Japanese charged into the newly bolstered Marine line, and they were beaten. The advancing Raider platoons sprang forward against spotty opposition. Shortly, Tetemara and the 3-inch coast-defense gun fell to Currin's force. Then the remaining defenders were flushed from the underbrush and caves.

The fall of Tetemara cost the 4th Raiders eight killed. The Japanese lost a confirmed forty-eight dead along with several heavy guns, a mortar battery, a fair-sized haul of small arms, and the base supply depot.

While the fighting around the village was still underway, the LSTs assigned to bring in the supplies for the proposed PT-boat advance base patiently stood offshore until a landing site could be cleared. The moment the village fell, the hulking ocean-going landing ships moved in, lowered bow ramps, and began disgorging cargoes and men from their gaping maws.

The Viru Occupation Unit plodded into Tombe on July 4, following a grueling overland march from Nono. Though the Raiders were then free to withdraw to Guadalcanal for a rest, Lieutenant Colonel Currin elected to await the landing of a larger permanent garrison force, which arrived on July 10.

The occupation of Viru Harbor cost the 375-man Raider force 13 dead and 15 wounded. Major Masao Hara's 1st Battalion, 229th Infantry, and attached units lost 61 confirmed killed and as many as 100 wounded in the defense of Tombe and Tetemara. An estimated 170 Japanese survivors hid out in the rain forest around Viru Harbor while, under orders from his superiors at Munda, Major Hara marched the main body of his battalion overland through the forest toward distant Munda.

6

The Allied occupation of Segi on June 21 was the signal for the Rabaul-based 8th Area Army and 8th Fleet to begin increasing planned defensive-type operations throughout the Solomons. Infantry and support units in the region were put on full alert. Aerial striking forces were rapidly built up at Buin, and naval surface units prepared to engage Allied forces anywhere in the Central and Northern Solomons. Beyond that, the Japanese could do little until Allied intentions became clearer.

Then, all of a sudden, the Japanese relaxed the alert. The failure of the Allies to quickly follow up the Segi occupation by any sort of offensive action led the Imperial Army and Imperial Navy command echelons in Rabaul to look upon the undertaking as an infiltration-in-force, or even a figment of some overwrought imaginations. In any case, it could be dealt with by local forces. The aerial force at Buin was dispersed, and 8th Fleet was ordered to resume normal operations.

On the night of June 29, a Japanese submarine on routine picket patrol near Gatuki Island reported sighting a large force of Allied ships. That same night, a force of Allied cruisers and destroyers bombarded the Vila and Buin airfields under cover of a driving rainstorm, which allowed the intruding warships to make off unhampered. As a result of the bombardment, the Japanese deduced that the submarine had sighted the warships. In fact, the submarine had sighted the Western Force on its way to Rendova. Luck and the elements combined to cause the Japanese to lose a full night's jump on the offensive they had been awaiting for many months. Meanwhile, Rear Admiral Kelly Turner's invasion force crept toward Rendova Bay under cover of the storm front that had screened the bombardment force to the north.

The movement of the Western Force from Guadalcanal was uneventful. The convoy left the anchorage off Koli Point at 1545 on June 29 and headed northwestward. Screened by a powerful destroyer flotilla, six transports and two destroyer-transports bearing the Western Landing Force moved past the Russells bases in a double column and made for Blanche Channel.

Shortly before dawn, the transports dropped anchor in the bay under cover of the weather front. The troops were already bordering the rails of their ships, awaiting the word that would send them into their landing craft for the uncertain run on the mist-shrouded beach.

Many of the infantrymen had been in on the Russells landings, which had been bloodless. But this was Rendova, close by a major air-base complex. And the Japanese had had a half year to prepare a hot welcome. Colonel David Ross's 172nd Infantry Regiment had already taken casualties when the transport carrying it to the Pacific from California had struck a friendly mine and sunk off Espiritu Santo the preceding October. How many more, those soldiers wondered, would be claimed by the war this day, and in the days ahead?

The immediate objective had about as good a beach as any in the New Georgia Group. Situated on the northern end of the twenty-by-eight-mile haunch-shaped island, the beaches were mostly marshy bogs set into a steep, irregular coastline. Most of them were badly fouled by patches of protruding coral heads. Rendova Harbor, a cove less than a mile in length that was protected by three barrier islets, was the best of the bad lot. There were two deep-water entrances, and the eastern one had been designated by reconnaissance teams as being the better.

Five fleet destroyers were echeloned along a 1,000-yard picket line to the northwest while three others blockaded Blanche Channel, to the east. The infantry units aboard five transports had been assigned objectives on the eastern side of Rendova Harbor. Two additional transports were to disembark infantry assigned to the western beaches.

At 0530, Major Martin Clemens, a former British colonial officer and former Coastwatcher, now the commander of a detachment of Commonwealth officers and native constabulary, looked toward the dawn-lit beaches. Visibility was virtually nil; a cloudy dawn mist hung over the entire vista.

Clemens had won a degree of local fame by staying behind on Guadalcanal when the Japanese drove the British out in May 1942. He had stayed on to help the Marines at Lunga until October 1942, when he was sent to Australia for a rest. He was elated to be meeting the Japanese on somewhat more equal terms. He was at Rendova to lead the initial assault of the Western Landing Force.

At 0630, Major Clemens and the two specially trained "Barracuda" companies he was to guide—C and G Companies, 172nd Infantry—disembarked from a pair of destroyer-transports. Clemens had with him a dozen native constables and Lieutenant F. A. Rhoades, all veterans of the Guadalcanal Campaign.

Things began going wrong as soon as the troop-laden craft reached the entrance to Rendova Harbor. The unusually inexperienced Navy coxswains had a miserable time even finding the passage, and the flimsy plywood craft went aground on the reef, one after another. After pulling off the coral, the coxswains attempted to find Kokorana Island, which they managed to do at length. Meantime, large infantry assault units of the 172nd Infantry Regiment were already nearing the beaches the Barracudas were to have secured.

Low in the water, American infantrymen were getting their first fitful glimpses of Rendova Mountain through the thinning mist. Then, through a rift in the opaque curtain, some could make out Rendova Plantation, hard by the beach, some 3,000 yards distant. Though the mist closed back in, many of the boat coxswains found the eastern entrance. The trouble was they all found it at once, which resulted in a fantastic traffic jam. After some maneuvering and no little cursing, the lead waves sorted themselves out and continued on the final run to the beach.

Major Clemens's scouts made it to the beach behind some boats carrying the 1st Battalion, 172nd, but just ahead of the bulk of the main landing force. Most of the Barracudas never reached the correct beach, but one of their boats landed near the plantation house, and Clemens rode another to the labor house, a little farther on. The Barracudas disembarked to carry out an attack in open order, with Lieutenant Rhoades and two scouts well in the lead.

The Japanese had had no idea that Rendova might be a serious Allied objective, so the island was not seriously defended. The defenders awoke too late to offer much resistance, and most made a run for it as soon as they saw what was coming their way. A number took to canoes and paddled to Munda as soon as the shooting started, and the rest headed for the hills behind the beach. Fortunately for the green American soldiers, only a very few Japanese chose to stand and fight. As it was, only about 180 Japanese were in the vicinity of the landing beaches, but very few of these were on hand to defend the beach in the opening minutes. Momentarily, soldiers from the leading boats gained the upper hand and seized the initiative. Major Clemens and Lieutenant Rhoades probably drew first blood by dispatching two Japanese they found kneeling in the undergrowth just back of the beach.

As the first boats carrying the main force disgorged several yards from dry land, disorganized groups of Japanese continued to tumble out of their grass shacks and open fire on the oncoming invaders. An even larger number of Japanese could be seen heading for the bush. That any Japanese were opposing the landing at all was a severe shock to everyone; the troops had been ordered to carry their own barracks bags ashore, so certain was the high command that *no* Japanese would oppose the landing. Despite its overwhelming might, the land force bogged down after making an average gain of fifteen yards.

Just off the beach, the soldiers around Major Bill Naylor, commander of the 1st Battalion, 172nd, all dropped their barracks bags in their boats, leaped into the shoulder-deep water, and waded to the beach. Naylor was gratified to see that there was no panic, but there was confusion about the location of the Barracudas, who were supposed to be out ahead. Bullets passing overhead were all going the wrong way—from inland toward the incoming boats.

While still cursing the Navy for dumping him in chest-deep water when, he thought, he could have been landed on the dry beach, Private First Class Stanley Grablick, of Headquarters Company, 1st Battalion, 172nd Infantry, plopped down at the water's edge with his squad leader, Sergeant Stanley Smith. There, Grablick dismantled his waterlogged rifle and set the pieces out to dry. No sooner done than the two heard several bullets zing by their heads. They ducked and cursed some more. Then there was a sudden flurry of heavy fire followed by a confusing silence. Since no more bullets seemed to be coming their way, Grablick and Smith ventured forth to see what they could see. A short distance from the beach, they ran into a knot of riflemen from B Company, 172nd, standing at the base of a tree. Secured by ropes high up in the tree was a dead Japanese sniper. Fortunately, no other snipers fired on the crowd of overexcited naifs of B Company.

Aboard Admiral Turner's flagship, transport *McCawley*, Vice Admiral Bill Halsey turned to a 43rd Division staff officer and asked when the division forward command post was scheduled to go ashore. The Army officer told Halsey that the assistant division commander, Brigadier General Leonard Wing, planned to

head for the beach right behind the 172nd Infantry. Against strong
and concerned advice, the area commander said that he wanted to
accompany General Wing. The command boat grounded about
fifty yards from the beach and all hands, including Admiral Halsey, were obliged to wade under sniper fire through hip-deep
water. Halsey never wavered. Wet to the belt, he inspected troops
on the beach in an unhurried, unruffled manner and, in due course,
left for *McCawley*.

Within the confined beachhead there milled Seabees with work
to do, straggling infantrymen, a few Marines who were supposed
to set up light antiaircraft batteries, and a very few individuals who
knew what they were doing but could not quite get it done. To add
to the confusion, overzealous boat crews rushed to carry reinforcements and equipment ashore in second and third round trips between the beach and the transports. The scene was mindboggling
in its disorganization.

The confusion became dangerous when groups of Japanese recovered and began spraying the entire beachhead from machine-
gun emplacements set through the interior of Rendova Plantation.
American counterfire was uncontrolled, sporadic, and generally
inaccurate. The infantry threw everything it had at the Japanese,
and the crews of beached landing craft zealously fired machine guns
over the heads of the assault troops, adding to the general confusion and terror by pinning the friendly infantry from the rear while
the Japanese took care of the front.

The situation became somewhat less anxious as a few officers and
noncommissioned officers, cooler than the rest, began taking some
initiative. In time, organized groups of infantrymen began mopping up the defenders. Hastily contrived skirmish lines advanced
along a general front through the plantation area. Snipers were
painstakingly flushed, and carefully concealed machine-gun nests
began falling to the slowly organizing American riflemen.

The Americans did not come up against any organized defenses
until they reached the Pengui River. There, a particularly accurate
fusillade greeted the leading elements. A base of fire was established by the stalled Americans along the riverbank and, for the
first time, mortars were brought to bear against the dug-in Japanese emplacements.

Miraculously, only four Americans were killed, and only five
were wounded. One of the wounded was Colonel Ross, of the

172nd Infantry, who was creased in the arm. Sixty-five Japanese, including the garrison commander, died.

The first word of the landings to reach Munda came by way of signal lanterns; all radio batteries on Rendova had been ruined by the heavy rains of the preceding night and morning hours.

With the Japanese on the run, ground action for June 30 ended. As soon as it was quiet, First Lieutenant Ben Sportsman, commanding F Company, 172nd Infantry, ordered his platoons to dig in a short distance from the beach. The entire 2nd Battalion was to develop a defensive cordon to screen the unloading of supplies and from which further advances into the interior might be launched. As soon as the troops began digging foxholes, Lieutenant Sportsman heard griping that the ground was so waterlogged that the foxholes immediately filled with water and collapsed. In time, the entire 2nd Battalion was ordered to head for high ground where, presumably, the water table was unreachable.

Japanese artillery emplaced around Munda contested the easy American victory by firing intermittently at the transport fleet. The only hit scored by these guns was in the form of a 4.7-inch shell that plowed into the main deck aft of destroyer *Gwin*. It killed three sailors. *Gwin* was ordered to retire; as she did, she laid a smoke screen to obscure the transports. Veteran destroyers *Buchanan* and *Farenholt* were sent in to engage the shore batteries, and did so with a vengeance, knocking out seven guns. Brief exchanges continued through the day, but no further hits were scored on the shipping in Rendova Harbor.

While the 172nd Infantry slowly expanded the beachhead against spotty opposition, shore parties were falling down on the job for the reason they had been falling down on previous jobs: combat troops were being used for beach labor details, a task to which they were, at best, apathetically inclined.

It was bad enough that the laborers looked down on laboring, but they had to labor to move material that bordered on the asinine. In addition to vital supplies and equipment, the unloading zone was soon cluttered to capacity with tentage, camp chairs, officers' locker boxes, barracks bags, and other personal items. That drove the cursing shore party mad, almost to a man.

Nature took her toll as well. As hundreds of sweating, swearing men hauled heavy crates over the rainsoaked beach, as heavy rolling stock traversed the cargo areas, the spongy ground was churned into an endless bog. Eventually, wheeled vehicles were skidding, then miring, then being abandoned. The culverts of the few crude roadways had been adjudged strong enough to support heavy vehicles, but they simply disappeared along with the mired roadway, vastly increasing the mayhem.

After a short time, the only vehicles getting through the mud were the 9th Marine Defense Battalion's tracked prime movers and semitracked trailers, the Seabee tractors, and the heavy tracked prime movers of several heavy artillery batteries. A detachment of the 24th Naval Construction Battalion found itself fighting to clear the western beach. Seabee bulldozer operators tried to open a road under intermittent sniper fire while other Seabees began felling trees and cutting them into twelve-foot lengths for corrugating the roadway. This expedient was fine for the tracked vehicles, but the spinning wheels of ordinary trucks and jeeps were soon throwing the logs in all directions as the trucks and jeeps sank into the mud. The Seabee bulldozers then had to be used to pull out the imbedded vehicles; the bulldozers were lashed to large coconut palms for traction before painstakingly winching each truck or jeep onto the semisolid ground beside the putative road.

Captain Hank Reichner's A Battery, 9th Marine Defense Battalion, was having a gruesome time setting in its four new 155mm guns. Again, it was the mud; despite intelligence information about "good" roads, it was almost impossible—even with tracked prime movers—for the battery to get through to its positions. In fact, so far as Captain Reichner could see, his battery's tractors and tracklaying trailers were the only vehicles moving, except for similar equipment that belonged to the Seabees.

Despite the Herculean efforts of the Seabees, the burden eventually fell to the backs of men. All ammunition, food, gear, defensive weapons, and assorted paraphernalia had to be manhandled to the proliferating dumps and defensive positions, bivouacs, and headquarters.

Conditions along the beach forced the longshoremen to wade up to fifty feet into the surf to unload lighters. Eventually, overworked bulldozers pushed coral fill into the water to provide shallow ramps for the movement ashore. In an effort to relieve some of the congestion on the main beach, many landing craft were rerouted to hurriedly designated points on the barrier islets. However, with very nearly all the heavy rolling stock out of service, the Navy transports in the harbor were soon ordered to secure.

Once again, the frightfully expensive lessons of Guadalcanal were overlooked, and there were consequences. But for the terrible condition of the ground, most of the problems might have been of rather less consequence. It was a very good thing for all concerned that the unloading did not take place under hostile guns.

For all the problems encountered in getting ashore, and for all the problems looming as a result of being ashore, the vital toehold had been seized. The main event had been a tactical success.

7

O nce the Rendova landings were well under way, twenty-nine AirSols fighters from Guadalcanal and Advance Base Knucklehead appeared overhead—right on schedule—to form the day's first combat air patrol. (There should have been thirty-two fighters in the initial relay, but two had had to abort and one crashed on takeoff, killing its pilot.) These friendly fighters, and relays from numerous land-based Marine and Navy squadrons, would be aloft over friendly beaches from dawn until dusk every day of the operation. As soon as Seabees could complete the proposed fighter strip at Segi, several friendly squadrons would move directly into the combat zone to provide on-call fighter protection.

On the down side that day was the news that Major General George Kenney's New Guinea–based Fifth Air Force had not been able to hit Rabaul's airfield complexes with more than twenty-five spoiling sorties in the five days preceding the landings. This disappointing turn of events was caused by poor weather. The result was that the powerful Japanese air groups based in the Bismarcks posed a serious threat to the fledgling operation. The counterpunch was not long in arriving.

The Rabaul-based 11th Air Fleet dispatched twenty-six twin-engine Betty medium bombers and eight single-engine carrier bombers shortly after dawn. This strike picked up seventy-two Zero fighters over Bougainville and made direct for Rendova.

The moment news of the approaching Japanese air strike was received by the invasion fleet from Coastwatchers occupying observation posts around Bougainville, the second relay of thirty-two Marine and Navy F4U Corsair and F4F Wildcat fighters scrambled to join the twenty-nine Marine and Navy Corsairs and Wildcats already on station.

Captain Bruce Porter was leading six other orbiting Corsairs from the early Knucklehead contingent when the Japanese strike approached the anchorage behind the 10,000-foot cloud ceiling over Rendova. The first inkling Porter had that Rendova was under enemy air attack came when forty or fifty Zeros suddenly emerged

from around the cloud cover right in front of his face. It happened
that fast.

The nine-plane Japanese fighter squadrons, arranged in vee-of-
vees formation, struck simultaneously from several directions. The
Japanese fighters all had the advantage of altitude and they all arrived from out of what little sun there was. American shipborne
radar had completely dropped the ball. Porter also saw bomber
formations slip through far below, but there was no way he or any
other Corsair or Wildcat pilot could attack the bombers when there
were so many Zeros to fend off.

The chatter in Porter's earphones overwhelmed his efforts to
exert any influence over his subordinates' actions. Initially, there
were only the twenty-nine Knucklehead fighters to challenge the
oncoming Zeros; it would take many minutes before the thirty-two
combat-air-patrol fighters could pitch into the battle.

The first individual Japanese warplane Captain Porter focused
on was a Zero, which was passing a dozen feet below his Corsair's
nose at high speed from left to right. The Zero was on the tail of
a smoking Marine Corsair. Porter, a superbly trained fighter pilot
who had scored his first kill in his first combat sortie over the Russells several weeks earlier, instinctively yanked around sharply to
his right to try to get on the Zero's tail, at least to scare him off
the damaged Marine fighter.

The Zero was less than 300 yards ahead and Porter was closing
when his reflector gunsight fell right on the Zero's nose. Porter
coldly squeezed his trigger for three seconds. Every third round
out of the Corsair's six .50-caliber wing guns was a tracer. He saw
a whole line of them fall right into the Zero's engine cowling. At
first, pieces of debris flew off the Zero's engine. Then the Zero
disintegrated right in front of Porter, and he flew through the
maelstrom of metal and burning fuel. The kill had taken less than
seven seconds from the moment he first saw the Zero flash by.

Porter had not yet recovered from his right turn when a blue
Corsair passed from right to left in front of his propeller disk. It
was his wingman, First Lieutenant Phil Leeds, who Porter had
shaken loose when he turned into the Zero seconds earlier. Leeds
was right at Porter's altitude and 500 yards to the left by the time
Porter boosted power to follow him. Only then did Porter notice
the twin streams of pink tracer that were chasing Leeds's tail. Yet
another Zero flashed into view from over Porter's left shoulder. He

was stunned by the size of the red "meatball" emblem set against the Japanese fighter's shiny aluminum fuselage.

Porter immediately reversed course by turning hard to the left, and quickly brought his reflector sight onto the Zero chasing Leeds. He had the Zero in the sight in a split second and fired a full four-second burst, which struck the Zero in the starboard side, in the engine and around the cockpit. The Zero stayed with Leeds, so Porter gave him another burst. And another. And a fourth. By then, Porter could see smoke trailing from the Zero's engine. He had an instant to see the Zero pull up, but he lost him when his attention was wrenched to thoughts of his own survival.

Porter's first inkling that his exposed tail had acquired a stalker came in the form of brief, bright flash to the right. Porter caught the 20mm round in the corner of his eye just as it blooped into his starboard wing and tore a two-inch hole between the aileron and the wing-gun magazine. The Corsair shook and jerked as dual streams of 7.7mm rounds also struck the Corsair's starboard wing.

Porter saw the Zero flick past his rearview mirror, but before he could do anything, a 7.7mm bullet passed through his Corsair's Plexiglas canopy, fortunately without causing any damage. He could not shake the Zero. The Japanese pilot followed move for move for agonizing seconds. Porter was growing desperate as he realized that only a lucky break could save him from being shot down and perhaps killed.

Without warning, the stream of bullets let up. Porter followed through with his next two or three maneuvers before he realized that the Zero was gone. He dared a quick peek into his rearview mirror and saw that Lieutenant Leeds was closing into his usual off-wing position. Clearly, Leeds had chased Porter's tormentor away.

The Zero's bullets had damaged the engine of Porter's Corsair so, after flying across the beach at Munda to verify the loss of one of Porter's closest friends, Porter and Leeds flew back to Knuckle-head.

Captain Bruce Porter was credited with one confirmed kill and one probable. Three members of his squadron were credited with three kills apiece. Japanese records indicated the loss of eighteen bombers and thirty-one fighters from this strike group.

Fortunately, the American fighters met the Japanese strike well

away from the transports. However, because the shipping was
forced to maneuver at high speed to avoid being hit, two hours of
precious unloading time were lost.

Admiral Turner called it a day at 1505. He had been as lucky
as he dared hope. His ships left with a combined total of 50 tons
of gear in their holds. This was far less than many of these same
ships had *themselves* hauled away on D-Day at Guadalcanal, less
than a year earlier.

Turner would have been gratified to know that one interested
observer labeled the movement ashore as "absolutely miraculous."
Major General Noburo Sasaki had watched most of the day's efforts from his command post atop Kokengolo Hill, in the middle
of the Munda complex, and he was mesmerized by the spectacle.

At about 1530, the transports were informed that a forty-nine-
plane Japanese air strike was on the way; twenty-four Betty medium bombers and twenty-five Zero fighters were looking for a kill.
Finding no shipping in Rendova Harbor, the Japanese continued
southward toward Guadalcanal in the hope of catching Turner in
open waters. In the meantime, an air liaison team aboard one of
Turner's escorting destroyers coached sixteen Marine fighters into
a collision with the Japanese. Amid shouts of "Go get 'em, boys!"
and "Protect your shipping," the Marine aviators destroyed several of the highly combustible bombers.

On the water, the double column of transports continued on
course with their high broadsides exposed to the incoming strike.
As the bombers commenced their attack runs, Turner ordered an
emergency 90-degree turn to starboard, which brought the narrow
sterns of the ships into the bombardiers' sights and gave antiaircraft guns more time to chew away at the shallow-diving formations.

Only about ten of the bombers succeeded in getting through the
Marine fighters. Aboard *McCawley*, which had carried Turner's flag
for over a year, Commander Robert Rodgers ordered vain maneuvers to avoid torpedoes coming in on his port quarter. *McCawley*
was struck high amidships, beside the engine room, and went dead
in the water.

Seventeen of the twenty-five Bettys were downed. For days to
come, ships plying these waters would pass the green-lifejacketed
remains of Japanese airmen. Altogether, Marine and Navy fighter
pilots claimed 101 kills for the day, but this number was reduced,

after a thorough investigation, to 66 confirmed kills and 15 prob-ables, plus two Japanese airplanes definitely damaged.

McCawley was dead in the water, her engine room and after hold flooded; a second hold was slowly filling with water. There was, thankfully, no fire. Admiral Turner and his staff transferred to destroyer *Farenholt* while destroyer *Ralph Talbot* took off most of the transport's crew, fifteen of whom had died and eight of whom had been wounded in the blast. *Libra*, a cargoman, passed a tow to the cripple and, with two escorting destroyers, continued the re-tirement with the remainder of the transports. Eight Japanese Val dive-bombers cut through the overcast at 1715 and planted bombs ahead of *Libra*, and three Japanese aircrews succumbed to ships' fire; one, in fact, fell to *McCawley*'s own after machine gun.

The small salvage crew aboard the stricken transport fought a generally downhill battle. The ship continued to settle by the stern. Finally, the salvage crew transferred to destroyer *McCalla*; the transport seemed to be a sure loss. Fleet tug *Pawnee* arrived from Guadalcanal to take the tow from *Libra*, but the line then parted. Admiral Turner, aboard *Farenholt*, was debating with himself over the need to scuttle the veteran transport, but the matter was set-tled for him when a pair of torpedoes struck the cripple. She went under at 2023. No one knew where the torpedoes had come from, though nearly everyone assumed they had been fired by a lurking Japanese submarine. The fleet hurriedly retired from the scene.

As to the source of the torpedoes that sent *McCawley* under, it is clear that they were fired by friendly PT boats on the way from Guadalcanal to New Georgia—a case of mistaken identity.

In the course of the first day's action, the Allies lost a total of seventeen fighters to enemy fire and operational accidents. Eight of the downed pilots were saved from the water by amphibian res-cue aircraft and PT boats. For all their efforts, Japanese aviators got an "assist" on *McCawley*.

American aircraft carried out numerous offensive strikes on D-Day, mainly in direct support of ground forces. Vila Field was struck by sixteen bomb-equipped TBF Avenger torpedo bombers and twelve SBD Dauntless dive-bombers, and an afternoon strike by twenty-five twin-engine medium bombers, eighteen Daunt-lesses, and eighteen bomb-equipped Avengers hit Munda Field. Damage from the two air-base strikes closed down both runways, which forced the Japanese air groups based in the north to mount their counterstrikes without the benefit of runways near the battle zone on which they could land damaged aircraft that might otherwise have reached safety. Lack of close-in emergency runways was precisely the factor that had turned the tide of the air war at Guadalcanal against Japan, and it was precisely the reason why the Japanese had built the two tantalizing Central Solomons air bases so close to Allied air bases.

During the night of June 30–July 1, the Rabaul-based 8th Fleet attempted to strike a blow against the beachhead. A strong infantry force was hastily assembled in the Shortland Islands for a counterlanding at Rendova. However, only five destroyers managed to make the rendezvous to pick up the troops. These ships moved southward around Vella Lavella and arrived off Rendova at about 0130 on July 1. The same rain squalls that had hung over the area all day were still relatively stationary, restricting visibility. The Japanese navigators could not find the point designated for the disembarkation of the infantry. After searching for as long as they thought prudent, the destroyer captains turned their ships about and made for safer waters.

Despite all the enervating setbacks encountered through the day, the Allies had achieved a very definite victory on June 30, 1943. What had been and would continue to be the very hardest part of an amphibious undertaking—getting the troops into a fairly secure foothold on an otherwise hostile beach—had been successfully accomplished. And all manner of counterstrokes had been blunted without drastic loss.

8

Among the jumble of side operations concurrent with the landings at Rendova was the mission against the Japanese garrison at Vangunu Island, which sits immediately east of New Georgia about one mile from Segi Point—astride the main supply route between the Russells and Rendova.

Although early reconnaissance revealed that Vangunu would itself be of little value as a base, it was lightly held and, as such, might present a danger to the flow of supplies required at Rendova. Wickham Anchorage, a well-situated sheltered harbor tucked behind a string of protective coral heads, lay immediately to the west of the island.

An amphibious scouting party sent to Vangunu in June reported that the proposed landing site at Oliana Bay, on the southeastern coast, was more than adequate for the task, and that the landing phase could probably be carried out in complete safety due to the sparsity of defenses throughout the island. In fact, occupying forces consisted of a single platoon of the 1st Battalion, 229th Infantry, and a company of *rikusentai*.

Rear Admiral George Fort, who was commanding this as well as other subsidiary D-Day operations, decided to land over a full battalion against Vangunu, mainly because the June reconnaissance team had been discovered and, it was assumed, the garrison was alert to danger.

Selected for the landing was Lieutenant Colonel Lester Brown's 2nd Battalion, 103rd Infantry. As the landing-force commander, Brown would have nominal command over an antiaircraft battery and half of the 20th Naval Construction Battalion. At the last minute, Admiral Fort also added the uncommitted elements—two companies—of 4th Marine Raider Battalion to Brown's command. Direct fire support was to be provided by B Battery, 152nd Field Artillery Battalion, and a medium weapons battery of the 70th Coast Artillery Battalion. Two fleet destroyers would be on hand to provide gunfire support.

The plan of action, which was a bit complex for a mixed force of novices, directed the Raiders to land at Oliana Bay before dawn from destroyer-transports *McKean* and *Schley*. The first men ashore were to establish contact with First Lieutenant James Lamb's three-officer scouting party, which had been left by a larger scouting party to mark the beaches. Thirty minutes after the Raiders had landed, seven LCIs were to haul in the leading echelon of Brown's infantry battalion. The remainder of the force would disembark from seven additional LCIs in midmorning.

Lieutenant Colonel Brown's infantry force was to strike inland to widen the beachhead. As the main body moved inland, Captain Irv Chappell's E Company, 103rd, reinforced by the battalion's 81mm mortar platoon, was to skirt the beach and advance eastward toward Vura Bay, which was reportedly the main Japanese supply base for the area. Chappell was expected to come up against about 100 Japanese at Vura.

The flotilla arrived on station without difficulty and, up to the point at which the destroyer-transports began debarking the Raiders—about 0230, June 30—the operation went quite smoothly. Soon after 0230, however, the plan began deteriorating into something only a bit short of chaos.

Amphibious warfare had not progressed by this stage of the war much beyond doctrinal theorems. Complex operations could not be carried out effectively by partially trained troops in the hands of inexperienced boat crews under the command of classroom trained officers operating with experimental plans.

Lieutenants James Lamb, Ellis Satterthwaite, and Frederick Burnaby, the three pathfinders who were to be picked up by the Raiders, had eluded the Japanese for several weeks so that their efforts might add to the success of the operation. They arrived at the appointed place right on schedule after enduring no end of privation and placed their signal lights in the proper positions. But their courageous sacrifices were for naught. The destroyers and LCIs arrived in the middle of a heavy downpour and the signal, a series of lighted dots and dashes, could not be seen from seaward.

In addition to the downpour, helmsmen were put off by the consistent chop of the sea. The weapons-laden Marines groped their way into their bobbing rafts and LCVPs, which the chop tossed out from under them. It was to be, in all ways, a blind landing. Radar, which might have eased some of the burden, was represented in its entirety by a crude old set aboard Admiral Fort's flagship, minesweeper *Trever*. The ships simply could not be brought to accurate positions relative to predetermined reference points ashore. Someone was bound to suffer.

Admiral Fort had every reason to suppose that the elements were going to destroy his operation, so he ordered the Raiders to stop what they were doing. This might have been the correct solution, but it was poorly transmitted. The Raiders continued to mount out for the beach.

At 0345, while the Raiders were right in the middle of the tricky disembarkation maneuver, the transport commanders decided that their ships were incorrectly positioned, so they moved them about 1,000 yards to the east. Once at the new station, more Raiders were sent over the sides of the transports. The result was a thorough dispersion of the landing craft. Regaining contact among and between small units proved a feat completely beyond the capabilities of the boat crews. Barely knowing which way the beach lay, the coxswains began putting their charges ashore at widely dispersed points along a seven-mile stretch of Vangunu coastline. This feat was topped only by the complete demolition of six landing craft in the pounding surf, miraculously without loss of life. Fortunately, the scattered groups of Raiders met no opposition and were able to regroup, after a fashion, within a relatively short time.

The first waves of the 2nd Battalion, 103rd, landed from calmer seas at about 0700. As it turned out, the landing of the battalion was, in the words of the battalion operations officer, "a screwed-up mess." Lieutenant Lamb's wristwatch, which was used to time the signal for landing, was five or ten minutes fast, and the LCI commanders missed the signal. After churning about in confusion, the LCIs landed the troops, who were badly seasick. This meant that the battalion was in no position to do anything useful until late in the day.

The remainder of the landing force—two antiaircraft batteries, a battery of 105mm howitzers, and the Seabees—began landing an hour after Brown's battalion. During that time, Lieutenant Lamb reported in to inform Lieutenant Colonel Brown that the Japanese had all moved from Vura Village to Kaeruka Village, about 1,000 yards northeast of Vura Bay, on another coastal indentation.

The main body of Brown's infantry force—half of Headquarters Company, 4th Raiders; N and Q Companies, 4th Raiders; most of H Company, 103rd Infantry: all of F and G Companies, 103rd Infantry; Brown's headquarters; and eight local guides—

would swing inland over a hopefully undiscovered Coastwatcher track to a high-ground position some seven miles from the beachhead. The hilly terrain just east of the Kaeruka River, about 700 yards from the objective, would provide a line of departure for the attack. Oliana Bay was left to the artillery and antiaircraft batteries and busy Seabees.

In occupying Vura Village, Captain Irv Chappell's E Company, 103rd, was opposed by sixteen Japanese armed with rifles and a pair of 7.7mm Nambu light machine guns. The company 60mm mortars quickly reduced this minor opposition and the company quickly established a base of fire from which the battalion's 81mm mortars could support the assault on Kaeruka Village.

The hard, driving downpour of the early morning had turned the Coastwatcher track into a slick, muddy jungle-walled gash, and the Vura and Kaeruka Rivers were rushing in shoulder-deep torrents. Strong swimmers strung heavy ropes across these obstacles at great personal risk, and the troops slowly crossed by pulling themselves hand over hand.

It took until 1320 for Lieutenant Colonel Brown and his officers to position the assault companies. The American force finally jumped off at 1405 without the planned initial 81mm mortar support because the rains had forced a shutdown in communications between Brown's headquarters and Chappell's mortars.

Q Company, 4th Raiders, moved in along the meandering Kaeruka with orders to cross farther south and turn the Japanese left flank. N Company, 4th Raiders, drove straight for the Japanese center. On the left, Captain Ray Brown's F Company, 103rd, began a partial envelopment of the Japanese right. G Company, 103rd, under Captain Ollie Hood, was in reserve, ready to exploit any weakness discovered or developed in the Japanese lines, and to strengthen and protect the assault force's flanks.

Off to Q Company's right, the Kaeruka River made a 300-yard loop eastward before turning south for a 350-yard run to the sea. This long bend partially enclosed the Japanese encampment, which was situated directly on the coast, and made the stream a formidable obstacle to be overcome by the Raiders.

Fifteen minutes after jumping off, Captain William Flake's Q Company began drawing fire from Japanese snipers concealed in trees and spider holes. As the Marines deployed to deliver their attack, they became targets for considerably heavier fire from prepared positions across the river. At 1445, Major James Clark, the 4th Raider Battalion executive officer and commander of the Raiders on Vangunu, ordered his Marines to begin crossing the river, reduce opposition as it was encountered, and carry out a direct assault upon the Japanese main line.

Flake's Q Company struggled into the water over the steep, slippery near bank, crossed the rushing stream, and struggled up the steep, slippery far bank. Captain Earle Snell's N Company, however, encountered so much Japanese fire that only one squad could make it to the opposite bank. The assault was stopped.

Contact between the Raiders and the adjoining Army unit had been broken. As Captains Flake and Snell sought to refuse their companies, patrols were dispatched to reestablish contact between the dangling flanks of the Raider companies and Captain Ray Brown's adjacent F Company, 103rd.

From its position on the left, Captain Brown's F Company tried to envelop several Japanese machine guns it had run into from its own right. This maneuver widened the gap between F and N Companies, so Lieutenant Colonel Brown ordered Captain Ollie Hood's G Company to fill the gap and thus restore the continuous front line. Hood's advance from the rear was carried out against light opposition.

Despite the groping to regain contact between the various companies, the Americans had succeeded in breaching the Japanese line. G Company slid between N and F Companies and reached ahead all the way to the beach. As soon as the Japanese realized that the attackers were now in their rear, those facing the Raiders and F Company, 103rd, gave way in complete disorder.

As the resistance in front of Q Company faded, N Company sprang rapidly ahead through the forest to exploit the confusion resulting from G Company's breakthrough. In the meantime, the assault broke free from the control of the force commander, whose command group was mired in the woods a good 1,000 yards behind the scene of the action, on the far side of the Kaeruka. Fortunately the action was nearing its conclusion. The Raiders drove southwestward from either side of the river and pressed on to the beach below Kaeruka Village. F Company quickly overcame the last of the opposition on its front and drove to the beach on the heels of the Marines.

Twenty-two American soldiers and Marines died in the drive on Kaeruka, and forty-three were wounded. The victors counted one hundred twenty Japanese corpses on the battlefield.

While the Army battalion's command group was struggling forward, Marine Major James Clark, the senior officer with the assaults units, established an all-around defensive perimeter between the beach and the east bank of the Kaeruka River. Clark immediately ordered out strong combat patrols to mop up straggling Japanese, but the onset of darkness forced them to return to the perimeter before any contacts were made. Lieutenant Colonel Brown's headquarters was obliged to spend a tense, eerie night in the rain forest on the far side of the river.

Japanese mortars fired sporadically on Kaeruka through the night, and the northern defenses were strafed by automatic weapons emplaced in the forest. However, the Japanese made no effort to infiltrate any American positions during the dark hours.

Major Clark's combat force hit the jackpot at about 0200, July 1. Troops manning the beach-defense line reported that three Japanese landing barges were approaching their positions. Major Clark assumed that this was a supply flotilla bent on bringing food and reinforcements to the now-dispersed Vangunu Butai. In fact, the barges had been sent before the American landings to evacuate the garrison in accordance with Major General Noburo Sasaki's wishes to concentrate all available forces in eastern New Georgia.

Tense, tired troop commanders on the beach quietly passed the word along the line of rifle pits near the water's edge: Wait. The Americans steadied up and awaited the order that would, hopefully, compound the success of the afternoon. The Japanese craft glided closer to the reception being prepared by Captain Hood's G Company, 103rd, and the 4th Raider Battalion's demolitions platoon.

A terse order was passed: "Fire!" A concentrated burst of small-arms and automatic-weapons fire erupted at the three landing craft, sending them foundering and drifting out of control. Japanese voices called out. The occupants of the barges were clearly certain that they were being fired on by friends, so they did not return the fire. The incoming tide moved the drifting barges closer to the beach. Next, Q Company Marines began firing rifle grenades. That was enough; the Japanese returned the fire in self-defense. Dark human shapes were seen vaulting the gunwales of the drifting craft, running through the shallow water. Most of these men were killed by hand grenades from the Raider demolitions platoon. One of the barges sank a few yards from the beach, its occupants silent. The others broached to in the surf.

The fight was over within thirty minutes. Out of an estimated 120 Japanese on board the three craft—mostly evacuees from other outlying bases—109 were killed, as were just 3 Americans.

In the morning, Lieutenant Colonel Brown established his command post at Kaeruka and dispatched combat patrols back into the surrounding forest to flush out snipers and stragglers. During the remainder of the day, patrols discovered that the remnants of the Vangunu Butai were beginning to concentrate in a defensive sector about 500 yards east of the Kaeruka River. After contemplating his prospects for holding his prize, Lieutenant Colonel Brown decided to march his entire force back to Vura Village so it could help defend the gunners and Seabees there. The artillery emplaced at Oliana Bay, together with available air support, could more cheaply neutralize the local Japanese force than could a direct infantry assault.

The march from Kaeruka to Vura on July 1 was disrupted at odd intervals by brief flurries of harassing fire from deep within the forest. However, the Japanese refrained from coming into direct, strong contact with so large a force of confident, victorious Americans.

As soon as Brown's main body had installed itself at Vura, strong combat patrols were again dispatched to reconnoiter and harass the main Japanese defenses near Cheke Point. The 105mm howitzers emplaced at Vura spent the day registering on the Japanese position, and they began firing in earnest on July 2. Also on July 2, Admiral Fort's flagship, minesweeper *Trever*, fired her 3-inch guns at the Japanese at Cheke Point. On July 3, eighteen Marine Dauntless dive-bombers ripped into the fight as Lieutenant Colonel Brown dispatched a strong infantry force against the Japanese base. Kaeruka was reoccupied without a fight, and the Cheke Point position fell after offering desultory opposition. Prisoners revealed that the main force had been safely evacuated the night before. Supply and ammunition dumps were destroyed and seven Japanese corpses were buried.

Major James Clark's force of Raiders was shuttled to Oliana Bay from Cheke Point on July 4. It rested there until July 9, then set off to Gatuki Island to confront a reported 50 to 100 Japanese based there; Clark's Marines spent two days fruitlessly searching an uninhabited island, though abandoned bivouacs attested to recent occupation. The Raiders were shipped to Guadalcanal on July 12 to be reunited with the portions of the 4th Raider Battalion that had been active at Segi and Viru.

Despite the confusion encountered at the outset, the occupation of Vangunu had been admirably acquitted.

9

On the morning of July 1, 1943, infantrymen of the 172nd Infantry Regiment began a cautious expansion of the Rendova beachhead against spotty opposition. As the infantry companies sought to clear a wider working area, static defense units, such as 9th Marine Defense Battalion, set to work on defensive emplacements thoughout the occupied areas of Rendova Plantation. Reconnaissance and command teams selected likely looking sites for weapons emplacements, command posts, observation posts, fire direction centers, fields of fire, ammunition and supply dumps, and bivouacs. Miles of a dozen different types of wire were strung over the area, and whole stands of palm trees were blasted up by the roots.

At the top of the agenda for defensive units was the siting of antiaircraft weapons as proof against the expected massive Japanese aerial effort against the invasion forces. This was a job at which American units excelled, even at this relatively early stage of the war. For example, the 90mm antiaircraft guns of E Battery, 9th Defense Battalion, were emplaced on Kokorana Island and in action against low-flying Japanese fighters by 1645 on D-Day, despite the temporary loss of the battery's gun director, which had to be rescued by tediously sifting through mounds of gear all over Rendova. The battalion's Special Weapons Group emplaced twelve 40mm, eight 20mm, and eighteen .50-caliber automatic antiaircraft weapons by the end of the first day.

The agenda for July 1 mainly called for the expansion of the area under Allied control on Rendova. Lieutenant Colonel Jim Wells's 3rd Battalion, 103rd Infantry, was chosen to take part in a mission that would nearly double the area under domination: As soon as resistance at the beachhead was overcome, plans called for a combat patrol to lay wire down the west shore of Rendova to Poco Plantation, a small farmstead about three miles to the south. The patrol was to clear the area of any Japanese and remain to cover the landing of the 3rd Battalion, 103rd, on the morning of July 1. On approach of the battalion in four LCIs, the patrol was to fire a green flare indicating the area was clear, or a red flare indicating there was resistance that the patrol could not overcome, in which case the troop-laden LCIs were to stand off. Lieutenant Colonel Wells felt that the last detail was vital because LCIs were not designed for attack landings; when the bows were run up on the beach, two gangplanks were lowered on either side of the bows and troops descended to the beach in single file. Clearly, enfilade fire from automatic weapons would make such a landing very costly, if possible at all.

Wells's battalion embarked at the Russell Islands on the night of June 30 and arrived off Poco Plantation at dawn on July 1. No signal of any sort was received from the beach. The commander of the LCI flotilla was anxious to discharge the troops and get out of the area before Japanese planes appeared overhead. The mission of the infantry battalion at Poco Plantation was to guard the left flank of the 43rd Infantry Division beachhead from an anticipated attempt at counterinvasion. Unless actually repulsed, therefore, it was necessary for Wells's battalion to land. The LCIs stood off just long enough for Lieutenant Colonel Wells's machine gunners to saw off the tops of rail stanchions so the pintles of their .30-caliber medium machine guns could be set on stable gunnery platforms from which they could provide at least some counterfire if the beach was occupied by the enemy.

Fortunately, the beach was clear. Within the first five minutes, gunners had set up two heavy .50-caliber machine guns on anti-aircraft tripods at each end of the beach. Less than fifteen minutes later, the battalion was strafed by eight low-flying Japanese Zero fighters, which also dropped light antipersonnel bombs. The .50-caliber machine guns got one of the Zeros, and the others did not attempt a second pass.

The brief attack scored no hits on personnel or equipment and barely held up the unloading of troops and gear. The entire battalion and all its equipment was safely unloaded in less than an hour. Some hours later, the combat patrol from Rendova Plantation arrived, laying its telephone wire. Somebody had forgotten to dispatch it the day before.

Also on July 1, the second transport echelon arrived off Rendova Plantation. LCIs and LSTs encountered problems identical to those encountered on D-Day. The shallow-draft boats and ships had to make slow-speed approaches until they grounded in mud quite far from dry beaches. Vehicles from the LSTs ran into the mud, from which they had to be winched by Seabee bulldozers.

The 155mm artillery battalion brought in on July 1 was towed by tracked prime movers, which ground the marginal roadways to mush; the big guns eventually had to be manhandled ashore when the roads gave way completely.

Then it rained. As the terrifying deluge continued to plague the occupation forces, all available personnel were pressed into stevedore service at the beaches. Rations, fuel, ammunition, personal gear, communications equipment, tentage, garbage cans, shovels, tent pegs, toilet paper—everything had to be hand-carried across the beaches and disposed of at central dispersal points, from which they were manhandled to priority dumps or collecting points further inland.

The Seabees were set to work rebuilding the butchered roadways in whatever ways they could. Huge, freshly cut twelve-foot palm logs were manhandled into place in an attempt to reset the corduroy foundation. Then pierced-steel Marston Matting plates were set over the logs. However, the weight of the matting combined with the mass of the prime movers slowly pushed the precarious roadways below the surface of the bottomless glop.

Preselected battery sites once thought to be on dry ground were often found beneath vast boggy expanses. Dispersion of troops was virtually out of the question; soldiers, Seabees, and Marines who attempted to dig foxholes throughout the beachhead area soon owned subterranean mudbaths. The vastly humorous quality of the total situation was, somehow, unappreciated.

Despite all the problems encountered in finding suitable sites and moving into them, 9th Defense Battalion's twin-battery 155mm Gun Group managed to come to some degree of order during July 1. Captain Hank Reichner's A Battery first had to cope with the incredible depth of viscous mud just to get to the battery site. Then the gunners had to cut down about 600 coconut palms so that the trajectory of the weapons was clear. There were communications difficulties, the requirement to get aerial observation for registration, and the necessity of digging foxholes for personal protection. Despite the problems, the four-gun battery succeeded in firing several test salvoes at Munda by nightfall. B Battery was temporarily emplaced by day's end, but it did not fire.

Two of 9th Defense Battalion's 90mm antiaircraft batteries were set up during July 1, and the Special Weapons Group command post was dug in near the battery sites. However, the Marines quickly discovered that underground shelters were impossible to maintain, so they went to work building rather formidable above-ground positions out of coconut logs and sandbags.

The 43rd Division's 192nd Field Artillery Battalion, a 155mm howitzer battalion, did a good deal better than the Marines. Based on Kokorana Island, the battalion gun crews found that the pre-selected battery sites were perched atop a solid coral substratum that could easily support the heavy weapons. And the fields of fire were unobscured by foliage, so the gunners did not have to cut down hundreds of trees. They manhandled the howitzers into po-sition, dug revetments, took general aim at Munda—only 13,000 yards distant—and began firing for effect late in the afternoon of July 1.

Throughout July 1, as artillery and support units struggled with the elements, infantry units continued to push outward. By the time the day's activities ended, the 172nd Infantry, with support-ing units, had beaten over half of Rendova against spotty opposi-tion.

Aerial activity on July 1 was limited. AirSols fighters were called upon to beat back only one attempted Japanese air strike. Twenty-eight bomb-laden Marine torpedo bombers and dive-bombers mounted a strike against Vila, which was rendered inoperable. Before returning to their Guadalcanal bases, fighters escorting the single-engine bombers worked over the Munda defense perimeter with their .50-caliber machine guns. Brigadier General Francis Mulcahy, who was ashore at Rendova and already hard at work as ComAir, New Georgia, organized a fighter sweep against Tombe Village in support of Lieutenant Colonel Mickey Currin's Marine Raider force. In fact, the Tombe strike was the first official strike occurring under Mulcahy's command auspices.

July 2, the third day of the operation, was much like July 1—the weather was bad, the infantry expanded the beachhead, and gunners brought more artillery to bear against the Munda defenses. The artillery fire went completely unanswered. The Japanese could not retaliate.

Shortly after 1330, July 2, the Japanese were finally able to put some figures on their side of the scorecard. The series of events leading to their success says little for their opponents' powers of observation.

The weather over Rendova and New Georgia steadily deterio-

rated in the hour after noon, with the result that the fighter combat air patrol was ordered to return to Advance Base Knucklehead
and Guadalcanal, both for safety's sake and because no one thought
they would be needed in such bleak weather. Next, the only early-
warning radar set in the beachhead was put temporarily out of
commission when someone poured in a load of diesel fuel instead
of the prescribed white gasoline. Finally, the Japanese 11th Air
Fleet had succeeded in scraping up several dozen aircraft with
which to launch a strike none of the aircrews frankly thought they
would survive.

Captain Hank Reichner's 155mm gun battery was firing registration when the first aircraft appeared over the beachhead. In the
course of one of the many delays that occur between rounds in a
registration operation, Reichner noticed a flight of what appeared
to be Army twin-engine B-25s coming in over Rendova Mountain.
An instant later, like others, he realized that they were Betty medium bombers. Reichner's initial surmise and belated recognition
were generally shared throughout the beachhead. A great number
of men were caught in the open when the steel started flying.
There were a few scattered yells of "Condition Red!" before bodies began hurtling for anything vaguely reminiscent of shelter.

Captain Reichner hit his battery executive officer's pit at the
same time as the exec and the battery gunnery sergeant. Though
the simultaneous arrival of the three men lacked dignity, they remained unscathed. However, three of Reichner's gunners were
killed when the battery area was blanketed by bombs a moment
later.

Japanese bombs ripped from one end of the beachhead to the
other. Hardest hit was a small promontory directly behind Reichner's 155mm gun battery. This promontory—known thereafter as
Suicide Point—was occupied by 24th Naval Construction Battalion, and was the location of a five-ton cache of dynamite. When
the TNT went, a lot of men went with it. The largest bulldozer
the Seabees had on Rendova was located near the center of the
blast, and survivors swore that it was tossed into the air, where it
disintegrated. Twenty-three Seabees were killed, many were
wounded, and most of the battalion's camp gear was lost.

The 169th Infantry Regiment, elements of which were just beginning to stage into Rendova from Guadalcanal, took its first casualties as a result of the raid.

Adding to the general mayhem, and no doubt to the loss of life, was the direct hit scored on 43rd Infantry Division's 125-bed casualty clearing station; available assistance to the injured was greatly diminished, though many of the wounded were rushed to ships in the bay for emergency treatment.

Early estimates regarding casualties varied greatly, a fact no doubt attributable to the shuttling of wounded directly to outbound ships without proper recordkeeping. In all, it was eventually verified that sixty-four men were killed and eighty-five were wounded.

Despite the appalling congestion of material on the beaches, damage was relatively light. Two Marine 155mm guns were chipped slightly by shrapnel, two 40mm antiaircraft guns were temporarily out of commission, and two Marine amphibian tractors were damaged and a third was totally demolished.

There were a number of reasons why the raid was so successful. Chief among them was the lack of surveilling radar, which was abetted a good deal by improper identification of the Japanese medium bombers; many men had mistaken a flight of B-25s for Bettys on July 1, and no one really wanted to be seen diving for his muddy foxhole without very good reason. There were large air-raid shelters near the beaches, but lack of time had prevented the placement of adequate protection only a short distance inland. This deficiency was corrected before long, and without much prodding.

During the night of July 2–3, the Japanese launched their first naval counterattack against the New Georgia Occupation Force and its accompanying transports. Light cruiser *Yubari*, a well-blooded old veteran of Wake and a half dozen engagements off Guadalcanal, led nine fleet destroyers into waters off Rendova, from which they all proceeded to pump many 6- and 5-inch shells into the rain forest and palm groves around and in back of the crowded beachhead. The Japanese guns did almost no material damage and caused few if any casualties. While retiring, the flotilla was spotted by a section of PT boats, but the crews of these swift attack craft were overly cautious in looking over prey because they were the same boats that had inadvertently sunk transport *McCawley* on D-Day eve. The Japanese flotilla commander dispatched four of his destroyers to take on the PT boats, and these fired furiously for some time as the Americans made off under smoke cover. Neither side scored on the other.

By July 3, the top Allied commanders had at least one important decision to make. From one standpoint, the Rendova landings had been an unqualified if untidy success, most of the initial objectives had been secured and, thus far, all but one of the Japanese reprisals had been beaten off or were unsuccessful in their own rights. On the other hand, as good as things looked, the most critical point of the undertaking had arrived. The Japanese had had three full days in which to gather reinforcements; more, even, if the count began with the Segi operation. Admiral Halsey's staff had no way of knowing that the original alarm had been cancelled, so it was highly likely that the first infantry reinforcements from outside the area were on the way to New Georgia. In fact, those with past experience viewed the *Yubari* bombardment force as a screen for the landing of reinforcements. Another view, not widely held, was that the *Yubari* force was keeping down the opposition while General Sasaki's entire force was being evacuated from New Georgia. No one knew.

Halsey's staff required that several conditions be met before the force on Rendova could be sent to New Georgia: The Rendova base had to be sufficiently established to support the New Georgia Occupation Force; the Japanese could not hold any of the preselected New Georgia beachhead sites in any strength; friendly forces at Segi, Viru, and Vangunu had to be in position to block any Japanese counterstrokes from those quadrants; local air and naval tactical superiority had to be assured; and ground superiority at the beachhead on New Georgia had to be in favor of the 43rd Division by a factor of at least two to one during the initial landing phase.

In answer to these conditions, South Pacific analysts saw the situation this way: At least a full infantry battalion, and more likely two, would remain on Rendova along with large numbers of combat-trained Seabees and artillerymen; the support base for the main show was very much a going concern despite grotesque early problems; Zanana Beach, the projected beachhead site on New Georgia, appeared to be undefended; Vangunu, Segi, and Viru were secure; local air and naval superiority had been established even prior to the commitment of ground forces to the area, and the

several minor Japanese successes of the past several days had only
served to heighten the awareness of aircrews and naval forces; and
the four or five infantry battalions that would be sent to Zanana
Beach would immediately outnumber available Japanese ground
units by a great deal more than two to one.

Everything seemed to be going for the New Georgia Occupation Force, which would be facing two thinly spread and understrength Japanese infantry regiments and less than a regiment of
rikusentai, almost no aerial opposition, and only a very few Japanese warships. In fact, the Japanese commanders in Rabaul had all
but written New Georgia off; they would commit very few aircraft and no warships larger than light cruisers.

Orders were cut on July 3: All available naval support and
transport was to stage into Rendova Harbor to pick up the initial
strike force of the New Georgia Occupation Force and put it ashore
on Zanana Beach. The move would be carried out under the direct control of the newly established U.S. Third Fleet. The pre-
cise date of the Zanana landing would be determined within a
matter of days, once the Japanese had revealed their intentions in
the area.

Lieutenant Colonel Henry Shafer's 136th Field Artillery Battalion, which had been detached from its parent 37th Infantry Division, was on its way to New Georgia. The 155mm howitzers and
the men who served them were loaded aboard LSTs at Guadalcanal on July 2 and spent the night and most of the next day under cover of the jungle growth hanging over the shore of an island
in the Russells. At 1700, the LSTs rendezvoused with several other
groups of ships to dash to New Georgia under cover of darkness.

Lieutenant Colonel Shafer climbed to the bridge of his LST to
watch the rendezvous and organization of the convoy—and what
appeared to be the start of a race. From where Shafer stood, the
bows of the LST seemed to be shaking and weaving like a reed in
a strong wind. The captain was fixing his gaze on an LST dead
ahead, which seemed to be getting farther ahead by the minute.
After a brief interval, the captain told the startled artillery-
battalion commander that he hoped that his ship could keep that
other LST in sight and that he was giving the engines all they
could take.

Shafer asked what would happen if they lost sight of the blacked-
out leading LST during the night, and the captain told him that

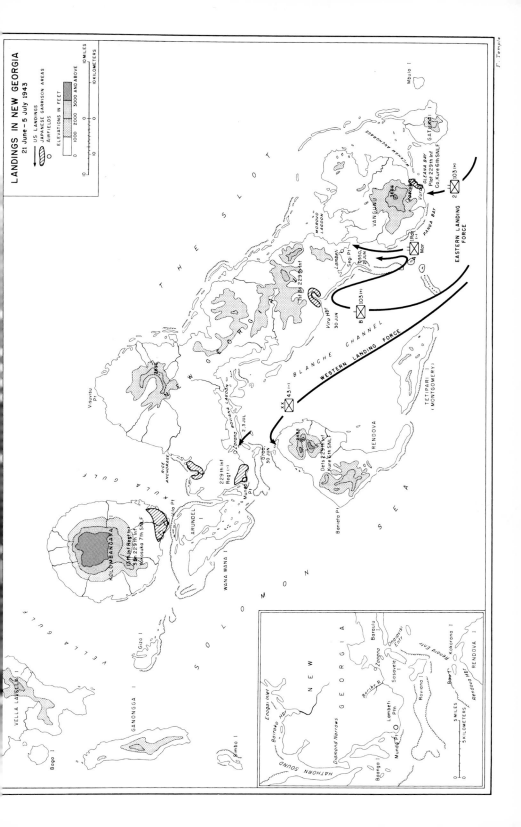

LANDINGS IN NEW GEORGIA
21 June – 5 July 1943

US LANDINGS
JAPANESE GARRISON AREAS
AIRFIELDS

ELEVATIONS IN FEET

| 0 | 1000 | 2000 | 3000 AND ABOVE |

0   10 MILES

0   10 KILOMETERS

F. Temple

Mbulo I

VURA OLEANA BAY
GATUKAI I
Plat 229th Inf
Co. Kure 6th SNLF

VUKELAI

2 | 103(+)

VANGUNU

EASTERN LANDING FORCE

Hd
Mor

PANGA BAY

THE SLOT

MOROVO LAGOON

Lambeti
Segi Pt

550
30 JUN

B | 103(+)

1st Bn 229th Inf

Viru Hbr
30 JUN

BLANCHE CHANNEL

WESTERN LANDING FORCE

TETIPARI
(MONTGOMERY I)

Visuvisu Pt

1875

XX
43(-)

ROVIANA LAGOON

RICE ANCHORAGE

2,3 JUL

Ozanga

0700
30 JUN

838

RENDOVA

SOLOMON SEA

Bonieta Pt

229th Inf Regt (-)

Munda Pt

Via Pt

ARUNDEL I

Dets 229th Inf
Kure 6th SNLF

WANA WANA I

KOLOMBANGARA

13th Inf Regt (-)
3 Bn 229th Inf
Kokosuka 7th SNLF

VELLA GULF

KULA GULF

Vella Lavella I

Baga I

GANONGGA I

Gizo I

Simbo I

NEW GEORGIA

Enogai Inlet

Bairoko Hbr

Diamond Narrows

HATHORN SOUND

Bangai I

Munda Pt

Lambeti Pln

Zanana

Barike R.

Sasavele I

Onaiavisi Entr

Baraulu I

Roviana I

Baanga I

Roviana Entr

Kokorana I

Rendova Hbr

RENDOVA

0   5 MILES

0   5 KILOMETERS

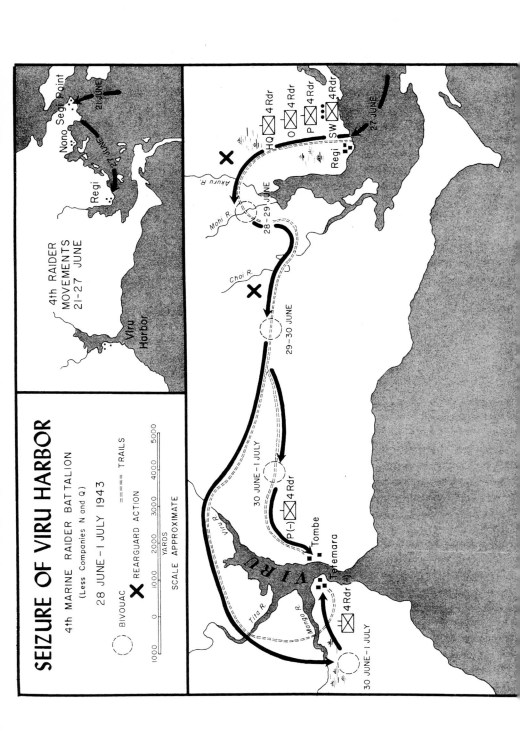

SEIZURE OF VIRU HARBOR

4th MARINE RAIDER BATTALION
(Less Companies N and Q)

28 JUNE - 1 JULY 1943

⊖ BIVOUAC   ✕ REARGUARD ACTION   ===== TRAILS

1000   0   1000   2000   3000   4000   5000
YARDS

SCALE APPROXIMATE

4th RAIDER
MOVEMENTS
21-27 JUNE

Nono   Segi Point
21 JUNE
27 JUNE
Regi
Viru Harbor

27 JUNE
SW 4Rdr
Regi
P 4Rdr
O 4Rdr
HQ 4Rdr
✕
Akuru R.
Mohi R.
28-29 JUNE
Choi R.
✕
29-30 JUNE
Vuru R.
Tita R.
Mango R.
VIRU
Tetemara
4Rdr
30 JUNE-1 JULY
Tombe
P(-) 4Rdr
30 JUNE-1 JULY
30 JUNE-1 JULY

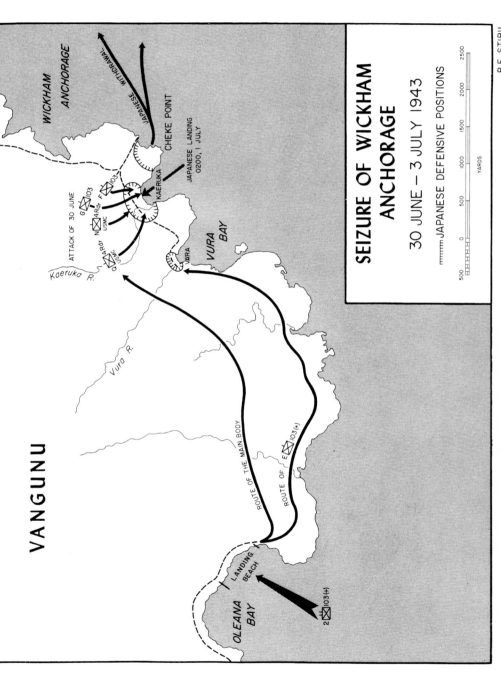

VANGUNU

WICKHAM ANCHORAGE

JAPANESE WITHDRAWAL

CHEKE POINT

KAERUKA

JAPANESE LANDING 0200, I JULY

ATTACK OF 30 JUNE

G 103
4 Rdr F 103 USMC
N USMC
4 Rdr Q 103 USMC

Kaeruka R.

VURA

VURA BAY

Vura R.

ROUTE OF THE MAIN BODY

ROUTE OF E 103 (+)

LANDING BEACH

2 103(+)

OLEANA BAY

SEIZURE OF WICKHAM ANCHORAGE

30 JUNE – 3 JULY 1943

˄˄˄˄˄˄ JAPANESE DEFENSIVE POSITIONS

500   0   500   1000   1500   2000   2500
YARDS

R.F. STIBIL

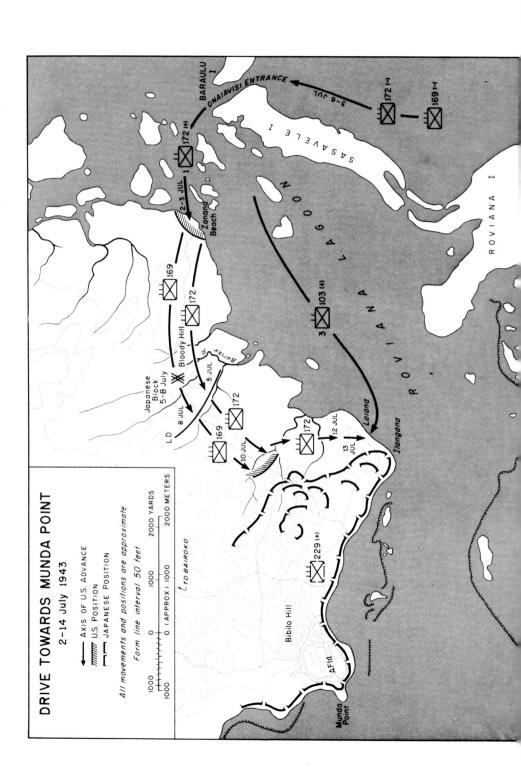

DRIVE TOWARDS MUNDA POINT
2-14 July 1943

→ AXIS OF U.S. ADVANCE
▨ U.S. POSITION
▥ JAPANESE POSITION

All movements and positions are approximate

Form line interval 50 feet

1000   0   1000   2000 YARDS
1000   0 (APPROX) 1000   2000 METERS

BARAULU I

ONAIAVISI ENTRANCE

172 (-)

169 (-)

3-6 JUL

SASAVELE I

ROVIANA I

1 172 (-)

2-3 JUL

Zanana Beach

ROVIANA LAGOON

169

172

Bloody Hill

3 103 (-)

Barike R.

Japanese Block 5-8 July

5 JUL

172

8 JUL

LD

169

10 JUL

172

12 JUL

13 JUL

Laiana

Ilangana

TO BAIROKO

229 (+)

Bibilo Hill

Afld

Munda Point

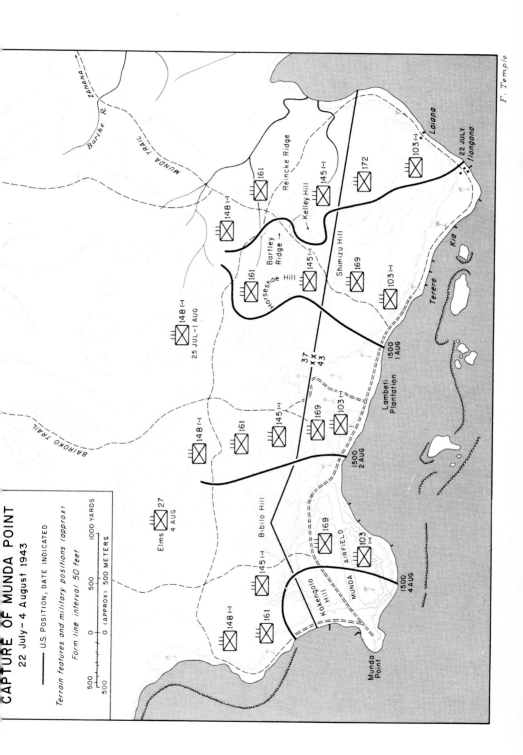

CAPTURE OF MUNDA POINT
22 July–4 August 1943

U.S. POSITION, DATE INDICATED

Terrain features and military positions (approx)

Form line interval 50 feet

500   0   500   1000 YARDS

500   0 (APPROX) 500 METERS

F. Temple

ZANANA

Barike R.

MUNDA TRAIL

BAIROKO TRAIL

148 (–)
161
Reincke Ridge
145 (–)
Kelley Hill
172
103 (–)
Laiana
22 JULY
Ilangana

148 (–)
25 JUL–1 AUG
161
Horseshoe Hill
Bartley Ridge
145 (–)
Shimizu Hill
169
103 (–)

Terere
Kia

37
x x
43
1500
1 AUG
Lambeti
Plantation

148 (–)
161
145 (–)
169
103 (–)

1500
2 AUG

Elms
27
4 AUG

Bibilo Hill

169
AIRFIELD
103 (–)
MUNDA

1500
4 AUG

145 (–)
Kokengolo Hill

148 (–)
161

Munda
Point

BGen Leonard Wing, RAdm Theodore Wilkinson, RAdm
Richmond Kelly Turner, and MGen John Hester aboard
U.S.S. *McCawley*. June 29, 1943.   *(Official Signal Corps Photo)*

A 105mm howitzer of the 152nd Field Artillery supporting the
2nd Battalion, 103rd Infantry on Vangunu. June 30, 1943.

(Official Signal Corps Photo)

A typical Japanese coconut-log pillbox (after camouflage has been stripped away). *(Official Signal Corps Photo)*

An 81mm mortar squad under fire. *(Official Signal Corps Photo)*

Members of the 43rd Signal Company string communications wire in the wake of the 172nd Infantry's advance from Zanana Beach. July 6, 1943.

(Official Signal Corps Photo)

An infantry battalion surgeon bandages a wounded soldier in a frontline foxhole. July 5, 1943. *(Official Signal Corps Photo)*

that would be "too bad." Shafer inquired about whether his ship
had a course to follow in that event. "No," the naval officer replied, but he had been to Rendova with another convoy a few days
before and thought he could find it again if he got left behind. Dusk
found the captain and the battalion commander straining
their eyesight through binoculars trying to see an ever-darkening
and disappearing silhouette. When the captain said, "I think I can
still see it," in the pitch blackness of night, Shafer decided to rest
the problem with the U.S. Navy—and proceeded below with vi-
sions of a Japanese submarine wolfpack pouncing on his ride to a
land battle he was better prepared to face.

On July 4, the Japanese determined to make one last attempt at
reducing the major supply points on Rendova and destroying as
much Allied shipping as possible. As the only major success of the
campaign had been through the efforts of 11th Air Fleet, the
Southeastern Fleet commander, Vice Admiral Jinichi Kusaka,
sanctioned another major aerial assault.

American radar was working this day, and the weather was fine
and clear. Of the 100 aircraft that formed for the mission, only 16
succeeded in bucking the huge Allied fighter umbrella to begin the
run on their targets.

Lieutenant Colonel Henry Shafer, who was in the process of
settling his 155mm howitzer battalion on Baraulu Island as this attack developed, witnessed the run of the surviving bombers. He
saw sixteen bombers fly out of the west and proceed right over his
head in a superb stepped-up vee-of-vees formation. They proceeded in a curve toward Segi, to the southwest. Shafer could not
yet identify the insignae, but since the bombers paid his battalion
no attention, he swallowed in pride and comfort, convinced they
were Americans. The bombers continued in a gentle curve from
Segi and made straight for Rendova, which was about five miles
south of Shafer's vantage point on Baraulu.

Beneath the Bettys' open bomb-bay doors was the last contingent of the 169th Infantry Regiment to arrive in the combat zone.
An entire stick of bombs landed between two of the LCIs, killing
two infantrymen and wounding eleven.

Then Lieutenant Colonel Shafer and his gunners had a ringside
seat to an incredible spectacle. Antiaircraft shells from Rendova and
Kokorana blossomed blackly within the bomber formation, and
Betty after Betty fell away in flames. None of the remaining war-

planes veered from its initial heading until only two were left. The antiaircraft fire ceased as the last two bombers flew out of range—right into the guns of waiting fighters, which destroyed them.

Ninth Defense Battalion's Special Weapons Group had set an all-time record. The Marine 90mm antiaircraft guns based on Rendova and Kokorana downed twelve Bettys and one escorting Zero fighter with only eighty-eight rounds. This was by far the fewest number of rounds per aircraft destroyed to date, and perhaps for the entire war.

The July 4 air strike was the last daylight attempt the Japanese at Rabaul made to shake the grip the Allies had on Rendova. Several attacks were later attempted by lone night bombers or observation planes. These kept men awake nights, but rarely hurt anyone.

With Rendova and its vast new logistics establishment secured, the second phase of the TOENAILS operation was about to begin.

PART III

*

Munda Trail

10

The Japanese had no idea what their adversaries were up to. Immediately after the occupation of Rendova Plantation, the intelligence sections of various commands comprising 8th Area Army, and most particularly 17th Army, found themselves more than a little confused. It was known, certainly, that American units had just completed the occupation of the larger barrier islands guarding Munda Field; it was obvious that the Americans were intent on ringing Munda. But there had been no major undertaking against Munda Field itself, other than a rising crescendo of artillery bombardments and air strikes against the runway, air-base facilities, and their immediate antiair and beach defenses.

There seemed to be a number of possibilities to the puzzling American strategy: There might yet be the expected direct assault against the airfield over the Munda Bar; Munda might be physically isolated by American artillery and air, and then left to rot; or a major infantry force might be landed somewhere between Rendova and Munda, then sent overland against the base. If Munda was left to rot while Americans built a major air base at Segi, the Japanese could not afford to commit infantry reinforcements that might be needed to counter American moves north of New Georgia. If the Americans were contemplating a direct amphibious assault against Munda Point, there would be no time to draw in outlying forces or bring in reinforcements. But if the Americans landed on New Georgia and attempted an overland drive against Munda, a defense in depth, with ample infantry reinforcements, might be feasible.

No one could be certain, but there was at least one strong indication that the Americans were thinking about an overland drive on Munda. On the morning of June 30, while attention was riveted solidly on the main landings at Rendova Plantation, two companies of American infantry occupied the pair of islands on either side of Onaiavisi Entrance, the channel leading from Wickham Anchorage to Zanana Beach, on New Georgia proper.

Landing from a pair of destroyer-transports during a lull in the rainstorms that plagued operations throughout the area, Barracuda Companies A and B of the 1st Battalion, 169th Infantry, occupied

Baraulu and Sasavelle Islets. There was no resistance, and the islands were occupied well within schedule. Thus the most vulnerable portion of the route from Rendova to Zanana was in American hands.

When news of the occupation of Baraulu and Sasavelle reached Major General Noburo Sasaki at his Munda headquarters, it appeared that he at last had an inkling of what the Americans were planning. Sasaki could not be certain, of course, but at least he had an event upon which he could draw a logical conclusion and to which he could react. Higher headquarters in Rabaul agreed, and reinforcements were ordered into Munda. At the same time, Sasaki was permitted to draw in specified outlying garrisons, and to assume direct command over Imperial Navy ground-combat and base units in his sphere of command. Thus, late on June 30, all Japanese units operating in eastern New Georgia were ordered to make their way to Munda for eventual redeployment. In addition, the artillery commander at Bairoko Harbor was ordered to dispatch two 140mm guns and two lighter field pieces overland to Munda, a company of the 229th Infantry was ordered in from neighboring Kolombangara, and landing barges were dispatched to pick up the garrisons at Viru and Vura Villages.

On July 1, from his vantage point atop Kokengolo Hill, General Sasaki watched intently as the Allied forces continued to strengthen their newly won prizes. As he watched, the sector commander was suddenly struck by the realization that the forces he had thus far ordered to Munda had not the remotest hope of successfully defending the airfield against a concerted effort by so many Americans. In view of this, he ordered the entire 3rd Battalion, 229th Infantry, to Munda to occupy a defensive sector.

General Sasaki's orders to his subordinates were brief: "Maintain alerted conditions throughout the night and guard against enemy landings; if the enemy commences to land, destroy him at the water's edge."

Major General John Hester had not yet made a firm commitment to land the main body of his division at Zanana Beach. Though that objective was certainly at the top of a very short list, developments during the days in which Rendova was to be turned into a major support base would determine the issue. In the meantime, Hester ordered portions of his force to proceed on the as-

sumption that Zanana would, in the end, be the site of the buildup
for the drive on Munda.

After spending a quiet night on Baraulu and Sasavelle, the two
Barracuda companies prepared for an active day. One B Company
platoon sent to Roviana Island encountered a ten-man Japanese
outpost. Three of the Japanese were killed in a brief fight, but the
remaining seven escaped. The main bodies of both American
companies warily dug in and awaited some effort by the Japanese
to drive them from their tiny prizes. A Company, 169th, drew the
big job. After spending most of July 1 preparing itself, the company was to move to Zanana Beach on July 2 to clear the way for
a landing by the entire 1st Battalion, 172nd Infantry.

Major Bill Naylor, the commander of the 1st Battalion, 172nd,
had first learned of his vanguard mission on July 1 when he was
ordered to report to a Navy commander to coordinate the movement of his battalion. The naval officer first asked Naylor if he
knew where the landing site was. Naylor admitted that he did not
know. Once the battalion commander was properly briefed, it was
decided to load the entire battalion into landing craft and start off
around midnight for the run to Zanana. All the preparations went
smoothly, and the loading was completed on time. However, at the
moment the battalion was getting under way, a red alert was
sounded. The loaded landing craft had to scatter to avoid an air
attack. The orderly company-size landing waves broke in all directions, imparting a delay of no-one-knew-how-long. The all-clear
was sounded in due course and Major Naylor moved in among the
milling boats to try to instill some sort of order. By the time the
boat groups were reorganized, it was raining quite hard.

To help matters along, General Hester's headquarters dispatched Sergeant Harry Wickham, the Coastwatcher, with a force
of canoe-borne islanders who would help guide the landing craft
through the narrow and treacherous passage to Roviana Lagoon and
Zanana. Wickham posted the canoes at regular intervals on both
sides of the channel, and the islanders were to display signal lamps.
Major Naylor's landing craft were well on their way to the beach
when all the islanders simply vanished. The orderly boat waves
came unglued the moment the signal lamps were extinguished.
First one, and then all, of the leading troop-laden landing craft
piled up on the reef. Instantly, boat crewmen got into shouting
matches with their fellows as the coxswains manning the lead-wave

boats reversed their engines at full power and started backing up into boats from the follow-up waves. The entire proceeding degenerated into a total fiasco.

Chaos reigned until Colonel David Ross, the regimental commander, who had insisted upon accompanying Naylor's battalion into Zanana, ordered everyone back to Rendova. As Ross was leaving, he turned to Major Naylor and said, "Naylor, you hop off at the next island, have a look at the situation in daylight, and make a recommendation." So Naylor left the command boat along with his driver, Private First Class Frank Porowski.

Daylight found Naylor and Porowski on dry land, afoot, in search of friendly faces. The first one of those they discovered belonged to Lieutenant Colonel William McCormick, commanding officer of the 103rd Field Artillery Battalion. He had landed with just one howitzer and its crew; the rest of his battalion had returned to Rendova with Colonel Ross and Naylor's battalion.

Major Naylor was able to hail a passing landing craft that was on its way to a nearby island with a load of troops. Naylor and Porowski hopped aboard and rode to the island, Baraulu. There, Naylor made his way to the command post of Captain William Smith, the commander of A Company, 169th Infantry, which was the force that was supposed to support Naylor's battalion on Zanana Beach. Naylor and Smith conferred and decided to reconnoiter the landing beach. They rounded up an islander who knew the channel and climbed back aboard the landing boat that had earlier conveyed Naylor to Baraulu.

Naylor and Smith, who were accompanied only by Private First Class Porowski and Smith's bodyguard, conducted their reconnaissance without difficulty. Zanana Beach and the immediate area were clear. The tiny command party reembarked and headed back to pick up Captain Smith's company, which headed straight to Zanana Beach in full force and in broad daylight.

Later in the day, Captain Edward Scherrer, the NGOF's assistant intelligence officer, landed with a small group of divisional scouts and, even later, Captain Charles Tripp, a New Zealander, landed with a small group of Maori scouts. Major Naylor radioed the 172nd Infantry's command post near dusk to report the situation and to recommend that no further night landings be attempted.

This is how the island of New Georgia was invaded.

                              *   *   *

Naylor's entire 1st Battalion, 172nd Infantry, landed without difficulty at Zanana on July 4 and cautiously advanced about 500 yards inland to establish an all-around defensive cordon. So far, there had been zero opposition, a fact considered crucial to General Hester's final decision to mount the entire New Georgia Occupation Force through Zanana Beach.

While Naylor's battalion developed beach defenses, the divisional and Maori scouts, plus Captain William Smith's A Company, 169th, conducted extensive patrolling between the beach and the Barike River; water points were marked, trails were blazed and mapped, possible artillery battery sites were plotted, and locations for dumps and bivouacs were selected. In addition, the patrols checked out likely looking defensive positions throughout the area in hopes of finding a useful key to destroying them in the event the Japanese moved in before major forces could be sent from Rendova.

All the activity did not remain unnoticed. The 5th Company, 229th Infantry, was dispatched from Munda to find out exactly what was going on around Zanana Beach. Shortly, Japanese patrols were shadowing American forces in the area in hopes of sending information to General Sasaki that would allow him to accurately divine American intentions. The Americans hadn't a clue that they were being watched.

At dawn, July 4, Brigadier General Leonard Wing, 43rd Infantry Division's assistant commander, left Rendova in a landing boat to establish a forward division command post at Zanana Beach. Immediately following the July 4 Japanese air strike against Rendova Harbor, the remainder of the 172nd Infantry Regiment was ordered to move to Zanana Beach to begin offensive operations. The 105mm howitzers of the 103rd and 169th Field Artillery Battalions were deployed on the barrier islets to directly support the advance on Munda, and the 155mm guns of the 136th and 192nd Field Artillery Battalions were registered for general support of the advance as well as for missions against Munda Field.

On the morning of July 5, A Company, 169th, was holding the right (northern) flank of the beachhead, and the 1st Battalion, 172nd, was deployed away to the southeast. While A and B Companies, 169th, operated as divisional units near Zanana Beach on July 5, Headquarters, C, and D Companies of the 1st Battalion, 169th, were designated the 169th Infantry's regimental reserve.

Elements of the rump battalion were set to work carrying out boat patrols to the barrier islets.

At about noon, shortly after the bulk of the 172nd Infantry departed Rendova for Zanana, Major William Stebbins's 3rd Battalion, 169th, turned over its defensive sector on Rendova and began its move to Zanana. While a Japanese air strike prevented most of the battalion from moving on time that day, L and M Companies did reach the newly established beachhead after nightfall and unloaded in a rainstorm in the dark. Unable to spread out as they had been taught to do and would have preferred doing, the fresh troops spent a miserable, scary night crowded together in the rain.

On July 5, his first night ashore at Zanana, First Lieutenant Ben Sportsman, commander of F Company, 172nd, was faced with the task of getting his troops safely deployed and dug in beneath an awesome rain shower. The unloading of the company's boats was accomplished only with the greatest difficulty due to the soggy condition of the ground. The only soil that was not saturated was around coral outcroppings. Lieutenant Sportsman managed to find such an outcropping, and he dug his own one-man foxhole there after seeing that his troops were properly deployed and fed. The feeding was a chore in itself. The company's field kitchens had been landed and it seemed like a good idea to lift morale with a hot meal. However, by the time the kitchen was set up and the meal cooked, it was quite dark, and the rain continued unabated. Everyone received dollops of warm, hearty food, but mess kits instantly filled with rainwater; it was hardly the sort of experience to lift spirits.

After eating and seeing that his troops were dug in and under tents to keep off some of the rain, Lieutenant Sportsman retired to his own sleeping hole, which despite its having been dug into porous coral was soon half filled with the chilly runoff of the higher ground on all sides. No sooner had Sportsman dozed off than he was awakened with a jolt by the loud booming of what he was certain were enemy mortar rounds dropping into the company area. Immediately, Sportsman was seized by a fit of uncontrollable trembling, for he knew that there was virtually no defense against the impersonal fall of high-trajectory mortar rounds. He clearly and strongly chided himself for the shaking, which he took to be a sign of cowardice. Though the urge to urinate soon overtook all other thoughts, he steadfastly refused to leave his foxhole for any reason, so certain did he become that he would be sliced to ribbons by shrapnel from the incoming mortar rounds. In time, the discomfort became so great that Sportsman threw caution to the winds and left his solitary foxhole. As soon as the company commander got above ground level he realized that the booming that had scared him so was the sound of outgoing friendly artillery located on the barrier islets just a few yards behind his beachside position. Still too shaken to see any humor in his travail, Sportsman nevertheless felt that his worst personal ordeal of the war was behind him, that he could face the worst the Japanese had to offer because he had already weathered the worst his own imagination had to offer.

The 43rd Infantry Division's drive on Munda Field was set to begin the next day, July 6.

11

A merican infantry units on Zanana Beach moved to the divisional line of departure at the Barike River on July 6. Nearly all of the 172nd Infantry was ashore as the lead files advanced through the silent rain forest toward their initial objectives.

Major John Carrigan's 2nd Battalion, 172nd, which was on the regimental left, beside the beach, jumped off with two companies abreast and one in reserve. The leading companies had only just started down the trail when they met the first Japanese to be encountered in the vicinity. The fighting, which ebbed and flowed through the dense rain forest on either side of the trail, lasted until the middle of the afternoon, when Carrigan's battalion finally captured its first objective, a tiny group of huts strung out along a creek that wound down from nearby hills.

First Lieutenant Ben Sportsman's F Company, 172nd, had been the battalion reserve through the day, but Sportsman had been ordered forward by the battalion commander to watch the action and attempt to get a feel for jungle operations. During the day, he heard that a close friend from Officers Candidate School had been killed in a sudden clash in the forest. It was therefore with some relief that Sportsman was ordered to lead F Company through the battalion front to pursue the Japanese who had been holding the tiny village and who were then retreating more or less down the nearby beach.

As Sportsman's company was mounting out, Sportsman was told to avoid a direct clash with the enemy. He was to see what he could see and report back in a few hours. Sportsman deployed two platoons abreast and one in reserve, just as he had been taught. Since Sportsman expected action on the beach, if there was any, and because the beach platoon was commanded by a staff sergeant, he remained on the beach. The troops were eager to prove themselves, and Sportsman was eager to avenge his dead friend.

The advancing company moved only 500 yards before Japanese mortar rounds began falling among the troops. It soon appeared that the rounds were the 57mm grenades fired by so-called "knee" mortars, a spring-activated grenade launcher. The troops, eager at first, were quickly demoralized, for the knee mortars fired without a sound; the first anyone knew of any danger was when a grenade landed nearby with its fuse smoking, about to detonate. The first man to panic was the staff sergeant commanding the beach platoon; he threw down his weapon and ran as fast as he could to the rear. Lieutenant Sportsman was so shocked that he was slow to realize that other soldiers were about to follow the noncom's example. As soon as Sportsman overcame his surprise, he stood in full view and bellowed as loud as he could that he intended to shoot the next man who attempted to break ranks and flee. The panic stopped right there and soon the knee-mortar barrage stopped. The beach platoon, and then the entire company, withdrew in accordance with its orders.

F Company, 172nd, returned to its battalion just before sunset. Lieutenant Sportsman had been planning to conduct a roll call to learn if there had been any stragglers, but it was impossible to do so in the dark. During the night, piercing screams were heard from out of the rain forest, but it was impossible to rescue anyone who might have been wounded and left behind, or even to determine if the screams were friendly troops or enemy soldiers hoping to draw out compassionate rescuers. A fearful, troubled night was spent by all.

While the 172nd Infantry moved ahead in its sector, the leading elements of the 3rd Battalion, 169th, were ordered to advance up the Piraka Trail to await the arrival of the combat elements whose leavetaking at Rendova had been disrupted by the previous afternoon's air strike. Unfortunately, the battalion's bivouac was located on the far side of the Piraka Trail's juncture with the Munda Trail, the axis of advance for the 172nd Infantry. The half battalion's logistics train became intermingled with a large rear-guard element of the 172nd Infantry. Since night was falling, both units claimed a football-sized field beside the trail junction, and both units—and others that had become enmeshed in the initial confusion—camped out there for the night. The vast assemblage that sat itself down in the open field would have been dead meat if the Japanese had been able to get their mortars or artillery working.

Also on July 6, Headquarters, C, and D Companies of Major Joe Zimmer's 1st Battalion, 169th, were sent to Zanana. After stopping off at General Wing's command post to pay their respects and pick up orders, Major Zimmer and his battalion operations officer,

Captain Harold Dunbar, set out alone to find the 2nd Battalion, 169th, which had been designated the division reserve after coming ashore on July 5. Zimmer had been told at the division forward command post to follow a pair of telephone wires to the battalion, which his own unit would be relieving on the perimeter the following morning. Trusting blindly, the two novice officers set out through an impossible swamp. Soon the two were attempting with little success to hop from one tiny dry hummock to the next, wondering all the while how anyone could have gotten a wheeled wire cart through terrain in which two unencumbered men could barely advance. The two eventually reached the end of the wire, smack in the middle of nowhere. All Zimmer and Dunbar could do was follow the wire back to the division forward command post. There, Zimmer was informed of a change in orders; his battalion was to bivouac in a direction wholly opposite to the one originally given. It was too late by then to do a thing, so the exhausted battalion commander marched his companies into the forest and established an independent perimeter for the night. B Company, 169th, was returned to the battalion that evening, but A Company was still held as part of the force reserve.

The day's disorganization left a thoroughly distraught Major Zimmer with the unshakable conviction that more surprises awaited him and his untested battalion. But he had not a clue as to what those surprises might be, or how he might prepare himself or his troops to meet them.

Nearer the beach that evening, the rear elements of Major William Stebbins's 3rd Battalion, 169th, were similarly unprepared for a night-long siege of disconcerting experiences. Late that night, a small group of Japanese soldiers crept to within a few yards of the half battalion's front and began shouting taunts at the Connecticut riflemen, telling them that their training days were long over and that life would be much changed. Then one of the Japanese called out a challenge to "First Lieutenant Marr, commanding I Company." The commander of I Company, 169th, was indeed First Lieutenant Aubern Marr. At that point, the Japanese departed, allowing the green troops time to ponder *that* lesson.

The entire 3rd Battalion, 169th, was re-formed at the Munda-Piraka trail junction early on July 7 to begin an advance directly up the Munda Trail. Following a cautious initial advance, First Lieutenant Aubern Marr's I Company, the battalion vanguard, was

fired on by a single machine gun emplaced to the right of the narrow trail where the ground rose sharply four or five feet and lev-
eled off to form a flat plateau. I Company's two leading platoons
were to advance another fifty yards before they were pinned down
and forced to deploy astride the trail. Immediately, Captain Howard Nelson's L Company moved in on its right and Captain Robert Fleischer's K Company was held in reserve. Then the entire
battalion bogged down.

As the action developed, the M Company commander, Captain
Jim Rankin, advanced to the front with the 81mm mortar forward
observer, Sergeant Frank Atwater. On the way to the forward I
Company platoon, Rankin and Atwater passed several wounded
soldiers, including the I Company commander, Lieutenant Marr.
Within minutes, two of the I Company platoon leaders were also
seriously wounded, and the company was temporarily unable to
continue its advance.

To the rear, the commander of the battalion's 81mm mortar
platoon, First Lieutenant Ben Lindquist, was already at work
clearing trees and overhead coverage from the gun-target line.
Lindquist well knew that the instantaneous point fuse of the 81mm
mortar rounds could detonate right after leaving the mortar tubes
if they struck even a leaf during their passage. It had been Lindquist's decision to bring up only two of the battalion's four 81mm
mortars so that extra hands could be put to use carrying a pair of
two-man crosscut saws and several axes. As soon as I Company
was stopped on the trail, Lindquist's gunners located a spot for
their tubes and went to work felling a large tree that would otherwise have blocked the passage of the mortar rounds. The overhead cover was cleared by the time Captain Rankin and Sergeant
Atwater arrived at the front-line positions. While Atwater went to
work guiding the mortars over a phone he had carried forward,
Captain Rankin reconnoitered the front. Between calls for mortar
fire, Rankin spoke to Major Frank Dorsey, the battalion executive
officer, by means of the mortar platoon's phone, which was patched
through to the battalion command post. Rankin suggested that I
Company hold in place while K Company put in a flank attack
from the left.

While Rankin conferred with Captain Fleischer at his observation post on the I Company line, the 81mm mortars were brought
on target and several of M Company's .30-caliber medium machine guns were rushed forward to bolster the I Company base of

fire. As L Company maneuvered on the battalion right, the Japanese machine gun fired a short burst, which killed Second Lieutenant Charles Kubin, the first of many of the battalion's company-grade officers to die on New Georgia.

K Company's flank attack jumped off. The advance was slow, hard, hot work. The troops were rattled but seemed eager to get on with what amounted to their first real taste of combat. As the fight progressed, Captain Fleischer took the forward elements of the company on a wide flanking move, but he swung out too far and then did not move far enough forward to get even with or beyond the Japanese position. The completion of the flanking move brought Fleischer between the Japanese and I Company's base of fire, which amounted to approaching the Japanese position frontally. In the end, K Company was beaten back to the I Company line. Captain Fleischer passed back through I Company clutching his bloody groin; he had been severely wounded and would die two days later.

Once Captain Rankin had submitted his recommendations for the battalion attack, he joined Sergeant Atwater in the latter's observation post, which was a mere thirty yards from the Japanese machine gun. The 81mm mortars pulverized the small clearing the tiny Japanese force had held through the day against assaults by a full infantry battalion. However, the battalion was unable to get rolling. Well before nightfall, the entire American battalion was ordered to backtrack 200 yards up the trail to establish a night bivouac at the base of a cluster of huge banyan tress. The 3rd Battalion, 169th, had been baptized at the cost of six killed and thirty wounded. Five of the dead and wounded American soldiers were company officers.

During the night, many of the haggard, sleepless troops of the 3rd Battalion, 169th, became convinced that Japanese snipers were ensconced in the banyan trees around which the battalion had established its bivouac. Weary and frustrated by the day's shadowboxing at what the troops were already calling Bloody Hill, many soldiers opened fire at alien noises. There was no general panic—that would come later—but the sleepless men convinced themselves that they were in mortal danger, and they succeeded in keeping themselves awake as much as any Japanese might have done. Elements of the 172nd Infantry, which had remained in place during the day and which were bivouacked nearby, reported no contacts with the enemy that night.

                                    *   *   *

The actual organized 43rd Division advance on Munda was set
to begin on July 8. However, since the assault elements of the
169th Infantry had not yet reached their line of departure, the divisional assault simply could not begin on time. The 3rd Battalion, 169th, was ordered to hold in place while the balance of the
regiment caught up. The battalion dispatched combat patrols to
probe Bloody Hill, and these reported that the Japanese had withdrawn, leaving their dead. It appeared that most of the Japanese
dead were the victims of the mortar fire.

While the combat patrols were still out, Brigadier General
Leonard Wing came forward to the battalion command post to ap-
praise the battalion's combat readiness. Everyone on the scene realized that some heads might roll: General Hester had assured his
superiors that the advance would begin on July 8 and, because of
the twenty-four-hour delay, he had had to go all the way to South
Pacific Area Headquarters to seek permission to establish a new
schedule. However, the permission was immediately forthcoming,
and no heads rolled that day.

Major Joe Zimmer's abbreviated 1st Battalion, 169th, which had
patrols out in the morning hours, was ordered to the front upon
General Wing's return to the division forward command post. The
battalion marched as far as Bloody Hill, but had to stop for the
night. As the troops were digging in, A Company, 169th, was detached from the force reserve and dispatched to Bloody Hill to
bring Zimmer's battalion to full strength.

In the late afternoon, Lieutenant Colonel John Fowler's 2nd
Battalion, 169th, was ordered up to positions just behind the regimental line. Fowler's troops would be the division reserve, and
Lieutenant Colonel Jim Wells's 3rd Battalion, 103rd, still on Rendova, was designated the force reserve.

The night of July 8–9 passed peacefully. The troops were pen-
sive over the promise of heavy fighting in the morning. Many had
not had any rest to speak of in over fifty hours, due to daylight advances and nocturnal disturbances. The gaps between training-
induced expectations and real-life performance against the Japanese were particularly worrisome. Sentries were drowsy, but tense;
sleeping men were restless, ready for anything.

———— 12 ————

As the 169th Infantry Regiment finally pulled into position along its line of departure during the afternoon of July 8, General Hester signaled his superiors and his subordinates that the New Georgia Occupation Force was ready to undertake the first phase of the drive on Munda. The advance was to commence early the following morning.

Private First Class Sam LaMagna, a member of the 60mm mortar squad of F Company, 169th, had dug a hole at sunset with his best friend, Private First Class Syl Bottone, and had debated with Bottone over whether they should both try to catch up on their sleep or stay awake in shifts. Their entire battalion had spent the day cutting jeep trails through the rain forest, and both men were exhausted. Neither had gotten more than a half-hour's sleep the night before because of disturbances throughout the battalion sector. In the end, the two faced one another in the hole, each grasping the other's left hand, each holding a heavy .45-caliber pistol in his right hand. After a time, in which there was not a hint of trouble, Bottone asked LaMagna if he wanted to nap. LaMagna said, "Hell no! You go ahead and sleep. I can't." But Bottone could not sleep either.

All of a sudden, LaMagna heard the detonation of a hand grenade. Immediately, the bivouac was filled with painful moaning and screams. LaMagna reflexively drew his knees up to his chest. The first thought that came into his head was that the Japanese did not have to hear him; he had the stink of fear around him, and they could find him by smelling him. Nearby, someone was moaning "Mama, mama!" over and over in the dark. After a very long time, it got quiet again, but LaMagna and Bottone got no sleep.

Someone fired a rifle in another isolated battalion bivouac. The troops later claimed that there were sounds of crawling things everywhere, and of people yelling that the Japanese had infiltrated in force. A few screams of pain followed, and the panic was on. After three nights of unbearable tension, the troops blew. The American infantrymen would later claim that a large number of Japanese had shouted, cursed, screamed, whistled, fired rifles, hurled hand grenades, slashed with bayonets, swung knives, tightened garrotes, jumped into occupied foxholes, and otherwise carried out swift bloody attacks upon the line and rear. After a night that sounded like a revolution in Hell, searchers came up with a number of lacerated American corpses. There were the dead, the wounded, the shocked, and the confused. And there were the braggarts. But there was not one Japanese.

The plan of attack for July 9 was conservative. The 169th and 172nd Infantry Regiments would move forward in line abreast from the Barike River to seize the high ground southwest of the river, then move in easy stages on the airfield. Colonel David Ross's 172nd Infantry was to advance astride the Munda Trail itself, with Major Bill Naylor's 1st Battalion on the left and Major James Devine's 3rd Battalion on the right. The move would be carried out with two companies from each battalion advancing abreast on a 300-yard front; one platoon from each of the four lead companies would stand back of the main line as reserves, and one uncommitted company from each battalion would follow in column farther back still.

Slightly to the north and east of Ross's regiment, Colonel John Eason's 169th Infantry would advance in lines echeloned right and rear to cover the division right flank. Major Joe Zimmer's 1st Battalion would be tied in with the 3rd Battalion, 172nd, while Major William Stebbins's 3rd Battalion deployed to cover a portion of the front and the flank. Lieutenant Colonel John Fowler's 2nd Battalion, 169th, was the division reserve. The antitank companies of the assault regiments were emplaced with Marine antiaircraft units in defense of Zanana Beach. The force reserve was Lieutenant Colonel Jim Wells's 3rd Battalion, 103rd, at Rendova.

Beginning at 0500 hours, July 9, every available gun of Brigadier General Harold Barker's Force Artillery Group fired on the jungle-covered hills and valleys facing the assault regiments; two 155mm howitzer battalions, two 155mm gun batteries, and two 105mm howitzer battalions battered the Munda-Barike area with over 5,800 high-explosive rounds. At 0512, four American destroyers eased up to firing positions just offshore and added a total of 2,335 5-inch shells to the effort. The fire continued high overhead for a full hour to get at rear areas and lines of communication, then it was pulled down closer to the American lines to soften the immediate objectives. As the artillery fire lifted just before H-Hour, eighty-eight Navy and Marine single-engine bombers worked over the immediate front with high-explosive and fragmentation bombs.

Suddenly it was H-Hour. The New England National Guardsmen of the 169th and 172nd Infantry Regiments opened the advance. Major Joe Zimmer reported a few minutes after 0630 that his 1st Battalion, 169th, was ready to move, but that the adjacent 3rd Battalion, 172nd, seemed to be stopped at the line of departure. Queries and responses flew from General Wing's command post to battalion and regimental command posts. There were reasonable excuses: the river was shoulder-deep, swamps were impassable, wrist-thick rattan vines had stopped or confused the vanguard, Munda Trail actually crossed the Barike River three times, ad infinitum. After three hours, General Wing had not yet heard that even one battalion had crossed the line of departure.

The entire area had been extensively patrolled by local guides, Fijian commandos, Maori and Tongan scouts, and American infantry. Everyone knew that it would be rough going. But maps were too general, and they had not been distributed much beyond battalion staff levels. No one knew what the next step might bring. It was impossible for platoons, or even squads, to advance abreast; forget about companies, battalions, and regiments! Columns of infantrymen were forced along clearly discernible paths. Japanese riflemen harassed the front and flanks in brief hit-and-run flurries of fire before scurrying off without so much as having been seen by the victims. Scouts roving ahead of the infantry battalions and pointmen leading the infantry platoons were being shot with sickening regularity. Only a few Japanese—probably only the 5th Company, 229th Infantry—were holding up nearly 4,000 American infantrymen. The Japanese main line was still 2,500 yards away.

The first unit to make it across the Barike was K Company, 172nd. By about noon, Major James Devine's entire 3rd Battalion, 172nd, had crossed the river and was pushing on into the rain forest. K Company managed to advance all of 100 yards beyond the river late in the afternoon. By nightfall, K Company, 172nd, was digging in 200 yards beyond the river; it was thus the farthest advanced American unit on the island. Major Bill Naylor's 1st Battalion, 172nd, was directly behind Devine's 3rd Battalion. In midafternoon, Naylor informed the regimental command post that his battalion was stopping 1,100 yards from its initial line. However, the estimate was off by hundreds of yards.

The 169th Infantry encountered heavier opposition than the

172nd Infantry, and it had a harder battle with the terrain and Japanese bushwhackers. Nevertheless, elements of the regiment did make some headway. The regimental command post moved forward as far as Bloody Hill at about noon, and the 2nd Battalion strung a perimeter defense around the hill. Neither the 1st nor 3rd Battalions advanced measurable distances.

The reasons for the rather sorry display of soldiering by the assault battalions on July 9 were manifold. The inertia of the troops must be explained in terms of a hundred variations of simple personal rationalizations—or else a bogged-down advance by 4,000 men against a mere handful of defenders would seem more absurd than it really was. The terrain was difficult, certainly, but the crux of the difficulty lay in the minds of men.

The troops were overtired and overwrought. The 169th Infantry's days and nights in the rain forest had unhinged the troops' confidence in themselves and in their units. Long nightly vigils had heretofore produced more conjurings than contacts with the enemy. The fault lay largely with the officers, whose impossible inexperience prevented them from doing more than uttering some platitudes they clearly did not believe themselves. Morale and discipline were bound to suffer, and they had.

Objectively, the lack of credible maps played an important role in the general trend toward collapse of unit integrity. Officers had only the barest information upon which to base their tactics. They could not pinpoint jungle stands, hill masses, watercourses on trails—much less their positions relative to these. They were confused and, as a result, a bit fearful. It rubbed off on their subordinates, who were barely repressing their own feelings of hysteria. The breakdown in unit integrity resulting from marching through jumbled, sound-deadening jungle terrain led directly to the dissipation of control by junior officers. Major Naylor's claim to an 1,100-yard advance was an honest attempt to calibrate a distance which was, in all likelihood, 1,100 yards of right and left twists and turns over a much shorter straight-line distance. Units up through company level became hopelessly entangled with the rain forest and with one another. Force Headquarters was not guiltless, believing as it did the erroneous reports passed up to it by erring battalion and regimental staffs. Officers and troops were well trained, to be sure, but not for the type of warfare in which they were then engaging.

*   *   *

The assault units settled in for another unsettling night. Their positions comprised a series of platoon- and company-size perimeters along a general front set through the rain forest on a northerly and then northeasterly heading. Haggard, sleepy sentinels in the sector of the 169th Infantry took up their posts while the men around them dropped off to restless sleep.

One could feel the tension lift from the sleeping men and take hold of the nervous, jumpy sentries, some of whom nodded off despite honest efforts to remain alert; they were invariably startled awake by the sound of something alien.

The 3rd Battalion, 169th, faced another bad night near Bloody Hill. As with nearby units, the troops were jumpy, ready to crack. Someone fired at a shadow or a faint sound, or nothing at all. Instantly, other scared men joined in. But then the entire battalion was stopped by a loud, ear-piercing Tarzan call. A little group from K Company's weapons platoon started laughing as Sergeant Ernie Squatarito jumped to his feet, thumped his chest, and let out another mighty jungle call. The laughter spread through the bivouac, and the panic ended—forever. Soon, scores of men found their voices and issued Tarzan calls at the lurking rain forest.

During the day, Private First Class Sam LaMagna, of F Company, 169th, was approached by his squad leader and asked if he would share his foxhole that night with a man who was not settling down. LaMagna was leery, but he agreed to help.

The two dug in well within the battalion perimeter and LaMagna told the other soldier to remain calm and, above all, not to yell or make any other noise. LaMagna admitted that he was scared, too, but that he knew enough to keep quiet. He showed the other man the .45-caliber pistol he kept in his right hand and the knife he held in his left hand. Sometime later, LaMagna drifted off to sleep, the first he had had in days. Suddenly, his foxhole buddy was whispering in his ear, "Sam! Look! A Jap is trying to get in the hole!" LaMagna looked up, startled, but saw only the canteen he had set on the lip of the hole. "Okay, Joe," LaMagna whispered, "Where is he?" The other man pointed to the shadow of the canteen. LaMagna pulled down the canteen. "There, Joe. See, it's only my canteen. Okay?" The other man grunted an acknowledgment.

An hour later, LaMagna felt something heavy on his left shoulder. He awoke with a start and found the two hand grenades he had placed on the lip of the hole. After checking the levers and pins to see that the missiles were safe, LaMagna gently prodded his sleeping companion and asked him if he had put the grenades on his shoulder. The other allowed as he had. "Why'd you do that," LaMagna asked. The other stuttered out a story about not wanting them to fall into enemy hands. LaMagna realized that he was nearing the end of his patience. He did not want to scare Joe, or get him more upset, however, so he said in his calmest voice, "Look, Joe, everything's fine. See how nice and quiet it is? You don't have to worry about any Japs. Here, you go to sleep and I'll watch." The man calmed right down. "Okay, Sam. But you be sure to wake me if you see or hear anything. Okay?" LaMagna agreed to do just that.

Around midnight, Private First Class LaMagna noticed that his buddy was beginning to breathe hard and shake in his sleep. LaMagna was about to touch the sleeping man, but he thought the better of it, fearing the other man might mistake him for a Japanese infiltrator. Before LaMagna could figure out what to do next, Joe shot up to a sitting position and began yelling, "You son of a bitch! I know you're out there! I can even smell you!"

As the half-awake man continued to yell into the peaceful night, LaMagna gripped the pistol in his hand and swung it around into Joe's mouth. Then he put the barrel of the pistol against the man's head and muttered in a dead calm voice right into his ear, "You feel that, Joe?" There was a brief nod. "Well, if I hear you so much as breathe, I will blow your head off. You understand?" There was a brief nod. LaMagna reached across the cramped foxhole and pulled Joe's weapons—rifle, bayonet, hand grenades, and knife—to his side. Joe slumped down in the bottom of the hole.

The yelling, which LaMagna had not stopped quite in time, set off other fearful men in the battalion perimeter. There were several shootings and more than a few stabbings as taut-nerved soldiers awoke suddenly and slashed wickedly at their buddies with the knives to which they desperately clung in their sleep. There was some solace in the fact that these Connecticut Guardsmen were finally learning to maim one another quietly.

Next morning, July 10, 360 soldiers were evacuated to Guadalcanal. All were or claimed to be "war nerves" cases. Major General Millard Harmon, the U.S. Army regional commander, was on hand to meet these men, and he saw to it that nearly 300 were re-

turned to their units. Whether these 300 were faking, as Harmon
later claimed, or whether they were really "war nerves" casualties, there was a bit of truth in all their tales. Certainly, they
were all close to folding under the effects of nervous strain and
exhaustion.

There had been very little research into the causes and effects of
"war nerves"—combat neurosis—prior to New Georgia. There had
been cases of maddening nighttime shootouts, which Marines at
Guadalcanal had called "jitterbugging." But these instances, as with
the case here, were matters of green troops adjusting to an intim-
idating new environment. Whether the adversary was a man, a rat,
or a hunk of rotting vegetation, the reaction would be the same:
Panic! The Marines had coped with the immediate problem by relieving junior officers, on the theory that they were not good leaders. As it happened, there had been few casualties during the
period of adjustment at Guadalcanal. But a lot of people got hurt
during the New Georgia baptism.

As it happened, war neurosis was just becoming recognized as a
legitimate, debilitating illness. Officers, from General Harmon on
down, were forced to balance the needs of individuals against the
embarrassing results of the first days of the offensive. Given the
effects the lagging advance might have on the careers of senior officers—most of the troops were National Guardsmen or draftees,
but nearly all the colonels and generals were Regular Army—it is
little wonder that a hard line was taken. As to this newfangled war
neurosis disease—well, the colonels and generals all felt they had
survived worse baptisms in France in 1917 and 1918; today's breed
of soft civilians just needed time to toughen up.

On the morning of July 10, the 3rd Battalion, 169th, was bypassed on the trail by its sister battalions. Upon recommendations
by General Wing and other notables, Major Stebbins was replaced by Lieutenant Colonel Fred Reincke, who had commanded
the battalion until just prior to its move to New Georgia and who
had been relieved apparently to provide Stebbins with a battalion
command. Morale in the battalion noticeably improved the moment Reincke's reinstatement was announced.

The unimaginably tired infantrymen of the 3rd Battalion, 169th,
were passed on the trail by the equally tired soldiers of Lieutenant
Colonel John Fowler's 2nd Battalion. Fowler's troops were unsure
about how they might fare when faced with a real fight. They had

weathered two full sleepless nights of sparring with phantoms.
The July 10 advance was smooth in the zone of the 172nd Infantry. Platoon leaders were soon reporting increased advances at
more rapid intervals. Even Zimmer's and Fowler's battalions of the
169th Infantry began taking ground.

Zimmer's 1st Battalion, 169th, crossed a small tributary of the
Barike by way of a pair of felled trees, then advanced as far as the
junction of the Munda Trail and a small track that curved away
toward the beach to the native villages of Laiana and Ilangana. At
1330, Zimmer's vanguard pushed on just beyond the trail junction, directly into the fire of machine guns manned and protected
by a large Japanese force built around the 9th Company, 229th Infantry. The Japanese base of fire was a camouflaged trail block on
a slight rise directly ahead of the American battalion, which instantly struggled to deploy in the dense undergrowth. One platoon of Japanese infantry, supported by a machine-gun section and
several 90mm mortars, held the strongpoint. To the rear was a full
battalion of 75mm mountain howitzers.

Major Zimmer reported the initial clash to his regimental headquarters, which decided to call in direct artillery support. Zimmer's troops obligingly pulled back 100 yards while regimental
mortars sought the target. Force Artillery soon joined with a concentration that would eventually consume 4,000 105mm and
155mm rounds. Nothing was heard from the Japanese manning the
trail block for some time, and observers concluded that they had
withdrawn or been dispersed. As soon as the bombardment ceased
the infantry began moving. However, the Japanese remanned their
guns and stopped the advance cold.

After the second unsuccessful attempt to breach the position,
Major Zimmer ordered his troops to dig in where they stood. The
remainder of the regiment did likewise, having gained a respectable, 1,500 yards during the day. It seemed that the Americans had
reached the beginning of an organized defensive belt and were
faced with fresh troops.

After repositioning several elements of his battalion, Major
Zimmer saw to the establishment of his command post at a bend
in the small stream the battalion had crossed earlier. A number of
staff officers gathered atop the end of a huge fallen log for their
dinner, and the battalion commander joined in their chatter as they
listlessly picked away at their cold rations. The officers turned in
as soon as it became dark. In the morning, a security patrol pried

a Japanese infiltrator out from under the log that had served as the battalion staff's dinner table.

The 2nd Battalion, 169th, had had a so-so day in the rain forest. The battalion encountered several Japanese snipers during the day, and Private First Class Sam LaMagna came across a dummy decked out in a Japanese uniform, which someone told him was meant to draw fire and thus pinpoint the Americans as they moved through the rain forest.

The battalion had had three terrible nights in a row in the forest, had sustained casualties from gunshots, slashings, and "combat nerves." That morning, LaMagna had recommended to his sergeant that Joe, his nerve-shattered foxhole buddy of the night before, be evacuated, but the sergeant had declined. This night, Joe was stuffed into an oversized foxhole between two sergeants. After a few quiet hours, LaMagna heard Joe begin to yell. Then shots were fired. Then one of the sergeants yelled, "Stop him! He'll kill us all!" Then there were more shots, and the sound of a scuffle. Before LaMagna could fit it all together, bullets were flying right over his head, hand grenades were exploding, and a large explosion engulfed his foxhole. Private First Class Sam LaMagna felt a sharp pain in his right shin, then his whole right side went numb and he passed out.

Much later, when LaMagna came to in a hospital on Guadalcanal, he found that the man in the next bed was one of the sergeants who had taken in Joe, the scared soldier. According to the sergeant, Joe went out of his head and grabbed the sergeant's .45-caliber pistol. As he yelled, "They're coming into the hole," he shot the sergeant in the chest and leg. The other sergeant had pulled out his own .45-caliber pistol and had shot the berserk soldier dead.

For some reason, that was the last bad night the 2nd Battalion, 169th, had in the rain forest. There was no more panic within the battalion lines at night.

After only three days of grueling but light combat, the 169th Infantry was badly under strength and nearly done in. The roads and tracks behind the front were overrun with wandering ambulatory wounded and shock cases attempting to find medical assistance or a consoling voice. These men created not only an immediate evacuation problem but further hindered progress at the front simply by being absent. Additional combat troops had to be withheld from the lines to lend a hand at hauling food, water, ammunition, spare parts, and weapons, all of which were needed to keep the assault forces moving.

Altogether, the 169th Infantry had had a remarkably harrowing collective experience. The regiment had lost many of its most qualified officers and enlisted men to cadres before leaving the United States. Excellent training had been constant in New Zealand, New Caledonia, and in the Russell Islands. However, the settings of all the training sharply differed from the unrelieved, closed-in, and totally *alien* rain-forest setting of New Georgia. A touch of patrol-style combat was experienced at Guadalcanal, but not enough for a good firefight; no doubt the infrequent contacts were with beaten stragglers who had missed the massive evacuation operation that concluded the Guadalcanal Campaign. The regiment next experienced a few scattered bombings in the Russells. So, for all practical purposes, the 169th Infantry faced its first real test at Rendova, where some units had gotten hurt by two successive Japanese air strikes while landing.

Many believed that fire discipline was poor at the start of the drive on Munda because visibility was poor. Anything that moved or made a noise was believed to be a Japanese bushwhacker. The terrain made movement very far in any fixed direction extremely difficult. Steep hillsides, swamps, streams a bit too wide to jump across, fallen trees, heavy underbrush that cut visibility to only a few yards resulted in a tendency for Americans out of their element to hug the rails. This natural channelization made advancing infantry units, large and small, extremely easy to waylay.

Generally, advance parties were ordered out of the battalion night cordons. These vanguards would step out in the required spread-out formations, but they invariably moved in too close to the trail. When the contact was made, the pointman was almost invariably shot through the head. And that would be the last of the advance for the time being. If the bushwhacked unit was able to pull itself together and close on the enemy, it never found more than a crude hunter's blind and, if anything more, a little pile of spent brass cartridges.

Since the American victims of these little hit-and-run skirmishes had to be evacuated along the overused trails, American infantrymen in follow-up units could plainly see the results of the jungle combat they would soon be facing. On the other hand, they seldom saw a dead or wounded Japanese.

13

The action on July 10 finally gave some needed clues regarding the nature of the Japanese pattern of defense. It was clear that General Sasaki's soldiers were occupying a sector consisting of a series of defensive lines dug into the jumbled mass of hills and ridges clear back to Munda. The New Georgia Occupation Force could count upon grinding away at strong lines of self- and mutually supporting pillboxes, bunkers, and rifle pits of coral-and-log construction. The Japanese were well armed, and they had a large number of 7.7mm and 13mm light and heavy machine guns. Batteries of 90mm mortars were dug into the rear, and 57mm and 75mm mountain guns could bring direct fire to bear on the advancing American columns.

That was the problem at the front. There were others to the rear.

Supply lines had to be maintained by overworked units of combat engineers, who had to build a traversable jeep track apace the advance in order to keep front-line units in contact with supply dumps. Local guides did their best to select dry routes, but these invariably descended into boggy terrain. They had to. The entire route was a muddy meandering mess that often ran parallel to the front for long stretches.

The engineers were constantly harassed by the Japanese. Several bulldozer operators were shot while far in the rear, and each bulldozer was eventually sent to the rear to be outfitted with a steel-plate shield for the operator's cab. Even this protection was insufficient, and armed patrols of at least squad strength had to be provided. These troops were often drawn from the engineer units themselves, thus cutting more deeply into the work force. Within a short time, the engineers were simply overwhelmed by their work and could no longer keep the roads open, much less apace the advance. That in turn affected the efficiency of the supply-starved infantry formations.

It was ultimately due to the bogged down road-building effort that General Hester decided to occupy Laiana Beach, fully 5,000 yards closer to Munda than Zanana. This was a highly controversial decision, not because it was taken but because it was made so late in the game. Laiana had been high on the list of possible sites for the initial landings on New Georgia, but had been turned down because of its proximity to Munda and the probability of its being defended in considerable force against amphibious assault.

General Hester might well have landed his infantry regiments at Laiana to begin with. Or, once the road to Laiana from Zanana was seen to be impossibly long, he might simply have halted the land drive, withdrawn a regiment or more from the Zanana front or Rendova and the barrier islands, and undertaken a direct amphibious assault at Laiana. But Hester did not see his options in those terms at the time. What he did see was that he had two infantry regiments that were just penetrating a built-up zone of defense from which they could not be easily withdrawn; he had, at best, barely acclimated combat troops on his front lines who might interpret a withdrawal for any reason as being a defeat at the hands of the enemy they might just be learning to overcome; he was still awaiting some sort of counterthrust by an enemy whose options were open, so he had to keep his reserves—the 103rd Infantry—in reserve; and he had sufficient reason to believe that a frontal amphibious operation against Laiana would be met at the beach by a determined defending force of considerable size. In the end, Hester seems to have made the only decision warranted by the information he then had. He ordered the 172nd Infantry to change the direction of its advance in order to take the defenses guarding Laiana from the rear; the 169th Infantry would continue its advance directly toward Munda.

There was one near misstep: The 3rd Battalion, 103rd, supported by a platoon of Marine light tanks, was ordered to make an amphibious assault on Laiana. After much scurrying and worrying, the battalion commander, Lieutenant Colonel Jim Wells, was told that his battalion would be landed at Laiana only after the beach had been secured by the 172nd Infantry. (Wells's battalion had several similar close calls of the same nature; it was at one time preparing to assault Munda directly over the Munda Bar, but was ordered to stand down at the last minute, an order that no doubt saved the battalion from suffering grave casualties.)

On the night before the drive on Laiana was to begin, the Japanese worked over the 172nd Infantry with artillery and mortars. Captain Edward Scherrer, the assistant NGOF intelligence officer, was severely wounded, as were several Maori scouts. Though his usual routine was to spend his nights at the regimental command post, Colonel David Ross, the grizzled Alabamian commanding the 172nd Infantry, elected to spend the night at the command post of Major Bill Naylor's 1st Battalion because he wanted to be on hand when the drive on Laiana began. As the tempo of the Japanese shelling increased, Ross grabbed the field telephone connected to the force artillery fire direction center and asked to speak to Lieutenant Colonel Ed Berry, the force artillery operations officer.

"Berry," Ross shouted into the phone above the din of falling shells, "I want some arty fire in my right flank."

"Sir, I can't deliver it there because it will endanger friendly troops," Berry explained.

"All right, give me the fire on my left flank."

"I can't deliver it there for the same reason."

"Then, goddammit, Berry, give it to me in the rear."

"I can't do that either," Berry sighed, "because it will endanger the division command post."

"Berry," Ross rejoined in a tired drawl, "I am prepared to sacrifice the division command post."

The 172nd Infantry disengaged from the Munda drive at 1000 hours, July 11, and came to a southward bearing for the drive on Laiana. The 2nd Battalion remained behind to hold a blocking position until the 169th Infantry could come abreast and seal the rear flank against infiltration. The 1st and 3rd Battalions, 172nd, conducted the beginning phase of the advance in line abreast.

Great care was taken to achieve tactical surprise, but the leading elements did not get far before Japanese combat patrols began making contact with them. The American troops, already slowed by knee-deep mud, next had to contend with a fairly constant rain of mortar shells. It was assumed that the two Japanese infantry battalions thought to be defending Laiana would be on full alert.

Before long, casualties were mounting under the steady mortar barrage. The wounded had to be carried with the regiment to conserve manpower and to keep the underdeveloped trails clear for resupply efforts. Often, the wounded had to be held aloft while stretcher bearers struggled through the hip-deep waters of mangrove swamps. This policy slowed the advance because infantrymen had to be detailed to carry the wounded, at least four to a litter but usually as many as eight, and even as many as twelve.

Colonel Ross reported in midafternoon that his companies had made gains averaging 450 yards and had come in contact with the first line of pillboxes yet encountered on New Georgia. There was some infiltration between the 172nd and 169th Regiments, but it appeared that the Japanese were content for the most part to remain within their prepared defensive emplacements.

There were no gains in the zone of the 169th Infantry. The regimental commander, Colonel John Eason, was relieved early in the day by General Hester, and his replacement, Colonel Temple Holland, of the 37th Infantry Division's 145th Infantry Regiment, spent the day familiarizing himself with his new command and getting a new regimental staff squared away; he brought the 145th Infantry's executive, operations, and intelligence officers and a dozen enlisted technicians with him.

On July 12, Colonel Ross ordered his 172nd Infantry to continue the advance on Laiana. It was hoped that the village could be occupied by nightfall. The troops moved out early and plodded on into the rain forest. Japanese machine guns and mortars firing from unseen or unassailable positions made every step a major undertaking, but the men trudged doggedly forward. By nightfall, the regiment's leading elements were still some 500 yards from the objective. Given the circumstances, it was felt that the regiment had turned in a superior performance. There had been little food brought in during the two-day advance, and carrying parties equaled nearly a battalion in strength. Safe drinking water had been virtually exhausted.

It was clear by the late afternoon of July 12 that Ross's battalions were facing a line of deep, interconnected pillbox emplacements. As this was a prepared line, there were grave fears that the emplacements would be of ferroconcrete construction, which would make the job of reducing them a horror.

Ross's soldiers passed a miserable night. Japanese mortars, which were in amply supply, had the range, and all hands were prevented from sleeping by a steady barrage. In addition to the bursting of mortar rounds, there was the sound of incessant tree-felling several dozen yards to the front; the Japanese were clearing fire lanes and building additional emplacements, an unhappy omen.

Colonel Ross was determined to have his isolated command in possession of Laiana by the end of July 13. Japanese patrols were roving through the regimental rear, though strong American combat patrols were doing an adequate job of fending them off.

As artillery batteries on the barrier islands opened fire to support the regimental advance on July 13, the tired, hungry, thirsty riflemen mounted out at dawn, right into an endless stretch of mangrove swamp. By nightfall, after hard fighting through the entire day, the 172nd Infantry was holding its objective. Strong combat patrols were out mopping up and consolidating the area and scouting Japanese defenses to the west. Somewhere on the trail to Laiana, the troops and their commanders realized, the 172nd Infantry had crossed the line; when it seized Laiana, the 172nd Infantry was a combat regiment manned by competent combat veterans.

During the night, a dozen food-and-water-laden landing craft set out from Rendova to resupply the haggard 172nd Infantry. However, because they were fearful of a counterlanding by the Japanese, soldiers on the beach refused to display a signal light of any sort. Since the regiment was out of direct radio communication with NGOF headquarters, there was no way to be certain that the milling landing craft were friendly. The relief force returned to Rendova fully laden.

On the morning of July 14, the 3rd Battalion, 103rd, boarded landing craft at Rendova and, accompanied by the organic light-tank platoon of the 9th Marine Defense Battalion, set out for the run to Laiana. Japanese artillery fired on the boats, but the landing took place without a casualty, although a heavy concentration of artillery smoke shells along the Japanese-occupied shore south of the beach did not materialize as planned. Lieutenant Colonel Jim Wells, commander of the 3rd Battalion, 103rd, could not understand why the Japanese did not open fire on the twenty or so vulnerable landing craft as they approached the beach. (Two weeks later, Wells obtained a copy of a report on the landing that was discovered in a captured Japanese company command post. It gave the date and place of the landing of 2,000 enemy troops, "more than half of which were wiped out during the landing operation." It was learned even later that Major General Noburo Sasaki informed Rabaul that thirteen out of seventy landing craft were sunk and twenty were damaged in a hotly contested landing—and that the Americans abandoned the effort.)

Once Wells's battalion and the Marine M3 light tanks were safely ashore, additional landing craft brought in engineers and their equipment, and a road from Laiana was pushed northward without delay toward the jungle-bound 169th Infantry. Once landed, Wells's battalion once again became the 43rd Infantry Division reserve. All hands in the 172nd Infantry received a full ration of food and water to alleviate the critical shortages encountered along the way, and the wounded were evacuated, some after three days on the trail. This alone restored the 172nd Infantry to respectable effective strength, for hundreds of litter bearers were returned to the infantry companies.

By the day's end, an underwater cable had been installed between the Force Artillery fire direction center and the beachheads at Zanana and Laiana. Within days, the fate of the Munda drive would rest upon this link.

On the morning of July 15, Colonel Ross prepared to get his battalions moving once again. To bolster his force, he borrowed L Company, 103rd, from the division reserve and sent it to plug a gap between his own 2nd and 3rd Battalions. Lieutenant Colonel Jim Wells objected strongly to the piecemeal commitment of his battalion but was forced to accede when Ross made clear his dire need. In any case, Ross had obtained permission from Brigadier General Leonard Wing to commit Wells's battalion as he saw fit. As it happened, L Company's commander was severely wounded by mortar fire. Late in the day, a 37mm gun crew from Wells's antitank platoon stripped down one of its light antitank guns and carried it to the front to destroy three pillboxes holding up the advance. However, despite assists from the 3rd Battalion, 103rd, the 172nd Infantry could make no headway. The regiment was right on top of the Japanese main line of resistance.

14

During the time it took the 172nd Infantry to secure Laiana Beach, the 169th Infantry ground its way slowly along its original axis of advance, getting hurt in attempts to overcome the extensive ridge-defense complex on its front.

On July 11, the day the 172nd Regiment wheeled southeastward, most of the 169th Infantry halted in place in order to settle the spooked troops, and so a thorough estimate of the situation could be effected by the new regimental commander and his staff. The regiment stood in line facing the forwardmost emplacements of the Japanese formal defense sector. In fact, in places, it had advanced a bit into those defenses. Directly to the front, on high ground and on both sides of the main trail leading through the area, were firmly entrenched Japanese units whose mission it was to keep the American infantry from reaching the junction of the Munda and Lambeti trails, which was a few hundred yards farther on. The seasoned Japanese veterans holding the ridges were emplaced in coral-and-log pillboxes and bunkers, which were at least vulnerable to supporting artillery fire and, up to a point, the 81mm mortars and 37mm antitank guns the American infantry was able to manhandle through the rain forest.

On July 11, Major Joe Zimmer's 1st Battalion, 169th, attempted to advance directly up the trail under cover of supporting artillery fire. The battalion cleared about 500 yards of its front when it was ordered to return to positions near the regimental command post, which was by then located on Bloody Hill. The troops were miffed, to put it mildly. And relieved.

Late on July 11, as Colonel Temple Holland was rounding out his first full day getting his new command into some sort of acceptable shape for its task of fighting, the division forward command post passed along an order directing the 169th Infantry to launch a ground assault at 0830 on the morning of July 12 in order to secure the high ground in the vicinity of the Munda-Lambeti trail junction. The 2nd Battalion was to take the lead, with 1st Battalion units echeloned to the right rear to cover the flank. The 3rd Battalion was released from Colonel Holland's control and would be assigned to holding the trail junction in force once the objective had been secured.

The regimental advance got off as planned, and on time. However, the elation the troops and their commanders felt was short-lived. Partly because of stiff opposition and largely due to its getting intermingled with the southward-turning 172nd Infantry, Holland's troops bogged down only a short distance from their starting line.

It took some cursing and shoving to get the troops back in order, but the redeployment was accomplished. Then Major Joe Zimmer's 1st Battalion sprang forward and made steady headway over 300 yards of hotly contested terrain. Meantime, Lieutenant Colonel John Fowler's 2nd Battalion was subjected to heavy enfillading fire from the northernmost ridge on its front, and it was firmly pinned.

Following heated discussions between Colonel Holland and his battalion commanders, the assault got under way once again. Artillery support was called, and the infantry was able to move forward behind a rolling barrage. The gains amounted to all of ten yards. The infantry proved itself completely incapable of keeping pace with the curtain of steel, and it fell far behind before coming to a complete standstill late in the afternoon. At day's end, Colonel Holland moved his command post forward and put in a request for close air support for the following day.

During the night of July 12–13, the Japanese attempted to infiltrate the regimental lines en masse. They were, for once, stopped cold by a close-in barrage put down by 105mm howitzers located at Zanana and the barrier islets.

The plan of attack for July 13 brought the entire 169th Infantry together in combat for the first time. Fowler's 2nd Battalion was to press home a frontal assault, Zimmer's 1st Battalion was to continue to move around on the right flank, and Reincke's rested 3rd Battalion was committed from the division reserve to flush out the Japanese on the left flank.

With the regiment's effective combat strength down to about 50 percent, the task facing the 169th on July 13 would be formidable. An intelligence estimate based on data pieced together from reports of the July 12 fighting indicated that the Japanese were securely emplaced along the entire front, and in considerable depth.

Several hundred yards out on the right front was a strongly developed defensive area; this was Zimmer's objective. On the left, and a bit farther into the dense growth, was another strongpoint; this was Reincke's objective. The ground to the immediate front was extensively developed in terms of construction, but probes had determined that the Japanese had been forced to withdraw considerable numbers of their soldiers in order to counter the move on the American right.

Fowler's 2nd Battalion jumped right behind an artillery preparation and began taking ground. G Company was in support while E and F Companies spread out on a more-or-less continuous front. After a short time, the lead elements began bearing too far to the left, bringing them into the friendly artillery-fire zone on that flank. A number of soldiers went down under the fire of their own supports, and the battalion began falling apart. It was impossible for troop leaders to maintain order under the terrific pounding, so they allowed their scared charges to stampede headlong to the rear in order to save themselves. These soldiers were met on the trail by Captain Jim Rankin, the commander of M Company, 169th, who was moving forward in advance of the 3rd Battalion. Rankin stood in the center of the trail and began collaring the retreating soldiers, who all obediently stopped. Then Rankin shook out several 3rd Battalion rifle platoons that were right behind him, and these were deployed across the trail, both to stop the retreating 2nd Battalion men and as proof against the Japanese breakthrough that seemed to be in progress. The panic was contained in less than an hour, and the 2nd Battalion men were all returned to their units.

Once it was committed, Reincke's rather more composed 3rd Battalion did a splendid job. Artillery fire had stripped away much of the concealing growth, greatly enhancing visibility. I and L Companies advanced over hazardous terrain for four full hours. The going was rough, but the advance was steady, if slow. At 1440, Lieutenant Colonel Reincke informed Colonel Holland that his battalion vanguard was at the base of a fairly large knoll overlooking the trail junction. Holland granted permission to Reincke's request that he be allowed to secure the hill.

Captain Howard Nelson's L Company deployed and advanced directly up the 200-to-300-foot hill. The weary troops flung themselves forward, scrabbling over the broken ground, climbing slowly toward clearer, cleaner air. About halfway up, the vanguard encountered very heavy fire, and that stopped L Company. During efforts by troop leaders to get the company moving again, both Captain Nelson and his executive officer were wounded and had to be evacuated. One of the two remaining platoon leaders, First Lieutenant Raymond Ewing, automatically took command of the company and applied pressure on the Japanese blocking his way while I Company approached the hill from the left at an angle. The combined efforts of both companies finally prevailed, and the battalion was able to occupy the hill.

As soon as the summit of the hill was secure, Lieutenant Colonel Reincke set all hands to organizing a stout defensive perimeter. The battalion was shorthanded—K Company had been detached the night before to guard the regimental command post—so the lines were on the thin side. It was clear that the Japanese would be back to reclaim their hill; they had obviously withdrawn for a bit to counter the assaults to the north.

From atop the hill, once they could look up from their digging, the American infantrymen caught their very first glimpse of the sea beyond Munda Field. They could not quite see the wide expanse of the runway because of intervening stands of high trees, but they could plainly see the channel beyond the ultimate objective. To be above the forest, in clear sunlight, was heavenly. For the first time in two weeks, the weary soldiers of the 3rd Battalion, 169th, felt a certain exhilaration that went down in unit journals as a marked increase in morale. All they had to do was hold.

To the north, Zimmer's 1st Battalion was having a difficult time. With A and C Companies in line and B Company in support, the battalion hit some of the most torn-up country it had ever seen. The area was a mass of shell craters and torn, twisted trees, all of which blocked routes of advance and provided cover for snipers.

The massive bombardment that had torn the ground so badly had forced the Japanese to retire to safer ground. But they had come back at the first sign of the American advance, and they now manned their emplacements with renewed vigor. Artillery support for Zimmer was out of the question; his troops were too close to the Japanese to allow the necessary margin of safety. The battalion commander was urged to order a bayonet attack. In the tradition of their Civil War predecessors, the Connecticut riflemen snapped blades to the barrels of their rifles, formed up, and, on orders from their officers, stepped into the fray. B Company was brutally cut apart as it crawled to the crest of a small rise on its front. The company commander and two platoon leaders were injured, but the survivors pressed home their spirited assault. For once, Japanese artillery and mortars were firing massed salvoes, and Zimmer's infantry took it hard. It was impossible to make headway in the close, hotly contested terrain. Zimmer was ordered to pull back before taking more needless casualties.

The successes of the day were uneven, but the 169th Infantry had taken ground. The troops seemed more responsive to the demands of their leaders than they had been, and they were certainly more aggressive in driving home their assaults, though the Japanese were meting out a heavy opposition.

By nightfall, the Japanese had come to realize the extent of their blunder in pulling troops from the southern flank to support units to the north. In front of the 3rd Battalion, 169th's hill—now officially named Reincke Ridge—was the defensive keypoint of the entire sector, Horseshoe Hill. South of the ridge was a large gap in the American lines, left by the turning of the 172nd Infantry. Colonel Holland's battalions were isolated, facing the largest concentration of Japanese infantry on New Georgia, a concentration made more dangerous by the need of its commanders to wrest back the ground they had given away in error. Lieutenant Colonel Reincke and Colonel Holland agreed that the 3rd Battalion was in a tight spot—500 yards into the Japanese main defense line and well ahead of its sister battalions—but the occupation of the high ground had appreciably raised morale, and it was providing an excellent artillery observation point. Reincke would stay.

The Japanese responded to Reincke's advance with a light artillery probe, followed by several light infantry probes. During these actions, First Lieutenant Neil Doyle, the regimental Catholic chaplain, was moving across the exposed summit, assisting the wounded and administering last rites. Caught in the open once too often, Father Doyle went down under a mortar concentration. In all, two American infantrymen were killed outright and nineteen were wounded. Father Doyle died two days later.

Though the Japanese artillery fire subsided at dawn, the battalion was kept busy fending off attempts at infiltration.

Antitank Company, 169th Infantry, was sent from Rendova to

Zanana on July 13. Its arrival was viewed by the regimental commander as a godsend. After leaving its 37mm guns on the beach,
the bulk of the company was ordered to take over much of the
supply and evacuation duties sustaining Reincke's 3rd Battalion.
This in turn released nearly all of the infantrymen who had been
pulled from the ranks of the fighting battalion to augment the inadequate service units. The burden placed upon the newly arrived
antitank troops had been made considerably easier in advance by
the opening of an engineer bridge across the Barike River on July
12 and the extension of the main supply route toward the regimental front.

With the regimental infantry units more than 50 percent understrength, Colonel Holland next ordered sixty antitank officers and
troops to join the 2nd Battalion as infantry, and twenty others
joined the 1st Battalion. Finally, combat patrols from the canni-
balized unit were ordered to cover the southern flank of the regiment, which was open.

Despite Colonel Holland's efforts to support his infantry battalions with fillers drawn from the regimental antitank company,
troop commanders, and perhaps the troops themselves, were painfully aware that Holland had by then permanently withdrawn a
full rifle company—in this case, K Company—to guard his regimental command post. Though Holland had many good ideas and
worked tirelessly to benefit his new command, he was held in
rather low esteem by his subordinates. One quirk that was considered dangerous by many and foolhardy by most was his standing
order that all communications wires leading to his command post
be severed at dusk each day to prevent Japanese infiltrators from
following them through the rain forest to his front door. In fact,
the simple expedient was a rather good precaution in a tight situation—it would be emulated by several of Holland's subordinates
in extreme emergencies—but it set a terrible example for a regiment that had come through so stormy a baptism as had the 169th
Infantry.

At 0800 hours, July 14, at tree burst erupted over the center of
the 3rd Battalion perimeter atop Reincke Ridge. The single Japanese artillery round killed four and wounded twenty-three, including Major Frank Dorsey, the battalion executive officer. That
so few died was due in large part to the efforts of Staff Sergeant
Louis Gullitti, the battalion's senior medic; in the absence of a

doctor, he and his small team of medics administered first aid, often radical aid, to the wounded while more Japanese shells struck the battalion perimeter.

Casualty rates surged upward on July 14. Two soldiers were killed and five were wounded by Japanese machine guns sniping from long range along the supply route to Reincke Ridge. The opening of a devastating barrage at 0200 hours, July 15, caught many members of Reincke's battalion in the open. Eight men were killed and twenty-six were wounded, including First Lieutenant Raymond Ewing, the last of the L Company officers. In fact, L Company was down to just fifty-one effectives. Just over one hundred casualties had been inflicted on the battalion in just over thirty hours. Staff Sergeant Louis Gullitti's shorthanded medical section continued to save lives despite the danger each medic faced in reaching, treating, and recovering the wounded from manifestly dangerous locations.

First Lieutenant George Mayo, the 3rd Battalion adjutant, was at the regimental command post when news arrived that Reincke Ridge had been virtually stripped of medical supplies. Mayo gathered all the volunteers he could dig up and loaded each of them down with the needed medical supplies. Then he led his party into the dark rain forest and advanced 500 yards to the base of Reincke Ridge. There he left the supply party and climbed the hill alone. As Mayo neared the summit, he called loudly, "This is George Washington Mayo. I have help for you." Wary riflemen called officers to the line, and the officers determined that the caller was indeed Lieutenant Mayo. They in turn shouted directions Mayo could home in on. He reached the summit safely and told his colleagues that the carrying party was at the base of the hill. Assured that the volunteers would not be fired on, Mayo returned to the base of the hill and led the carrying party into the 3rd Battalion perimeter.

Once the excitement died down a bit, Mayo revealed that he had acted on his own when news of the shortages arrived at the regimental supply depot, where he happened to be spending the night. The wire to the depot was the only intact wire leading back from Reincke Ridge to a regimental agency; all the others had been severed at dusk on orders from Colonel Holland. Indeed, the link to the supply depot had been maintained against the regimental commander's express orders.

During this night's barrage, word spread among the troops that they were being fired on by friendly artillery. Next morning, in response to news of the rumors, Brigadier General Harold Barker, the NGOF artillery commander, came up to Reincke Ridge and rooted through several fresh shell craters. At last, he came up with a large piece of shrapnel that bore Japanese characters. The general saw to it that the evidence was passed around among the troops, thereby dispelling the notion that they were receiving anything less than perfectly accurate support. The troops were impressed that a general took the trouble.

15

On July 16, Colonel David Ross's reinforced 172nd Infantry Regiment prepared to begin a westward sweep along the southern coast of the Munda Peninsula. For the moment, Ross's four-battalion force was to make limited assaults to bring continuing pressure to bear upon the elements of Major General Noburo Sasaki's Southeast Detached Force that were defending the coastal strip—the main body of Major Giichi Sata's 2nd Battalion, 229th Infantry. In addition, the high ground directly in front of Laiana was to be wrested from the Japanese in order to form a line of departure for a proposed sweep all the way to Munda by regiments from both the 43rd and 37th Infantry Divisions.

Initially, Colonel Ross was to employ only his 2nd and 3rd Battalions. Major Bill Naylor's 1st Battalion, 172nd, was to be the regimental reserve, and Lieutenant Colonel Jim Wells's 3rd Battalion, 103rd, was still the 43rd Division reserve. However, for additional support, the assault battalions would each draw three Marine light tanks that had come ashore with Wells's battalion when Laiana Beach had been secured.

Use of the tanks was made primarily for experimental purposes. Although armor had been employed at Guadalcanal to a small extent, the results had been disappointing or inconclusive. The terrain around Laiana was poor, although the tankers felt it was within bounds for a trial run. The nature of the Japanese defenses warranted whatever risks the experiment engendered.

To make the task somewhat less onerous for the tankers, each vehicle was to be assigned a six-man infantry escort. The escorts were to attempt to point out targets that could not be seen in the closeness of the rain forest from a buttoned-up tank. Also, the escorts were pledged to keep Japanese armed with explosives away from such blind spots as the lightly armored rears of the tanks.

The regimental attack commenced, as planned, on the morning of July 16. In the zone of Major John Carrigan's 2nd Battalion, 172nd, the tank-infantry combination made rather good progress. Initially, the lumbering vehicles had a fairly well-defined track to follow. This helped maintain a steady advance, but when the track petered out the clumsy tanks had an extremely hard time describing a straight line. Upended logs and shattered stumps left in the wake of recent artillery barrages made forward movement a tricky proposition. The tanks had to stop constantly and back up or tow one another out of shell craters and brush-obscured ravines. Frantic calls from the infantry escorts kept them out of more dire predicaments. The 2nd Battalion, 172nd's advance slowed to a crawl to keep pace with the tanks.

Major Carrigan and his staff were despairing of taking any of the day's objectives when, all at once, after losing much time, the advance burst into an extremely rapid seventy-five-yard thrust over ground that had been thoroughly cleared by devastating artillery concentrations. For once, visibility was excellent.

When a pillbox was easily spotted at the far edge of the cleared area, the infantry called up the armor to take it out. The three tanks lumbered up in wedge formation and blanketed the emplacement with fire from their 37mm main guns. As the tank guns slowly, methodically swept the trees around the pillbox, still more vegetation was torn away, thus revealing additional emplacements. When several Japanese machine guns opened fire from a cluster of nearly invisible grass shacks, the tank gunners switched to canister rounds and cut large swaths through the shacks and their occupants.

The tanks had entered the fight with their hatches open and commanders peering out. This was to aid visibility since a buttoned-up tank relies upon a periscope with a very limited traverse and highly distorted vision. As the armored vehicles fired on the grass shacks, one Japanese machine-gun crew set up its weapon off to one side and opened fire on the tank turrets. This sudden outburst caused a rapid shift in sighting methods as all the turret hatches promptly clanged shut. The tank turrets were quickly traversed as the gunners sought the hidden machine gun. The Japanese gunner was killed, but another man sprang to his place. He, too, died, but a third man took over. This went on and on until, at length, the machine gun itself was destroyed and the surviving bushwhackers were sent scuttling to the relative security of a nearby pillbox. The three tanks lumbered up on their heels and narrowly missed following them into the emplacement, which none of the drivers could see. The tanks backed up and the pillbox was mauled by their 37mm guns, as were two other emplacements the tankers stumbled upon. Supporting infantrymen moved in behind

the tanks and hand-grenaded the three emplacements into complete silence.

Inland, on Carrigan's right flank, Major James Devine's 3rd
Battalion, 172nd, was having a far rougher and far less rewarding
go of it. In Devine's sector, the advance by the infantry and armor
alike was severely impeded by sharply rising ridges.

To offset the blinding characteristics of the rain forest on the
buttoned-up tanks, the infantry escort teams had outfitted themselves with large quantities of tracer ammunition. Whenever a
hidden pillbox was located, the tracer-equipped riflemen fired at
the embrasures to help the tank gunners pinpoint the target. The
results were adequate, but there were too many pillboxes to be
handled efficiently. The action soon became an outright duel between the half-blind tanks and the many-horned forest. Every
opening in the thick living mat seemed to be the fire lane of one or
more hidden guns. Moderately armored, the light tanks stood up
very well to this form of opposition, and the gunners coolly fired
their little 37mm guns at the coral-and-log emplacements, destroying or at least neutralizing many of them.

After taking one extremely troublesome hill, Major Devine decided to call it a day. He ordered the tanks out and had his infantrymen establish a defensive perimeter on the newly won ground.
The advance, while successful, had been grueling.

On the way to the rear, Gunnery Sergeant Charles Spurlock, the
leader of the three-tank force, was driving his own vehicle when
his leg was snapped by a log that pushed its way through the trap
door beneath the driver's seat. Other than that, the tankers suffered no casualties in destroying a respectable number of Japanese
emplacements and their occupants.

After Carrigan's 2nd Battalion, 172nd, stood down for the day,
the Americans had their first real opportunity to carry out a detailed inspection of the type of emplacements with which they
would be faced for the rest of the sweep against Munda.

Of primary concern was the materials the Japanese had employed in constructing the pillboxes and bunkers. Emplacements
taken earlier in the campaign had been of coral-and-log construction, but they had been hurriedly contrived in the face of the
American offensive. The emplacements taken with the assistance
of the Marine tanks on July 16 had been constructed weeks, per-

haps months, prior to the landings at Zanana. As these were not of ferroconcrete construction, it was presumed—hoped—that the New Georgia Occupation Force would not be faced with the much more complex task of reducing ferroconcrete emplacements for the rest of the way to Munda. Morale was positively affected by this surmise; at least it appeared that the infantry had a fighting chance with the weapons available.

Close inspection of the bunkers and pillboxes was made in the hope of discovering methods by which similar emplacements farther on might be cheaply and efficiently reduced. Nearly without exception, the emplacements were built of weathered coral and heavy logs, though some were built of earth and logs. Each was in the neighborhood of twelve feet square and, in general, ten feet deep. Depending upon the lay of the land, each was about 70 percent underground. There were either one or two firing apertures for light or medium machine guns, and several loopholes for riflemen, who manned a packed-earth firing step on the forward wall. Each bunker's walls were found to be two or three layers thick, constructed of logs packed with raw earth and coral. The roofs were each five or six layers thick, depending upon natural overhead concealment.

Interspersed around the bunkers and pillboxes were numerous one- and two-man foxholes and spiderholes. A number of these were more or less in the open, protected only by intricate camouflage. In the main, however, the Japanese made thorough use of the terrain and the thick growth, setting many of these infantry emplacements within the thick, protecting roots of banyan and other large trees.

Construction was outstanding, and camouflage was superb. The natural roll of the land was used to full advantage in hiding the outlines of the emplacements. Earth, grass, vines, palm fronds, trees, bushes, rocks, stumps, logs, and leaves were extensively used to help conceal each position. Because of the incredible regenerative qualities of the rain forest, much of the natural growth destroyed during construction had grown back to conceal many positions as no man might have done. The effect was simply astounding. Americans had an incredibly hard time locating these emplacements, even where concealment had been torn away by artillery barrages. More often than not, the presence of a pillbox was discovered only when an advancing rifleman inadvertently stepped into its foot-high firing lane without knowing a thing until a quick machine-gun burst would cut him down at the shins; a second burst would be fired through the hapless victim's head, or the machine gunner might wait to bag the men who came to rescue the wounded man. Americans reported that the emplacements were harder to find visually than by the smell of the occupants.

On the morning of July 17, the three Marine tanks supporting Devine's 3rd Battalion, 172nd, were again ordered to push through the Japanese holding the ridge country north of Laiana. The three tanks, each with its six-man infantry escort, cautiously moved around the base of the hill taken on July 16 and pushed through the artillery-ravaged rain forest toward the next hill. The Marines fired a heavy concentration of high-explosive and canister rounds as they crawled forward. Opposition was scattered. Follow-on infantry units, which were closely following the tanks, poked into the cleared areas and secured the new ground by hand grenading each emplacement before actually crawling inside to check for dead and wounded defenders and to loot stores of weapons, food, and ammunition. In the afternoon, K Company, 172nd, intercepted and ambushed a heavily armed Japanese patrol well away from the main axis of the advance. It was clear from the Japanese patrol's movements that the American battalion's lines were being infiltrated.

The three Marine tanks supporting the advance of the 2nd Battalion, 172nd, avoided direct frontal attacks in order to save time; they moved on the Japanese right near the coast to come in on the blind sides of the emplacements along their route of advance. The envelopment worked well; a 200-yard swath was cut through the defensive network. The advance was proceeding extremely well when the tank commander noticed that his infantry escort had vanished. He immediately ordered his tanks to return to the line of departure. The armor was immediately ordered to spearhead a second assault, but the massed infantry stepped off right into a heavy mortar concentration, sending everyone diving for cover before the battalion had advanced ten yards.

Impervious to the mortar fire, the tanks forged ahead of the infantry, madly traversing their guns to keep the Japanese at bay. As the infantry could not remount their attack through the chillingly accurate mortar barrage, the tanks again returned to the starting point. While attempting to disengage from the losing struggle, each vehicle was rocked by heavy explosions. The rear tank was blasted twice and knocked out while the others sustained minor damage. For the first time anywhere, the Japanese had employed magnetic antitank grenades.

The tank turrets began traversing; 37mm canister rounds and machine gun fire spewed death and destruction into the moving underbrush on all flanks. Maneuvering erratically to throw off the opposition, the tanks managed to extricate themselves from the ambush and crawl back to friendly lines.

Movement on the coast ceased for the day.

As a result of the two days of armor-supported infantry assaults, which were thought to be generally successful, 10th Marine Defense Battalion, based in the Russell Islands, was asked to ship its light-tank platoon to New Georgia. These were the only additional tanks available anywhere near the combat zone.

The problems and frustrations encountered by armor in the rain forest were innumerable. The greatest problem was the matter of tank-infantry cooperation, which was something neither branch had had much training in. It is true that infantrymen are vulnerable to bullets while tanks are not, but tankers are by nature a paranoid breed, for they are easily broiled if their vehicles are set on fire. Buttoned up, the Marine light tanks were nearly blind, even in the open. Since the view of the drivers, gunners, and tank commanders was so limited, particularly in closed-in terrain, the tanks were extremely vulnerable to attack. Without infantry support, the tanks could not safely operate.

For a wide variety of reasons, including rivalry between Marines and soldiers, and rivalry between tankers and infantrymen—but mainly because neither side explained its imperatives to the other—a great mutual loathing was ignited in the wake of the first two days of the tank-infantry advance. Each side accused the other of cowardice.

The tankers were themselves generally happy with the results of two days of fighting, though they were perturbed by the lack of cooperative training among the infantry. The 37mm guns with which the tanks were armed were found to be adequate for the task of going up against coral-and-log bunkers, both when firing canister and high-explosive rounds. Ferroconcrete bunkers would undoubtedly require 75mm armor-piercing shells. The ability of the tanks to attack through virtually any jungle obstructions met with highly enthusiastic reports. It was found that the tanks were very rarely out of first gear in the jungle, a factor that would require ongoing maintenance. Resupply of fuel and ammunition was of vital importance as the small vehicles carried relatively little of either; depots were established as close to the front as possible to shorten the time required for replenishing these vital stocks. Recovery of damaged vehicles in the rain forest was another problem to be considered. By the time the campaign drew to a close, nearly all the Marine tanks were disabled, though very few of these were permanently lost.

Carrigan's 2nd Battalion, 172nd, was relieved on the night of July 17–18 by Lieutenant Colonel Jim Wells's 3rd Battalion, 103rd, which was to renew the tank-infantry advance in the morning. Just before dawn, however, Wells's battalion, which was together in combat for the first time, was itself assaulted by Major Giichi Sata's 2nd Battalion, 229th Infantry. The attack was easily routed, but the troops were a bit shaken by the unexpected turnabout so close to their own first combat sally. Sporadic gunfights between Wells's troops and Sata's continued near the coast until dawn, then abruptly ceased.

As the firing on the infantry line was dying down, five Marine light tanks moved up behind Wells's battalion. To ensure ample protection, the battalion commander agreed to provide thirty of his riflemen for each tank, a considerable investment in manpower. Captain Robert Blake, the Marine tank-platoon commander, stated that he would not move forward, and might even withdraw, if this protection was not in evidence at any time during the assault. The near loss of three tanks to Japanese infantry the day before was quite fresh in Blake's mind. With only eight tanks on the entire island, losses could not be sustained.

The attack fell apart in the face of furious opposition almost as soon as it jumped off. The tankers spewed out a great volume of machine-gun fire, but the Japanese only increased their opposition. Rifles and machine guns fired from carefully hidden blinds all along Wells's front. Ricochets caroming off steel tank hulls whizzed through the infantry formations, dropping several soldiers in their tracks.

But Wells's well-trained, well-motivated soldiers continued to grind forward. Individual infantrymen waded forward to locate and point out the Japanese machine guns for the armor. The advance continued, but very slowly, and the tempo of fire steadily increased. There were few positive results, but Wells's troops kept wading into the furious action.

Then the Japanese added a new twist. As Captain Blake maneuvered his tank in close to the main Japanese lines, he suddenly became aware that he and his tank were being doused with flamethrower fuel, which, fortunately, did not ignite. The assailant was quickly flushed and killed, but everyone involved was badly shaken, for fire is the tanker's worst enemy, and his worst fear. The fire hazard from flamethrowers was psychologically devastating to the tankers.

Despite their size and the zeal of the troops, the thirty-man infantry escort teams were quite ineffective in the close terrain. As the tanks ground forward, Japanese soldiers literally flew out of the trees in suicidal efforts to plant magnetic grenades on the steel hulls. The third tank in line caught one and, after the explosion ripped a gash in its flank and injured two crewmen, the tankers convinced themselves that the infantry had again run for cover. Covering one another, the armored vehicles moved slowly to the rear, pulling the damaged tank at the end of a tow chain. With that, the attack of 3rd Battalion, 103rd, petered out. Faced with widely conflicting information by day's end, higher headquarters directed the tanks to abstain from further action until further notice.

16

As early as July 6, the various command echelons in the South Pacific Area responsible for overseeing the conduct of the New Georgia campaign concluded that the objective would not be as easily wrested from 8th Area Army as had originally been anticipated. The first step toward rectifying the error of optimism was, in the mind of Major General John Hester, the immediate re-inforcement of his 43rd Infantry Division by no less than a fresh regiment of infantry, hopefully two.

From the beginning of the planning phase, General Hester had foreseen a number of administrative problems associated with op-erating the NGOF headquarters. When the operation was first planned, Hester's division was selected for the job and heavily reinforced. The larger force was all placed under the division commander, but the division staff was not augmented. Hester asked for more staff officers, but only one was furnished. There was one Army corps—XIV Corps—stationed at Guadalcanal at the time, and it occurred to Hester that it should run the operation so that he could oversee the operations of just his own division with his own staff, which would not be obliged to oversee far-flung op-erations by 43rd Division units, Marine Raiders, Seabee battal-ions, Marine defense battalions, even a PT-boat squadron. The result of Hester's retention of full responsibility for overseeing so many missions by so many additional units was that 43rd Division itself was administered through two weeks of action by an insuf-ficient number of relatively inexperienced and extremely harried officers.

On July 6, to ease the burden upon Hester's operating regi-ments, XIV Corps obligingly ordered Headquarters Company and the 1st and 2nd Battalions of 37th Infantry Division's 145th Infan-try Regiment to begin moving to Rendova for eventual deploy-ment on New Georgia. In addition to the 145th Infantry, the 148th Infantry Regiment, another 37th Division unit, was ordered to stand by for a move to Rendova should the initial reinforcement prove insufficient. Fortunately, some changes were also contem-plated for the command structure of the New Georgia Occupation Force.

On July 5, Major General Millard Harmon had joined Major General Oscar Griswold and Rear Admiral Kelly Turner to discuss the strategy and chain of command of the NGOF. During these talks, which took place at Guadalcanal, Harmon radioed a request to Vice Admiral Bill Halsey asking that a forward echelon of Griswold's XIV Corps headquarters be dispatched to Rendova on or about July 8 for the purpose of taking over administrative and logistical operations for the duration of the campaign. It was felt that General Hester's limited staff could no longer cope with the monumental problems of the effort.

Harmon's request had a further motive, the result of Admiral Turner's Old Navy idealism. The admiral felt that, as commander of the South Pacific Amphibious Force, he had a right to assume direct and tactical control over the NGOF, which was *his* landing force; this, on the presumption that the landing force was an extension of, and therefore subordinate to, the amphibious force and consequently the amphibious force commander. The annals of the Guadalcanal Campaign are steeped in controversy over this very point, and Harmon was quite concerned that the adverse developments already encountered in the New Georgia effort would be in no way enhanced by a renewed flurry of interservice rivalry exacerbated by top-echelon bickering.

In a letter to the Army's assistant chief of staff in charge of the Operations Division of the War Department General Staff, Harmon forthrightly stated that Admiral Turner was "inclined more and more to take active control of land operations." The insertion of Griswold into the equation was the only answer. As a corps commander, Griswold would be able to sidestep Turner's adherence to age-old naval tradition. XIV Corps was a land-based command organization directly responsible to Harmon, the regional Army commander. Harmon, in his turn, was directly responsible to Halsey, as was Turner. Inasmuch as Hester would report to Griswold and Griswold to Harmon, Turner would be cut out of the line of command; the ground echelon of a naval command would become the operating echelon of a land command.

On July 6, Halsey informed Harmon that he could make any staff and command changes or augmentations he thought might be beneficial to both the operation at hand and the overall strategy aimed at bringing Rabaul into the Allied sphere. The admiral's only stipulation, and a shrewd one, was that Harmon discuss such changes with him prior to implementing them.

On July 10, General Griswold was ordered to board an amphibian plane the next day with six members of his staff and fly to Rendova. The remainder of his corps headquarters staff would follow by Navy transport. On orders from Admiral Halsey, which he had intended to issue *after* the fall of Munda, Griswold was directed to assume command of the NGOF and to make recommendations for the commitment of reinforcements. Admiral Turner's authority over the NGOF thus ceased. General Griswold arrived as scheduled, on July 11, just as John Hester was ordering the drive on Laiana.

For his part, General Harmon, based at Guadalcanal, had only the reports of his subordinates to go on, and they said that all was well. However, on the night of July 13–14, he received a message from General Griswold that radically changed his views: "From an observer point of view, things are going badly. Forty-three Division about to fold up. My opinion is that they will never take Munda. Enemy resistance to date not great. My advice is to send up 25th Division to act with what is left of 37th Division if operation is to be successful."

This message had a catalytic effect upon the bits and parts of decisions then in process. Halsey met with Harmon and informally named the Army officer as his deputy area commander. Harmon was then ordered to "assume full charge for ground operations in New Georgia" and to "take whatever steps were deemed necessary to facilitate the capture of the airfield."

Before General Griswold had left Guadalcanal, he had been assured that infantry formations of significant size would be made available to him, at least three regiments. The 148th and 145th Regiments (both understrength by one battalion) had already been alerted for the move, and one regiment of the veteran 25th Infantry Division was to be placed at Griswold's disposal but was not immediately ordered to the battle zone. As a significant portion of the 37th Division was to be sent to New Georgia, it was recommended that the division commander, Major General Robert Beightler, be sent to Rendova with an element of his staff.

As soon as General Harmon had returned to Guadalcanal from his Noumea meeting with Halsey, he ordered Major General J. Lawton Collins, the 25th Infantry Division commander, to ready one regimental combat team for possible movement to New Georgia. Collins passed the word to the commander of the 161st Infantry Regiment, adding that the unit was to prepare to mount out within twelve hours of receiving its travel papers. Thus, the Washington-bred 161st Infantry was to be the first veteran regiment committed to New Georgia; it had turned in a superior performance when blooded late in the Guadalcanal Campaign.

On July 15, Admiral Turner was ordered to assume command of the newly formed Fifth Amphibious Force, which was preparing for offensives in the Central Pacific; Third Amphibious Force went to Rear Admiral Theodore Wilkinson, Turner's deputy through the dark days of Guadalcanal and the growing pains of 1943. Turner, undeniably a brilliant amphibious force commander and strategist, would be missed by even his severest personal critics.

Also on July 15, General Griswold was definitely ordered to assume responsibility for commanding the NGOF and directing group operations on New Georgia. Griswold's position was far from ideal. He was faced with his first command situation involving any army corps immersed in combat. He had not been in on tactical level planning, and had not had time to familiarize himself completely with the zone of action. Turner, for all his cantankerous brilliance, was gone, John Hester had been downgraded, the offensive was stalling, two frontline regiments were folding under fatigue and losses, supply was impossibly fouled up, the Japanese were growing increasingly determined and were, despite efforts to stop them, bringing reinforcements into the combat zone. About all Griswold had going for him was the fact that he had fresh troops in the offing, even if most of them were untried.

PART IV

———— ✳ ————

Counteroffensive

17

For all his competence as a defensive tactician, Major General Noburo Sasaki could not stem the tide of the American advance by remaining in a defensive posture. It had been growing increasingly apparent that the only true victor on New Georgia would be the side that could destroy the opposition through tough, relentless, intelligently planned *offensive* action.

Though any sort of action General Sasaki took would be rooted in a defensive strategy, he had only to reverse the American tactics that had been so useful at Guadalcanal: Attack! There was no better defense than a mobile offense.

As Sasaki cast about for a solution that would take into account the extreme shortage of troops faced by his command, he ruled out a direct assault by all available units because he desired to continue to man fully the defensive lines in front of Munda. He therefore settled on a middle course, a compromise. An attack would be marshaled against the American right flank and would be delivered by fresh infantry units from the Upper Barike region, while the units already manning the barrier before Munda played a holding game. The assault would be coordinated with a powerful naval attack. Roles would be reversed; Sasaki would be the victor.

Even as Sasaki struggled to bring outlying detachments and reinforcements into the ring around Munda, he had no idea what the strategic limitations on his planning might be. This had to come from higher authorities. All Sasaki could do was take the initiative at the tactical level, directly within his own sphere of control.

From the start, there had been two courses open to 8th Area Army concerning the type of campaign it would wage on New Georgia. The first course involved a strategic offensive employing massive infantry, air, and fleet units bent upon a decisive regional outcome. The second course involved a slow withdrawal or holding action to allow more time for adding to existing defenses farther north in the Solomons and around Rabaul. It is doubtful that anyone at 8th Area Army Headquarters thought there might be a victory before Munda. However, there was just a chance that a decisive battle might badly cripple enough of the Allied combat capability to buy time for marshaling a later all-out counterblow that might contribute to a strategic victory. Whether the defense of Munda or a limited offensive went awry, 8th Area Army would have to pull back in any event. The extent of the gamble rested upon what the Imperial Army could afford to put up as stakes. If the best it could do was withdraw to strengthened bases to the north, then it was clearly better to do so with its total available fighting strength intact.

There was at least one consideration in favor of the grand gesture. General Sasaki's badly outnumbered command had already exacted a fearsome toll from the Americans at very little cost to itself.

On July 3, while the Americans were consolidating their gains on Rendova, General Hitoshi Imamura, the 8th Area Army commander, had passed direct orders to Colonel Satoshi Tomonari requiring the colonel's 13th Infantry Regiment to stage into Munda via Kolombangara. The veteran regiment of the 6th Infantry Division, then based in the Shortland Islands, was to be heavily augmented by artillery, antitank, mountain artillery, medical, engineering, and communications units and detachments, as well as several uncommitted elements of the 229th Infantry. To aid in transporting these reinforcements from Kolombangara, Rear Admiral Minoru Ota, who had relinquished command of his *rikusentai* units in favor of organizing a naval support command, was to receive a number of light landing craft along with several new armored troop-carrying barges.

Colonel Tomonari's brigade-size force was to be the first reinforcing unit to enter the Central Solomons. It would be the only one, unless higher command ordered a general buildup. Much of the Guadalcanal-bloodied 230th Infantry Regiment had already staged into New Georgia from its Kolombangara bases, and several additional companies of the 229th Infantry had already been transferred directly from the Shortlands to Munda.

Also on July 3, General Imamura and Vice Admiral Jinichi Kusaka decided to put all of their efforts into the Central Solomons. The 18th Army, in New Guinea, was advised to continue with its operations there but not to expect support until the Central Solomons fighting had been decided.

The 13th Infantry was fully assembled on Kolombangara by July 8. On that day, Colonel Tomonari ordered Major Takeo Ohashi to move his 2nd Battalion, 13th, to New Georgia via the large *ri-*

kusentai base at Bairoko Harbor, which was on New Georgia's northern coast, directly across from Munda. The remainder of the regiment was to follow on successive nights in 1,200-man increments.

Ohashi's battalion arrived at Bairoko during the night of July 8–9, then passed quietly into the rain forest to the south—without a hitch. On the following night, Admiral Ota's barge flotilla landed the second increment at Bairoko, and it too landed and marched southward undetected by a large American force operating in that area. The remainder of Colonel Tomonari's troops passed through undetected on the next two nights.

The 13th Infantry was nearly ready to begin its crushing flank assault by the morning of July 13. Cleared plantation areas several miles north of the 169th Infantry's dangling right flank—safely away from aggressive 1st Fiji Commando patrols—were filled to capacity with fresh, optimistic Japanese infantrymen. All was ready, but the never-failing flaw in Japanese might had been unavoidably woven into the fabric of General Sasaki's best plan.

The Imperial Navy chose this crucial juncture to go its own way. The severe naval losses taken at Guadalcanal had made the admirals wary about committing ships larger than light cruisers to action in contested waters. Though the Navy had originally acceded to Sasaki's request for naval supports, the promise was withdrawn just as the attack was to be delivered. The land forces would have to make an unsupported assault.

18

On the morning of July 15, Major Joe Zimmer led a small combat patrol through the lines of his 1st Battalion, 169th, and cautiously advanced into the rain forest, making for a small patch of high ground about 400 yards southwest of Reincke Ridge. This high ground was Zimmer's battalion's next objective, and the battalion commander wanted a close personal look before he planned the assault. The inspection revealed no Japanese; it appeared that the move would be uncontested. However, it was noted that the objective was liberally covered with pillboxes and bunkers that, to Zimmer, smelled of recent occupation.

At 0800 hours, July 16, the 155mm howitzers of Lieutenant Colonel Henry Shafer's 136th Field Artillery Battalion fired a preparatory barrage against Zimmer's new objectives. The 81mm and 60mm mortars emplaced atop Reincke Ridge assisted the heavy artillery batteries.

As the barrage got under way, Zimmer's troops gulped down a hurried breakfast of hot coffee and fresh donuts. Then, as the bulk of the battalion passed in the shadow of Reincke Ridge, a reinforced platoon from C Company pushed off ahead of the main body, moved quickly around the western slope of Reincke Ridge, crossed the thickly overgrown flat between the hills, and assaulted uphill along the objective's eastern slope. The machine guns accompanying the lead platoon were immediately deployed on the crest to cover the advance by the battalion's main body, which trudged up the slope from the south. The entire forward move was made without making any hostile contacts.

As the battalion command group established itself in a spacious bunker that had apparently served the Japanese in similar fashion, the troops cautiously poked into the numerous shell craters, pillboxes, and bunkers throughout the area. They found, among other salvageable equipment, numerous rifles, a small number of operable light machine guns, and a large number of damp Japanese hand grenades.

The new hilltop position was fully consolidated by 1530 hours. The captured Nambu light machine guns were doled out to the rifle platoons along with captured 7.7mm ammunition, and the damp hand grenades were set out in the sun to dry. Ammunition for the battalion's own .30-caliber machine guns was in short supply, as were other essential stores and equipment, but Major Zimmer anticipated a large resupply effort to commence the following morning. In the meantime, he felt the battalion had absorbed enough captured weapons and ammunition to offset the shortages.

The vista was breathtaking. Zimmer's battalion could see the channel beyond Munda beach, its first clear view of the objective since landing on New Georgia on June 30. The airfield itself was obscured by intervening stands of trees, but the clarity of the vista had an immediate and noticeable positive effect upon morale.

The 1st Battalion, 169th, had its first brush with the Japanese at 1650. A small Japanese infantry patrol that had been sent to investigate the sudden bustling activity on Zimmer's hill blundered straight into the newly laid defenses. A brief firefight ensued, then Japanese artillery and mortars proceeded to pound Zimmer's battalion. The barrage quickly escalated to major proportions, and fourteen Americans were killed, including Second Lieutenant John Kelley, for whom the hill was named.

As soon as the battalion was pinpointed, Major Zimmer initiated the first of repeated calls to the regimental command post to urge the immediate dispatch of .30-caliber ammunition to replenish his unit's depleted supply. When it became evident that the Japanese were going to continue to harass the fresh American positions on Kelley Hill through the night, Zimmer ordered his communicators to disconnect the field-telephone wires and heave them into the jungle flats; this, to keep ubiquitous Japanese infiltrators from following the lines straight into the command bunker. The direct result of Zimmer's order was to prevent his battalion from communicating with supporting artillery and mortar units. However, Zimmer was more than willing to take the risk.

At precisely 2345, the Japanese mounted a major infantry assault. Captain Bunzo Kojima had ordered his 3rd Battalion, 229th Infantry, off Horseshoe Hill hours earlier and had directed it to move across the heavily wooded flat separating it from Kelley Hill. The assault was mounted as soon as the Japanese companies could deploy.

The Japanese attacked directly into the interlocking bands of American .30-caliber and former Japanese 7.7mm machine guns that had been emplaced around the crest of the hill during the late afternoon. The massed fires caused the lead assault files to recoil in shock. Captain Kojima met his retreating soldiers at the base of Kelley Hill and forcefully reformed them. Then he sent them around to the north face of Kelley Hill to resume the attack.

The second assault was beaten back as handily as the first, again by the numerous machine guns emplaced around the top of the hill. Captain Kojima was again on hand to reform the shattered assault files, and he ordered them around to the eastern face of the hill, directly in Zimmer's rear.

The Japanese assault files took off to deliver their third assault upon Kelley Hill, perhaps with a bit less alacrity than they had earlier mustered. And, for the third time in a row, they ran into unexpectedly heavy concentrations of .30-caliber and 7.7mm machine-gun fire, not to mention many of the hand grenades their countrymen had carelessly left for Zimmer's troops. Kojima's infantry was thus defeated for the third time. The stubborn Japanese battalion commander conceded the loss of Kelley Hill and ordered the survivors of the counterattacks back to Horseshoe Hill.

On the morning of July 17, Lieutenant Colonel John Fowler was ordered to work his 2nd Battalion, 169th, into the low-lying flat between Reincke Ridge and Kelley Hill. Fowler's troops jumped off in good order, but the Japanese on their front withstood the advance with a grim determination, forcing the battalion to yield its gains and pull back to the base of Reincke Ridge. About the only good that was accomplished in the wake of Fowler's abortive attack was that the 2nd and 3rd Battalions remained in direct physical contact at the end of the day. However, Zimmer's battalion remained cut off from the rest of the regiment. To point up that grim fact, a carrying party evacuating twenty wounded soldiers from Kelley Hill to Reincke Ridge was ambushed between the two positions.

Wire communications were restored to Kelley Hill, but conversations originating from Major Zimmer's headquarters were constantly interrupted by breaks in the line. Wire parties sent to investigate and repair the breaks were often ambushed. All in all, however, the regimental headquarters had a fairly good notion about what was going on atop Kelley Hill.

Water, food, and ammunition were all in very short supply. The troops were forced to draw stagnant rainwater from the many shell craters that dotted the summit of the hill. Understandably, this supply did not go very fast despite the vicious heat. Many of the troops became sickened when word got around that a pair of Japanese corpses had been found at the bottom of one of the larger craters. To add to the general misery, Japanese snipers peppered the cleared hilltop and, in the course of the day, wounded eight men who exposed themselves to fetch water.

A relief party under Captain Dudley Burr, the regimental Protestant chaplain, got through in the afternoon with litters, plasma, food, and the contents of three cases of .30-caliber ammunition. The troops perked up somewhat, though the actual benefit was minimal. Burr's party carried several of the wounded out on the return trip.

After dispersing his fresh battalions throughout the region of the Upper Barike, Colonel Satoshi Tomonari had calmly awaited the order that would send his regiment into combat. The order was not long in arriving. "The 13th Regiment will immediately maneuver in the area of the upper reaches of the Barike River; seek out the flank and rear of the main body of the enemy who landed on the beach east of the Barike River, and attack, annihilating them on the coast."

Even as Tomonari was receiving his orders from General Sasaki's headquarters, Colonel Genjiro Hirata's 229th Infantry Regiment was preparing to turn its defensive holding action into a deadly offensive sweep. To coordinate his assault with Colonel Tomonari's, Colonel Hirata had had to withdraw a number of his key defending units to staging areas beyond the reach of American patrols. This meant weakening the defenses, a factor leading to the quick, bloodless seizure of Kelley Hill on July 16 by Zimmer's battalion.

The Japanese assault units on the front and open right flank of the New Georgia Occupation Force were ready to jump off by nightfall on July 17.

19

A t 1635, July 17, General Hester received a message from Major General Oscar Griswold aimed at adding muscle to the faltering offensive: "Hold your present position. Make no more attacks. . . . Conduct active patrolling. Rest your tired troops. Make every effort to complete [the] road from Laiana. Prepare plans for a coordinated attack along your entire front using troops of the 37th Division. Target date about July 21. Until further orders, all troops in [the] Munda area [are] under your command."

During the course of July 17, and despite intricate precautions to offset premature discovery, elements of the 43rd Division Reconnaissance Troop, which was screening the New Georgia Occupation Force's open north flank with the assistance of the 1st Fiji Commando, reported that a large body of fresh-looking Japanese infantry numbering between 200 and 300 men was moving on the rear of the division. A single platoon of the reconnaissance troop set up a hasty ambush in the hope of holding the Japanese column. The ambush, however, was too little and too late. The Japanese smashed through without losing stride. The 13th Infantry was moving in for the kill.

The New Georgia Occupation Force was not in the best of defensive deployments. Security forces covering the right flank were inadequate, as evidenced by the necessity of employing a single reconnaissance platoon against nearly 300 Japanese. The meandering, broken front of the 169th Infantry was particularly vulnerable to flank and rear assault. But this was nothing compared to the predicament of the rear-area troops. Aside from a few small combat units, such as the 43rd Reconnaissance Troop, there were virtually no organized armed units. The men behind the lines were mainly clerks, gunners, medical personnel, service and supply troops, communicators, technicians, and ordnancemen.

Shortly after sunset on July 17, the 13th Infantry launched a more or less coordinated assault against many rear-area and beach installations in the Barike-Zanana sector. In most cases, the only opposition to the assault was a number of hastily contrived efforts by small security detachments. For their part, the large Japanese formations generally splintered into platoon- or section-size elements, a factor that caused widespread confusion among the surprised American forces, but which also diminished the real gains of the effort. Still, these small groups of assaulting Japanese infantry met initial success. Several defensive points were easily overrun; others held long into the night before caving in; more held firm as untrained, terrorized technicians manned the firing line in order to preserve their own lives. The installations behind the front were very well dispersed, a two-edged sword in that the Japanese had a hard time locating them while the defending troops found it impossible to organize a coordinated or mutually supporting defensive effort over a large area. Many isolated forest campsites were missed entirely, though the Japanese found many installations simply by following communications wire to any terminus. Litter parties encumbered with wounded soldiers on their way to rear-area casualty clearing stations were particularly vulnerable. Many of the wounded were injured again, and many were killed. Litter bearers were also injured while they and the ambulatory wounded did their best to carry the litter cases to safety. No one was safe, whether caught in the rain forest outside defensive perimeters or caught behind defenses undermanned by inadequately trained noncombatant technicians.

Tragically, a number of casualty clearing stations were themselves overrun. There, the Japanese bayoneted helpless patients while medics and physicians fought like demons to protect their charges. These men lived or died alongside the men they sought to save.

Headquarters and outposts were hit and sent reeling. Here and there, soldiers ran from their posts to save themselves, but most of the rear-area troops grimly clung to their camps and fought off the darting attacks that struck from out of the totally darkened rain forest. Command posts still in operation were flooded with calls for help, but many of these were having trouble enough coping with their own defensive measures. Lateral supply trails were mainly uncompeleted, so what there was in the way of pools of reserve troops could not be expeditiously dispatched. Relief columns often came under attack in the rain forest; far from being of assistance, they often drew yet more needed reserves when they called for help themselves. In the main, there was no cohesive effort by large forces in any one sector. Efforts at countering the stinging, confusing assaults were fragmented and spasmodic. There was nowhere to rally, and no one to rally. Noncombatants learned the instincts of veteran riflemen on the fly; those who could not learn quickly enough were maimed or killed in short order. Confusion was rampant. No one knew what was going on.

At 2030, General Griswold received a message from General Hester: "Force estimated to be 75 to 200 Japs approaching command post on north flank about 800 yards distant." Hester, who was on Rendova recuperating from a flare-up of his stomach ulcer, was referring to the 43rd Division forward command post, on Zanana Beach.

Communications with the division forward command post, which was under Brigadier General Leonard Wing, the assistant division commander, and Lieutenant Colonel Elmer Watson the division operations officer, became increasingly hard to maintain. Lines were going dead, one by one, as the Japanese closed in. It was too risky to send out wire teams to make repairs. In the end, all the lines were severed except the underwater cable to Kokorana Island, which was tied in with the Force Artillery fire direction center. At 0300 hours, 43rd Division Artillery relayed a message to XIV Corps Headquarters: "Division CP under attack. Request one infantry battalion [on the] beach [at] daylight. Medics and engineers in grave danger." The fight was on. Division clerks were infantry.

Fighting holes were hastily dug around the command post, which was astride the Munda Trail, and a pair of machine guns removed from jeeps were set up to cover the trail, one forward and one in the rear. In the end, there were neither rifles nor soldiers enough at the command post to hold off a determined assault. But there was a team of artillery forward observers, and these men were in direct touch with Force Artillery.

In an amazing burst of foresight, someone had rung up the fire direction center of the 136th Field Artillery Battalion about three hours before the division forward command post came under attack. It was a bare minimum. The big 155mm howitzers had to be retrained 90 degrees from their fixed battery sites on Baraulu Island in order to fire northward against Zanana. A high stand of trees masked that flank. A Battery was closest. Gunners from other batteries pitched in to cut down the trees and relay the guns.

Throughout, Lieutenant Colonel Henry Shafer berated his men for their lack of aggressiveness. When the Japanese first threatened the division forward command post, a single platoon of A Battery—two howitzers—was set to fire.

As usual, Brigadier General Harold Barker, the force artillery commander, was at the division command forward post. When the attack began, Barker joined a forward-observer team—Captain James Ruhlin and a Private Chamberlain—and began directing the fire of his sole supporting howitzer platoon. It was impossible to rely on sight detection of targets, so Captain Ruhlin expertly corrected the guns by sound alone—a dubious method except under the most extreme circumstances. He cooly and rapidly shifted fires to bring them in as close as he dared. The gunners on Baraulu fired as fast as they could juggle the heavy shells and powder charges into the hot breeches. One by one, more of Shafer's heavy howitzers were turned to lay on the target. Captain Ruhlin fired at all possible staging areas on all flanks, then slowly walked the fire back toward the tiny headquarters perimeter, stopping when he had set a neat curtain of bursting shells around himself and his fellows. While the artillery kept the Japanese at bay, the inexperienced rear-echelon troops manning the perimeter exchanged shots with the attackers. The only casualty at the command post was the 43rd Division operations officer, Lieutenant Colonel Elmer Watson.

At the height of the action, General Griswold rang up the forward command post from his Rendova headquarters to say that the newly arrived 1st Battalion, 148th Infantry Regiment, was expected to arrive on Zanana Beach by daylight.

In the morning, twenty Japanese corpses were recovered from cleared areas on or beside the trail leading to and from the command-post perimeter.

Among the hodgepodge of splintered support units on and near the beach was the 3rd Platoon, G Battery, 9th Marine Defense Battalion, a fifty-two-man automatic antiaircraft gun unit under the command of First Lieutenant John Wismer. The deadly automatic weapons belonging to the platoon had to be kept from Japanese hands to prevent them from being put to use against American units defending the area.

As the sound of gunfire drew nearer to the beach, Lieutenant Wismer decided to leave half of his detachments on the guns while he established a short defensive line about 150 yards off the beach, on a small promontory just down the trail from the 43rd Division forward command post. On the way to the new line, Wismer's weapons experts picked up a half dozen broken .30-caliber machine guns from a salvage dump they happened to be passing. From these, the Marines fashioned two workable machine guns, for which they scrounged several chests of ammunition.

Once the line was selected, a platoon of antitank gunners from the 172nd Infantry moved in on Wismer's right. On the left was a heterogeneous group of Army service and artillery troops, armed for the occasion but obviously a bit sheepish over the prospect of action. The ranking officer was an Army captain, a lawyer who wisely decided to allow his troop commanders to handle things warlike; he would be around to take responsibility.

The Marines set their two machine guns a short distance apart near the center of the line. The rest of the Marines were armed with rifles, as were the soldiers on either flank. Everyone slid into hastily dug rifle pits and behind bushes and trees to wait. But not for long.

About 100 Japanese were spotted on the trail from the 43rd Division forward command post at about 2100 hours. Fingers itched painfully on trigger guards, but the moment had not yet arrived. Then Lieutenant Wismer fired. The line jumped into self-sustaining life, and a murderous fire caught the totally unprepared Japanese. After milling in confusion for a few moments, dropping off clumps of dead and wounded, the crowd of painfully surprised Japanese infantrymen pulled back out of sight. There were frantic bursts of argument coming from the forest as the Marines and soldiers settled back to take a beating.

The trail and surrounding fringe of jungle were alive with the crackling of twigs and hoarse yells as the Japanese bounded forward to fulfill the national death wish. The forwardmost American positions gave way as dazed individuals made for the safer rear. Then nearly everyone—Marines, antitankers, service troops—ran pell-mell toward the line of friendly antiaircraft guns on the beach. The 20mm and 40mm guns had been turned to face inland, their muzzles fully depressed. As the retreating Marines and soldiers flopped down in front of and among the antiaircraft guns, every one of them, and the gunners, searched the front in hopes of seeing the first Japanese soldiers step onto the beach from the dark forest. But no Japanese came.

After waiting a bit, Lieutenant Wismer led several Marines back to the line they had earlier vacated. Over 100 Japanese lay dead on the forward slope of the slight rise. Here and there, wounded Japanese soldiers bemoaned their bloodstained agony. But there were no Japanese capable of opposing Wismer's little probe. There had been no apparent reason for the Japanese to withdraw; Wismer's troops had been routed.

The found Private John Wantuck beside his machine gun. There was no ammunition left in the chests beside the gun. It was clear that Wantuck had died in his place after what looked to have been a wild hand-to-hand brawl. He had been knifed to death, and grenade shards were all over the place. It took somewhat longer to find the other machine gunner, Corporal Maier Rothschild. He was bleeding badly, but his wounds were relatively minor. He was under a bush several yards from his gun, which, like Wantuck's, had no ammunition left to fire.

Shortly after midnight, Captain Bunzo Kojima began massing the tired remnants of his 3rd Battalion, 229th Infantry, in the low-lying jungle flat between Horseshoe Hill and Kelley Hill. When the Japanese companies were all in place, at about 0015, Kojima ordered a brace of machine guns on Horseshoe Hill to begin firing into the perimeter manned by Major Joe Zimmer's hungry, thirsty 1st Battalion, 169th.

As Major Zimmer's troops instinctively ducked under the hail of fire, Captain Kojima ordered the advance to begin. The Japanese infantry charged straight up the western face of Kelley Hill. After the initial reflex, American observers stared back along the arching lines of pink Japanese tracers to try to spot the positions of the harassing machine guns. The 1st Battalion mortars, with an assist from the 3rd Battalion 81mm mortars located on Reincke Ridge, began blasting the machine guns while Zimmer's riflemen placed their full attention on Kojima's frontal assault.

The Americans had nowhere to go. Every flank was the front. They could only hold. So, with a grim, fear-induced determination, the American riflemen and machine gunners waited for targets or fired blindly. The oncoming shadow ranks waded into the fire, then faltered, then fell back. Snipers and ambulatory wounded Japanese soldiers left on the slope kept up the lively fire from where they lay.

Japanese officers at the foot of Kelley Hill formed the retreating infantry into solid ranks. Captain Kojima berated them for their lack of heart, led them around to Zimmer's northern flank, and cursed them onward. They moved at a dead crawl. Zimmer's troops waited, then fired into them with M1 rifles, BARs, shotguns, Browning and Nambu machine guns, and Japanese-made Arisaka rifles. The crawling ranks of Japanese infantry crumbled.

Then a small group of attackers discovered that it was in a dead zone. The peculiarly breaking terrain made it impossible for any American gun on the crest to bear on this narrow, sloping hollow. The news passed down the Japanese line. Moving freely, unencumbered by the natural fear of being hit, Japanese soldiers crawled safely toward the American line. Close now, they tapped their cylindrical hand grenades on their mushroom-shaped helmets, made certain the fuses had ignited, then leaped to throw. They could not miss. It went well for a while, but the American mortars emplaced on Reincke Ridge found them. In minutes, detonating 81mm and 60mm shells were raking the dead zone. Even Zimmer's mortars, set only a score of yards behind the infantry lines, began scoring against the packed mass of bodies that had sought safety in what had so quickly become a slaughter ground.

Their hope gone, the Japanese began pulling back. Within minutes, most of them were charging headlong down the hill, through the beaten zone. Many were bowled over as chance bullets sent them careening off balance in their downward plunges, piling them up like so many rag dolls. It ended shortly thereafter. At daybreak, Zimmer's weary riflemen counted 102 bodies on the slopes of Kelley Hill.

While Captain Kojima's 3rd Battalion, 229th, was licking its wounds on Horseshoe Hill, the remaining two battalions of the regiment were active at widely separated points. Major Giichi Sata's 2nd Battalion, 229th, which had seen heavy action during the preceding several weeks, launched a massed assault near dawn against the lines of Lieutenant Colonel Jim Wells's 3rd Battalion, 103rd, which was fairly fresh and well prepared. The assault was stopped cold.

On the Barike River, at a spot known as the Engineer Water Point, a number of American litter cases were piling up due to the disruption of the evacuation routes. The water point was defended by a single rifle platoon from E Company, 169th, under First Lieutenant Nicholas Kliebert. After several hours of calm, Kliebert's thin defensive line was hit full force by nearly 200 members of Major Masao Hara's 1st Battalion, 229th, which had blundered into the area while nearing the end of its long retreat from Segi, during which it had been out of contact with the events of the past several weeks.

It proved impossible for Kliebert's handful of riflemen to hold, so the Japanese were soon swarming over the defenses. They found a group of immobile casualties who were ripe for the slaughter. Private First Class John Patrizzo, a member of the regimental service company, was working among the wounded when a hand grenade landed in the midst of three litter cases. Instantly, Patrizzo flopped over the explosive missile and absorbed the full impact of the detonation with his body. Then he lay quietly as numerous Japanese made their way through the area. Amazingly, he would survive.

Other survivors of the brutal assault on the Engineer Water Point lay doggo and quietly hung on into the morning, until the Japanese tired of the game and pulled out. Just after sunrise, a patrol from the newly landed 37th Division Cavalry Reconnaissance Troop moved into the area to help the emerging survivors bury seventeen of their fellows on the spot.

About 150 Japanese made their way to a supply dump established by the newly landed 145th Infantry Regiment, near Zanana. First Lieutenant Thomas Battles, the supply officer of the 1st Battalion, 145th, had a dozen men on hand to hold the dump. Corporal James Miller was manning the only machine gun, which was perched in an exposed position in the bright moonlight. As the Japanese moved on the dump, Miller fired short bursts into the lead ranks. The Japanese momentarily recoiled, then stomped over Miller's emplacement, bayoneting the gunner to death. The dump was taken.

Collecting Company B of the 43rd Division's 118th Medical Battalion, which was not harassed all night, dispatched numerous litter teams to look for wounded soldiers along the network of trails radiating from its encampment. One such group found that the trail it had been probing for some time had been interdicted both front and rear by strong groups of Japanese. The only way into the clear was through the rain forest, but the Americans were burdened with ten litter cases. The group meandered through the dense bush all day without encountering any Japanese, but it ran into trouble just before sunset, July 18. The Japanese were held for a few minutes, but the exhausted litter bearers were soon overwhelmed. Several of the wounded were killed, as were two medics. Two other medics went missing and were never found, and three litter bearers were wounded.

Fights and scraps continued throughout July 18, but the force of the Japanese counteroffensive petered out by dawn that day. The action cost both sides many lives and badly disrupted the rear areas of the New Georgia Occupation Force, but it failed, utterly. No major objectives were permanently secured, and the Americans emerged from the ordeal full of fight.

PART V

*

Corps Offensive

20

B y the morning of July 18, many large elements of the 37th Infantry Division had been on Rendova for as long as a week. After the Japanese counteroffensive petered out, Lieutenant Colonel Richard Crooks was ordered to march his 1st Battalion, 145th Infantry, up from Zanana Beach to occupy a defensive cordon around the 169th Infantry's regimental command post. The move was accomplished without any hitches, and a pleased Colonel Temple Holland placed a battalion of his former regiment under his command once again; these were fresh troops he had trained himself.

As had been promised during the attacks on the 43rd Division forward command post, the 148th Infantry Regiment—two rifle battalions and regimental headquarters and service units—was alerted for a move from Rendova. Shortly after arriving at Zanana, Colonel Stuart Baxter, the regimental commander, was ordered to march Lieutenant Colonel Herbert Radcliffe's 2nd Battalion, 148th, from the beach to the northern flank of the 169th Infantry, where it was to begin replacing the sparse divisional units screening the open NGOF right flank. The entire 169th Infantry was to be relieved in place. The truncated 148th Infantry (its 3rd Battalion, and the 3rd Battalion, 145th, were operating with a force of Marine Raiders around Bairoko Harbor, in the far north) was to assume control of the northern portion of the 169th Infantry's sector as well as to extend the NGOF battle line northward. The truncated 145th Infantry was to take over the southern portions of the 169th Infantry's front. As soon as the 169th Infantry had been relieved, Colonel Holland was to resume command of his own 145th Infantry. Plans allowed four days for the shuffle to be completed.

As additional elements of the 37th Infantry Division arrived from Rendova, they were fed into the northern end of the NGOF front. On July 22, Major General Robert Beightler was directed by General Griswold to resume command of all 37th Division units on New Georgia, with the exception of the 136th Field Artillery Battalion. The 25th Infantry Division's veteran reinforced 161st Infantry Regiment was ordered in from Guadalcanal, and it arrived on July 22. This unit was placed under General Beightler's temporary command pending the arrival of additional 25th Division units and the division forward headquarters.

The large 37th Infantry Division units on New Georgia were operating at something of a disadvantage in that the division was not organically sound. The division's own 129th Infantry Regiment was on garrison duty in the New Hebrides and could not be committed to New Georgia. In addition, the two operating regiments, the 145th and 148th, were each missing their 3rd Battalions, which had joined with Marine Raider units in a special mission to interdict Japanese lines of communication in northern New Georgia. Thus, the division's main infantry increment comprised a pair of two-battalion infantry regiments. The addition of the 161st Infantry helped fill out the division, but the two truncated regiments would be operating at a distinct disadvantage, and the senior officers of the 161st Infantry were unknown to the 37th Division commander and his staff.

The 37th Division Artillery Group, commanded by Brigadier General Leo Kreber, was given administrative control over its own and several 43rd Division 105mm battalions. However, the remaining artillery formations, including two Marine 155mm gun batteries, remained under the control of the 43rd Division Artillery Group, whose commander, Brigadier General Harold Barker, headed the entire NGOF artillery groupment.

With General Griswold's approval, General Beightler established his division boundary on a line about 1,300 yards north of Ilangana Village. The 43rd Division was to operate south of the line to the beach while Beightler's mixed command would operate north of the line. Corps troops were made responsible for rear- and northern-flank security.

Due to the nature of the terrain and the Japanese defenses, the 37th Division could be assigned no specific frontage in the northern portion of its zone of operations. The division's extreme-right-flank elements were to expand and contract their frontage in relation to Japanese defenses found along the way. The 145th Infantry was assigned a very narrow front, and only the 2nd Battalion was initially placed on the line; the 1st Battalion, 145th, was to hold Reincke Ridge and Kelley Hill. The 161st Infantry, which was not scheduled to arrive on New Georgia until July 22, was to be assigned a 500-yard front immediately to the right of the 145th Infantry's zone. The northernmost unit would be the two-battalion 148th Infantry, with no fixed frontage.

Some shuffling was taking place in the 43rd Division zone. Colonel Daniel Hundley was relieved of command of the 103rd Infantry on July 22 and posted as the 43rd Division chief of staff. His relief was Lieutenant Colonel Lester Brown, who had commanded the Vangunu operation and who was spot-promoted to the rank of full colonel. Major Ray Dunning was named to replace Brown as commander of the 2nd Battalion, 103rd, which was transferred from Vangunu and placed on the NGOF battle line between the 3rd Battalion, 103rd, and the 2nd Battalion, 172nd.

General Griswold's two-division command was thus expanded from seven operating rifle battalions to twelve, eight of which were fresh.

Administration of logistics for the two-division offensive had to be thorough and smooth. Because supply services had been marginally run with far-reaching effects prior to the assumption of XIV Corps command, General Griswold called for a number of sweeping changes. Rather than use one main supply dump for both divisions, a new dump was activated on Barabuni Island for use by 43rd Division; Kokorana Island was the site of the main 37th Division supply depot. Cargo-carrying vessels and landing craft arriving from the south were to land supplies at one or the other, or at designated New Georgia beaches such as Laiana, for direct replenishment of supply of units on the battle line.

General Hester's shift to Laiana was beginning to show dividends. The swampy ground encountered there had initially hindered landing craft, but the 43rd Division engineers had overcome the problems; goods were flowing swiftly across the beaches. The hard-working engineers had put down 600 yards of dry roadway by July 17 and by July 20 the entire road net serving 43rd Division units was open. General Hester optimistically reported that elements of his division were no longer dependent upon tricky, inaccurate air drops for replenishing their supplies. As proof of his confidence, Hester moved the 43rd Division forward command post and most of the divisional support and supply units and installations from Zanana to Laiana on July 21.

It was anticipated that heavy casualties would be sustained during this last massive drive on Munda. Fortunately, a number of state-of-the-art changes were just then catching up with the New Georgia Occupation Force. Thus, the medical-delivery situation was considerably altered during the preparations for the XIV Corps offensive.

Only several hours after assuming command of the NGOF, General Griswold radioed his superior, Major General Millard Harmon, to request that the 250-bed 17th Field Hospital be moved from Guadalcanal to Rendova. Harmon approved the request, and the hospital staff was immediately ordered to move. At the same time, Harmon acted on a specific recommendation by Griswold concerning the composition of the field-hospital staff. Griswold pointed out that a large number of the older doctors serving with the infantry and rear-area medical staffs were physically and mentally folding under the duress of jungle warfare. Harmon asked his medical subordinates to weed out doctors who might fail under the strain and replace them with younger, more athletic men. Also, the XIV Corps chief surgeon asked the Navy to provide larger medical staffs aboard LSTs charged with evacuating casualties from the combat zone; the Navy moved immediately to fulfill this request.

While modifying the quality of medical service being provided, Colonel Frank Hallam, the XIV Corps surgeon, began taking action with respect to the alarming upsurge in combat fatigue cases. Rest camps were established on several of the barrier islets, for it had been found that many of the men afflicted with fatigue could be returned to their units after a good rest away from the pressures and filth of the rain forest. Next, screening centers were established; every man leaving the battle area because of professed combat fatigue was thoroughly interviewed before permission for a rest was granted. Most important, definitions and standard procedures were established. "Combat fatigue" came to be understood as meaning *physical* exhaustion; "war neurosis" was given to mean emotional depletion.

A great deal had been learned about the nature of war neurosis in the weeks following the near collapse of large elements of the 169th Infantry, and more remained to be learned. A great deal of the problem had to do with environment. The rain forest was *totally* alien to the Americans manning 43rd Infantry Division. Soldiers recruited from varying locales across the United States could not relate to anything quite like New Georgia's rain forest. Months of duty on other Pacific Islands, which were nothing like New Georgia, had not prepared them for combat in such a closed-in environment.

The Regulars among them, and there were few, liked to think

that draftees and Guardsmen reflected the softness of the society at large. This perennial argument did not hold up under scrutiny. Of the thirteen infantry regiments that had taken part in the Guadalcanal Campaign—six Marine and seven Army—five had been National Guard outfits from Illinois, Ohio, Washington state, South Dakota, and Massachusetts. The incidence of combat fatigue and war neurosis in these units had been minimal, and was no higher than in the two Regular Army regiments, and only slightly higher than in the six Marine regiments. The fact that 43rd Division had been in its first fight was of no consequence. *No* unit serving at Guadalcanal had ever been in a fight prior to that campaign.

The enemy was less a factor than might be thought. The 229th Infantry, it is true, had served on Guadalcanal; it had suffered grievous casualties while being run off the island. The Japanese on New Georgia were good fighters, it is true, but not nearly as good as those in units that had served on Guadalcanal—all undefeated veterans who had all just participated in the most successful military venture their country had ever supported, a venture the equal of the most audacious military efforts before and since. But those Japanese had been defeated at Guadalcanal, and a significant remnant of the survivors was being whittled down on New Georgia.

It was not so much the real fighting qualities of the Japanese that put off the green American infantrymen early in the drive on Munda; it was their *imagined* fighting qualities. The misinformation circulating among 43rd Division troops and their officers was virtually, but not quite, beyond belief. For example, one of the 169th Infantry's chaplains had taken quite seriously a news article relating the induction of "monkey-men from Borneo" into the Japanese units fighting on New Georgia. The report indicated that these beings could scuttle unseen through the treetops and had been trained to pounce on Americans at night from their arboreal perches. It is no wonder, in the face of such fictions, that the inexperienced soldiers suffered from mass nocturnal delusions and their natural consequence, panicky nocturnal fratricide.

Lieutenant Colonel Jim Wells, commander of the 3rd Battalion, 103rd Infantry, had an eye-opening personal experience pertaining to the loss of personnel to the ravages of war neurosis. After dispatching a precious squad of riflemen to help evacuate casualties to the beach, Wells noted that most of the squad failed to return. He decided to walk to the beach to find out why. The rain forest thinned out as this Regular Army officer—a West Point graduate—got nearer to the shore. Soon, Wells found himself walking through a number of manifestly secure rear-area encampments. At length, the battalion commander burst out of the trees and was confronted by a wide, clear, sunswept beach inhabited by a knot of frolicking, laughing swimmers. The effect was instantaneous and discomforting. Lieutenant Colonel Wells had to force himself to continue walking. He felt an almost overpowering desire to strip off his filthy, reeking clothing and hurl himself into the warm, clean water; to hell with his duties, his rank, his career. There was no longer any question about what had become of the riflemen; they had succumbed to that sudden, overpowering urge to seek security; they had broken. At the end of his trip to the beach, Wells learned, without much surprise or chagrin, that the division surgeon had had them shipped to Rendova for a rest.

To preclude the spread of anxiety neurosis at night, which was the period of highest incidence, Lieutenant Colonel Wells provided the best possible reward for *bona fide* killings of nighttime infiltrators: a twenty-four-hour rest in the rear in return for a dead Japanese body. Such means of obtaining release from the rigors of combat made infiltration almost welcome. The troops in the battalion became the hunters rather than the hunted, even if the hunting was done by sitting in a foxhole waiting for the prey to come within reach. But that was not all. Under Wells's terms, the killing had to be done *quietly* if the pass was to be awarded. In restricting the award of time off to silent killing, Wells licked another problem. He had learned, as had all unit commanders, that nighttime shooting was infectious to the point of panic; if one man opened fire, then everyone opened fire, and with very little concern about who was being shot at. By restricting the "right" to fire to certain designated outposts and individuals, Wells removed the basic ingredient for panic. Going along with the system of rewards was a system of punishments. The battalion's perimeter was silent at night, and the incidence of war neurosis—and combat fatigue—went down because those who were supposed to be sleeping during any given period of time were left to do so in peace and quiet. The battalion, which suffered heavy casualties in daytime fighting, did not lose a man at night, and even showed a marked increase in all-around efficiency because the troops were rested and less apprehensive.

This insidious problem, far from beaten, was getting under control.

The air war was not going to win the New Georgia Campaign, but it was making the infantry's job a bit easier. Matters improved dramatically after July 10, when the Segi Point fighter strip was completed. Continuing efforts against Japanese airfields north of Munda could be more effectively escorted by short-range fighters using Segi, and infantry units operating in front of Munda could rely upon on-call fighter support at short notice.

Each day, between 0700 and 1630, formations of Navy, Marine, and Royal New Zealand Air Force fighters prowled overhead, initiating strafing runs when they had targets and going to the support of ground forces when called. The Allied fighters withstood the largest post-invasion-era Japanese air strike on July 15 by destroying forty-five of seventy-five Japanese aircraft against the loss of three American lives. The Japanese attempted no more daytime raids.

Although its resources were relatively limited, Aircraft, New Georgia, was a going concern capable of handling whatever was asked of it. On July 16, 84 Navy and Marine torpedo bombers and dive-bombers struck Lambeti Plantation with nearly 150 500-pound, 1,000-pound, and 2,000-pound bombs. Later that same day, many of the same aircrews struck Munda with a dozen each 1,000-pound and 2,000-pound bombs and assorted smaller ordnance. A similar raid on Munda on July 19, for example, caused serious damage to the air base and its defenses. Such raids increased in tempo as the time to begin the XIV Corps offensive drew closer. Strikes against tactical objectives near the corps battle line continued right down to H-Hour.

General Griswold's efforts removed much unnecessary pressure from infantry-unit commanders in the nine days following his assumption of control of the New Georgia offensive. The Japanese were certainly still there, but they had been turned by Griswold into the main problem. There were sufficient combat troops on hand for mounting an offensive; enough, in fact, to allow the more depleted battalions a chance to rest and refit. A passable network of roadways was in, and air support was becoming a more reliable factor in the fighting. The war neurosis and combat fatigue prob-

lems were being solved. The reinforced and reconstituted New
Georgia Occupation Force was ready.

Plans for naval support of the XIV Corps offensive called for
seven fleet destroyers under Commander Arleigh Burke to bom-
bard Lambeti Plantation shortly before H-Hour. In order to facilitate this mission, Commander Burke arrived on Rendova on July
23 to inspect shallow, reef-strewn Roviana Lagoon and to select
visual checkpoints, which he considered mandatory in such restricted waters.

Air support would be provided mainly by Marine and Navy
land-based dive-bombers and torpedo bombers based in the Russells and at Guadalcanal. In addition, Army Air Forces multien-
gine bombers would launch bombing strikes in the area between
Lambeti Plantation and Ilangana Village. Several light observation
aircraft had been acquired and based at Segi; these would be employed to direct artillery fire.

Artillery support would be under the overall direction of Brigadier General Harold Barker. All of his battalions were in competent hands, and most of them had been on the job for some time.
Each operating regiment was assigned one 105mm battalion for direct support, and one each of the two 155mm battalions was assigned to 43rd and 37th Division for general support.

Munda Field and Bibilo Hill were the corps long-range objectives. Ultimately, the Japanese were to be driven into the sea. The
37th Division was to envelop the Japanese left (north) flank and
drive to Bibilo Hill. The 43rd Division was to drive through Lambeti Plantation and on to Munda Field.

XIV Corps would exercise direct control over all Marine Corps
units on New Georgia. Major General Robert Beightler's 37th Division headquarters would oversee seven infantry battalions (two
each from the 145th and 148th Infantry Regiments, and three from
the 161st Infantry) plus their supports. Major General John Hester's authority was restricted to just five operating infantry battalions (all three battalions of the 172nd Infantry, and the 2nd and 3rd
Battalions, 103rd), plus their supports. The 3rd Battalion, 169th,
which received numerous replacements and much new equipment
in the days leading up to the XIV Corps offensive, was designated
the 43rd Division reserve. The 1st and 2nd Battalions, 169th were
designated the NGOF reserve, although their first order of busi-

ness was resting and regaining strength. The 1st Battalion, 103rd, was left with the responsibility for guarding Wickham Anchorage. Despite the arrival of the XIV Corps forward command post, most of the 43rd Division's staff was retained by the NGOF headquarters. Thus, Hester's divisional command post continued to be run by assistant department heads and severely reduced clerical and technical staffs.

D-Day was set for July 25. The day's fighting would open at 0610 with a thirty-minute bombardment by Commander Arleigh Burke's seven fleet destroyers. An air strike would begin at 0635. The line of departure would be identical to the front lines held at H-Hour, except in the case of the 161st Infantry, which would have to contain and reduce several strong positions on the way from its bivouac to its line of departure.

The primary tactic to be used in the offensive was the frontal assault. There would be no stopping to reduce troublesome pockets; these would simply be contained, then reduced as time and manpower became available.

$\mathbf{T}$he Japanese were waiting.

As of July 22, Major General Noburo Sasaki's main line of resistance ran some 3,200 yards from the sea in a northerly direction. At the time, only the remnants of the 229th Infantry were manning the lines. However, the fresh 2nd Battalion, 230th Infantry, was scheduled to move in soon.

Supporting the Japanese infantry battalions were various types of artillery units: the 38th Infantry Division Antitank Battalion; the 2nd Independent Antitank Battalion; a detachment of the 2nd Battalion, 10th Independent Mountain Artillery Regiment; and two *rikusentai* 75mm antiaircraft-artillery batteries.

Defenses were of the nature already encountered by the 43rd Division around Laiana. They ran solidly from the beach through the hill country and terminated just to the right front of the 161st Infantry's zone of action. The strongest concentration of prepared defenses lay in the vicinity of Shimuzu and Horseshoe Hills, facing the 172nd and 145th Regiments, straddling the divisional boundary. The 2nd Battalion, 230th Infantry, was in the process of extending the defensive line northward from Horseshoe Hill. Several companies of *rikusentai* from the Yokosuka 7th Special Naval Landing Force were in reserve and would be committed as needed in piecemeal fashion.

It was clearly understood by the various Japanese regional headquarters in Rabaul that these relatively few Japanese combat infantrymen and their meager support were capable of sustaining an obstinate defense, but not of winning.

The XIV Corps intelligence section slightly overestimated the number of Japanese available immediately at the front, but it made no allowance in its estimates for the remnants of the 13th Infantry that were bivouacked about 4,900 yards north and west of Ilangana Village. General Sasaki planned to use this still-powerful force for a renewed counteroffensive against the XIV Corps's open right flank. In fact, the 13th Infantry was ordered to launch its assault on July 23, but the regiment's preparations ran afoul of the intense preparations by the Americans for their offensive, and the attack did not come off.

In twenty-six days of fighting, General Sasaki had committed 4,500 soldiers and *rikusentai* to fight in front of Munda. Over 1,300 Japanese had been killed, and over 700 had been wounded and treated. Only a handful had been captured. The 13th Infantry's gamble had failed. Sasaki's main base, centered around Kokengolo Hill, at Munda, had been mercilessly pounded, forcing the general and his staff to seek more peaceful surroundings at a plantation north of the shattered air base.

The defense of New Georgia was failing, and the security of bases on Bougainville was of considerable and growing concern to the Japanese high command. On July 22, a seaplane tender escorted by five destroyers attempted to land troops and equipment on Bougainville. Sixteen SBD Dauntless dive-bombers, eighteen TBF Avenger torpedo bombers, and sixteen Army Air Forces heavy bombers stopped the mission cold, killing all but 189 of the 618 troops aboard the seaplane tender. Also lost were twenty-two medium tanks and large stores of ammunition and infantry weapons destined for New Georgia.

The noose around Munda was tightening. The 230th Infantry, which had not yet made good grievous losses sustained at Guadalcanal, could advance only 400 soldiers to New Georgia from Kolombangara in the face of the Allied naval blockade.

General Sasaki knew that he was losing; he was a realist. He was also quite envious of the material wealth his adversaries were able to bring to bear against his meager resources. Sasaki realized that he had been beaten as much by lines of supply as by lines of infantry. Yet, like many Japanese who encountered America's wealth in the Pacific and Asia, he was highly critical of the individual fortitude of the American fighting man who was attempting, with increasing success, to pierce his defenses. Sasaki later wrote:

> They awaited the results of several days' bombardment before a squad advanced. Positions were constructed and then strength increased. When we counterattacked at close quarters, they immediately retreated and with their main strength in the rear engaged our pursuing troops with rapid fire. The infantry did not attack in strength, but gradually forced a gap and then infiltrated. Despite the cover provided by tank firepower, the infantry would not come to grips with us and charge. The tanks were slow but were movable pillboxes which could stop and neutralize our fire.

As a counterpoint to the manifold serious problems encountered by American troops on New Georgia, this is a fascinating appraisal. More than anything, it points up the contrasting availability in each army of manpower and firepower. Each side used most of what it felt it had most to use; firepower in the case of the Americans, whose culture forbade the needless slaughter of soldiers if material means could be found for doing the job; manpower in the case of the materially poor Japanese, whose cultural ethos was based upon the concept of dutiful personal sacrifice in behalf of the homeland and its imperial godhead. The minds of America's war leaders were fixed firmly upon the allocation and use of seeming limitless industrial output on far-flung battlefields; the minds of Japan's military leaders were rooted in ancient wars, in personal honors, in spiritual virtues that had no earthly place on a mid-twentieth-century battlefield.

22

An hour before noon on July 18, Colonel Stuart Baxter, commanding officer of the 37th Infantry Division's 148th Infantry Regiment, received orders from Major General John Hester to relieve the 169th Infantry Regiment on Reincke Ridge and Kelley Hill. Under normal circumstances, the relief would have been a simple matter. However, the 148th Infantry was green, it was operating under unfamiliar command, and the relief was to be carried out in the wake of the terror-filled nocturnal Japanese counteroffensive. The Ohio National Guard regiment was in for a bad time.

Colonel Baxter's first reaction to his orders was to ask if Munda Trail was open all the way through to his new positions. NGOF headquarters, which was located on Rendova, had only fragmentary and inconclusive reports upon which to base its response, but Baxter was assured that the trail was clear.

Baxter ordered his regimental operations officer, Major Carl Bethers, to lead a motorized patrol up the trail to Reincke Ridge. Bethers and the regimental intelligence officer, Captain Edward Nicely, picked up a truck and a squad of infantry, and set out up the trail.

Munda Trail was *not* clear; Bether's patrol fell victim to a carefully concealed ambush about 800 yards from the 43rd Division Water Point. Tracers punctured the truck's gas tank, setting it alight and killing the driver. Another man was killed before Major Bethers ordered the survivors to flee for their lives through the rain forest. Four wounded men were carried to safety by the survivors. It was a good lesson, but a costly one.

As soon as Major Bethers had reported the ambush and its consequences to Colonel Baxter, it was decided that the 148th Infantry could not use Munda Trail until it was cleared. NGOF headquarters agreed, and the regiment was ordered to bivouac for the night.

On the morning of July 19, F Company, 148th Infantry's 3rd Platoon, hiked out ahead of the regiment to establish a march outpost several hundred yards beyond the site of the Bethers ambush. No one had told the patrol leader, First Lieutenant Sid Goodkin, that he would find a burned-out truck and dead Americans on the roadway, so Goodkin stopped his patrol in its tracks when the grisly discovery was made. The lieutenant, who was both the F Company executive officer and nominal commander of the 3rd Platoon, was trying to figure out what to do when a shot rang out up ahead. Minutes later, a New Zealand sergeant who had been leading a patrol of Fijian commandos ahead of Goodkin's patrol, arrived to tell Goodkin that his scouts had flushed a sniper.

Minutes after the New Zealander went back up the trail, Colonel Baxter arrived with his intelligence officer, Captain Edward Nicely, and the F Company commander, Captain Herald Smith. Lieutenant Goodkin had nothing to report; anything he might have said was plain to see. The colonel ordered Goodkin's platoon to carry the dead soldiers to the side of the road and cover them with ponchos, something that had not occurred to an embarrassed Lieutenant Goodkin in all the excitement. Then Colonel Baxter embellished his practical advice with a sign of bravado: "And if you find any Japs, well, kick them in the balls and, uh, cover them up, too."

Captain Smith ordered Lieutenant Goodkin to set up right where he was, that the rest of the battalion was returning to the beach, but that the remainder of the regiment would be along soon. Then Smith joined Colonel Baxter and Captain Nicely to venture farther up the road. None of the three seemed to hear Goodkin's warning concerning the sniper flushed by the Fijians. However, the colonel and the two captains returned shortly. Captain Smith stopped off to order Goodkin to remain in place, then rushed after the colonel.

Shortly after the senior officers left Goodkin's platoon, another shot rang out from the forest, then a Fijian rushed into view. The short, stocky commando, who had been shot right through the calf, stopped to have his wound dressed by Goodkin's platoon medic and allowed himself to be helped to the rear by one of Goodkin's riflemen.

The Fijian had barely hobbled out of sight when one of Goodkin's men reported that a large column of soldiers was thrashing through the rain forest about 100 yards to the right of the trail. No one had a clue about who those people were, so Goodkin and two of his men strode into the forest to find out. Though the three could hear noises they thought might indeed be men marching through the woods, nothing whatever was found in the first fifty yards. Goodkin was loath to advance farther, so he called out, "Who's there?" There was no response, so he yelled, "Halt or we'll shoot." Again, there was no response.

"Okay, boys," Goodkin whispered, "let 'em have it!"

Goodkin fired a full magazine of .45-caliber bullets from his Thompson submachine gun, one of the others ripped off a full magazine from his BAR, and the third pumped out eight rounds from his M1 rifle. Goodkin thought he saw several forms leap through a break in the trees, but the shooting was followed by dead silence.

The three backtracked to the trail, where they found the New Zealand sergeant, who asked what the shooting was all about. After a brief discussion, Goodkin, the New Zealander, and an American sergeant moved cautiously into the woods. The three passed the pile of brass cartridges left from Goodkin's previous attempt and went on another thirty yards. Sure enough, a large force of men was moving through the trees dead ahead. From a safe distance, Goodkin could see that some of the men were small and some were large. Many seemed to have twigs and leaves affixed to their helmets, a known Japanese camouflage technique. The three decided they were Japanese. Goodkin also estimated that at least a company had passed in the fifteen minutes since his last trip, and there were many men still on the move. The three therefore rushed back to the road so Goodkin could call up the machine-gun section attached to his platoon, but he learned that the guns had been ordered back to the beach during his absence; all he had to stop the Japanese was his platoon of riflemen.

Goodkin was trying to figure out a reasonable course of action when a column of strangers was heard thrashing through a wooded gully to the left of the trail. Goodkin called down and saw several men jump at the sound of his voice. These turned out to be American combat engineers who had been sent to open a new road. This news raised concern that Goodkin had earlier fired on friendly soldiers to the right of the trail.

Goodkin took one volunteer back to the right and ventured as far as he had on his last trip. Still keeping his distance, the lieutenant called out, "Who's there?"

The entire forest in front of Lieutenant Goodkin erupted in gunfire, mainly machine-gun fire. As Goodkin was thinking about dropping to the earth, he recognized the high-pitched rattle of a

Nambu light machine gun. Before he could further ruminate on
his situation or even reach a prone position, he felt like he had been
hit in the groin with a club. Then he sprawled on his face.

The machine gun fired several short bursts into the damp earth
less than three feet from the wounded lieutenant's face. Then the
firing stopped and a voice reached out from the trees: "Me kill. Me
kill."

Goodkin placed his helmet in front of his face for the little extra
protection it might offer, thumbed the safety of his tommygun, and
reached down to his pocket for a hand grenade.

A twig cracked, breaking the ominous silence. Overhead, green
ferns swayed in an unfelt breeze. A warm, wet sensation crawled
down Goodkin's thigh from the wound near his groin. The only
sound he heard was of his own breathing.

He laid aside the tommygun and unbuckled his cartridge belt.
Then he pulled the pin from the hand grenade and placed the pin
between his lips so he would not lose it. Then he went to work
disengaging his left leg from a clump of vines in which it had become entangled; that took precious minutes and precious strength,
but he accomplished the task without making a sound, which
somehow seemed important. After listening to the silent air for
another minute, Goodkin eased away from the spot on his belly.
Then he listened for another minute, and eased away some more.
After stopping and starting several times, he cautiously rose to his
hands and knees and slowly crawled back toward the road, which
was at least eighty yards away in a straight line.

As Goodkin neared the road, he was struck with the fear that
he might be shot by his own men. After due deliberation, he
whistled aloud. It took a moment of effort to arrive at a mellow
pitch, then he blew out the notes of "Yankee Doodle"—what
else?—followed by "You Are My Sunshine." After otherwise
breathless minutes, he heard an answering whistle.

"Don't shoot! It's Goodkin!"

A tall American shape stepped from behind a tree up ahead.
Goodkin stood up and stepped forward, right into the arms of two
of his relieved subordinates, who helped him stagger to the road
and laid him down to probe and dress his wound. A stretcher was
improvised from a poncho and two cut poles, and the lieutenant
was placed across the back of the platoon's jeep. The shot of mor-
phine administered by the platoon medic took blessed effect before the jeep got rolling. On the way to the battalion aid station,

the doped lieutenant unknowingly passed the long overdue main body of the regiment.

The order of march of the main body of the 148th Infantry was A Company in the vanguard, 1st Battalion, the regimental command post, Headquarters and Service companies, most of Antitank Company, motorized detachments, and a rear guard comprised of a single platoon of Antitank Company. The 2nd Battalion was left to guard Zanana Beach.

On the way out, the green troops from A Company began getting itchy. One of the inexperienced soldiers panicked when he spotted some moving leaves, and he cut loose. Most of the men around him opened fire—at nothing. The best targets they could find were clods of moss in dead branches. Colonel Baxter rushed forward and dressed down the malefactors, telling them that they had found the key to unlocking the war-neurosis nemesis.

After marching several miles, the column vanguard came upon a bridge from which the trail abruptly swung westward up an easy slope about 100 yards long. The point carefully picked its way over the bridge and signaled the main body that it was safe to advance. As the main body of the column turned sharply at the end of the bridge, Japanese soldiers strung out on either side of the trail opened fire with machine guns and rifles.

As soon as Colonel Baxter heard the firing, he rushed forward from the regimental command group. Baxter later told subordinates that while he rushed to find out what was happening his chief concern was how he would act under fire. Baxter had served in France in 1918, but he had not been shot at for a quarter century; he wanted to know if he could still take it. The colonel got as far as a big tree where the road turned. There, he found everyone prone on the ground, including several injured soldiers. The Japanese were not firing, so he carefully peeked around the tree and spotted a lieutenant hugging the ground in a rut on the near side of the road, about fifty feet ahead. In response to Baxter's query about where the Japanese were, the lieutenant responded, "Right ahead on the hill. And look out! You're right in the line of fire!" At that moment, the Japanese opened fire again and put a few rounds into the earth very close to the regimental commander, who went prone behind his tree. When the flurry of firing subsided, the colonel eased his head out from behind the tree and ordered the lieutenant, who was completely in the open, to roll to the left into the forest. The younger man, who had been calm to that point, replied, "I can't, Colonel." Baxter presented the option as an order, so the lieutenant rolled into the trees. His only injury was a tiny crease in his left shoulder. Colonel Baxter was extremely happy with his own performance.

Shortly after the colonel arrived at the ambush site, the 1st Battalion commander, Lieutenant Colonel Vernor Hydaker, loped down the trail to take charge of the vanguard infantry squads clearing the area. Captain Orville Wendt, the A Company commander, made his way back from the point of the main column to assist. It was known by this time that only a handful of Japanese were manning the ambush. The officers ordered a squad to cut through the forest on the left, then sent a second squad to the right. A hot little firefight ensued.

To end the fight, First Lieutenant Steve Losten was ordered to work his rifle platoon around on the left behind the left squad. Losten's platoon moved out immediately and soon had one machine gun pinpointed. The Americans picked off the machine gun's entire crew and several of the supporting riflemen. However, before Losten's platoon could press its advantage, the sun set with disquieting speed and the action had to be stopped. The five engaged American rifle squads moved back to the main body. There had been no casualties. The 1st Battalion's 81mm mortar platoon registered on the Japanese position across the bridge and supporting artillery was plotted in. However, the night passed without incident.

Early on July 20, Lieutenant Colonel Herbert Radcliffe's 2nd Battalion, 148th, was ordered to proceed from Zanana Beach to the 169th Infantry's sector by an alternate route. Hydaker's 1st Battalion, 148th, and supporting units were to force the trail block.

At 0915, Lieutenant Colonel Hydaker moved to the head of the 1st Battalion column to direct the area sweep. He was immediately fired on by several snipers and had to take cover until they could be flushed. C Company was stripped of one platoon and ordered to cut through the jungle to establish a blocking position to the north. Following a fifteen-minute mortar and artillery preparation, the detached C Company platoon swept ahead to begin reducing pockets of Japanese survivors.

While the 1st Battalion was clearing its front, the 2nd Battalion was trudging over the Old Barike Swamp Trail toward Reincke

Ridge and Kelley Hill. The battalion vanguard reached Reincke Ridge in mid-afternoon, and the battalion was in position by 1630.

The 1st Battalion advanced in force at noon. Ninety minutes later, C Company was in possession of the high ground 500 yards west of the bridge, and the remainder of the battalion moved ahead to join it. The rain forest was extremely thick in this area, so the inexperienced Ohioans moved with so much extra caution that they were still in the open, far from their objective, when night fell. A defensive cordon had to be established in the forest.

Next morning, July 21, a patrol from Radcliffe's safely ensconced 2nd Battalion arrived at the 1st Battalion bivouac to guide the main body of the regiment to its new lines. Transport bogged down and a bulldozer from C Company, 117th Engineer Combat Battalion, arrived to bail it out. The infantry battalions were joined by nightfall, and the regimental command post was established.

It had taken the 148th Infantry Regiment four days to secure its rear.

23

The 2nd Battalion, 103rd Infantry, arrived on New Georgia on July 22 to assume its place on the XIV Corps line. Major Ray Dunning, who had replaced Lieutenant Colonel Lester Brown as battalion commander, immediately led his staff to the command post of Major James Devine's 3rd Battalion, 172nd, and undertook a survey of the battalion's area of responsibility. Dunning's portion of the line was about 500 yards in length, most of it across a rise known as Gooslaw Hill. On the left, by the coast, was Lieutenant Colonel Jim Wells's 3rd Battalion, 103rd, and on the right was Major John Carrigan's 2nd Battalion, 172nd.

With the start of the XIV Corps offensive still days away, Dunning took great care in stringing his rested, blooded companies over Gooslaw Hill in a defensive deployment. Gooslaw Hill commanded all the ground to the left flank, toward the sea. To the right front was a small ridge that partially obscured the vistas in that direction. Lambeti Plantation, the immediate regimental objective, was approximately 3,000 yards to the front. Gooslaw Hill itself was not badly overgrown, but all the thick woods on the flanks and front were assumed to conceal many Japanese strongpoints.

Dunning's battalion sent out its first strong combat patrols on July 24. Platoons from E and F Companies moved off the hill into the rain forest and advanced up to 150 yards to the front. Despite expectations, no contacts were made and no Japanese defensive emplacements were discovered.

The remainder of July 24 was spent correcting the regimental boundary on Dunning's right. The 2nd Battalion, 172nd, was to be squeezed out of the line some days into the corps offensive; Major John Carrigan's troops had been on the line for three solid weeks.

July 25, 1943, dawned fair and clear. Visibility on land was excellent and, for once, there was no forecast of rain. Seven American fleet destroyers entered Roviana Lagoon at 0600 and two of them commenced firing at 0610 against targets around Lambeti Plantation. The remaining destroyers joined in at 0614. Visibility from the sea was adequate, though an early-morning haze still hung over the plantation. The haze lifted at 0629, but the dense smoke caused by a number of blazes ashore hung directly over the target. The destroyers secured fire at 0644 and made for more open waters.

A total of 254 aircraft of all types swept in over New Georgia between 0630 and 0700 to deliver over a half million pounds of aerial ordnance to a target area only 1,500 by 250 yards some 500 yards west of the lines manned by the 103rd Infantry's two operating battalions.

At 0700, 43rd Division Artillery opened with the first of over 100 fire missions for the day. In the initial fire missions, the 105mm howitzers of the 103rd and 152nd Field Artillery Battalions fired some 2,150 rounds. This fire was augmented by 1,182 155mm rounds put out by the 136th Field Artillery Battalion.

As the initial air strikes came to an end at 0700, and with artillery fires shifting westward, the infantry rose from their fighting holes. Right on schedule, riflemen headed out to begin prying the Japanese from their jungle warrens.

The leading riflemen in the 172nd Infantry's zone began making their way toward Shimuzu Hill, the defensive keystone in the sector. The going was especially hazardous for Major John Carrigan's 2nd Battalion. At 0810, Major Carrigan reported that his companies had advanced about 200 yards from the line of departure. However, headquarters of the 2nd Battalion, 103rd, on Carrigan's left, claimed that he was advancing more slowly than he thought. A line of pillboxes in front of F and G Companies, 172nd, had stopped Carrigan completely by 0830.

At 0832, Major James Devine informed the division command post that his 3rd Battalion, 172nd, had pushed forward 300 yards through heavy mortar fire and across numerous defensive emplacements. At that point, Devine reported, he had sustained only one man wounded. A bit over a half hour later, at 0910, Devine reported that three pillboxes on his left front were under infantry attack supported by fire from 37mm antitank guns and mortars.

At 0920, E Company, 172nd, was moving against a pillbox directly to its front. According to Major Carrigan, contact was being maintained with Dunning's 2nd Battalion, 103rd, on his left flank.

The 43rd Division riflemen were grinding into an extremely strong defensive sector, concentrated in a very small area. No advance continued for long before at least one pillbox opened on the lead troops. There was no way to employ artillery support in that terrain because the forest was too thick for the sort of infantry movement required. Moreover, the Japanese were all over the place, and it was as likely for a maneuvering unit of Americans to back into a defensive line as it was to advance on one.

F and G Companies, 172nd, cleared line after line of pillboxes and waded through dozens of barbed wire-entaglements. At 0920, the company commanders reported that yet another line had been uncovered, and they urgently requested that 37mm antitank guns be brought forward to provide direct support. The 900-pound guns were manhandled through the thick underbrush and emplaced only yards from the Japanese. Their fire eased the pressure a bit. G Company was left to maintain the fight while F Company broke off to swing to the right in order to regain contact with Devine's 3rd Battalion.

In the meantime, Major Carrigan called regimental headquarters for tank support. The request was approved at about 0950 and Marine Captain Robert Blake ordered Sergeant Robert Botts to lead his four-tank section into the fight. The tanks were formally released to Carrigan's battalion by XIV Corps at 1100. At that time, the infantry battalion commander received word that the tanks would be ready at 1150 and committed at 1210. B Company, 172nd, was released from the regimental reserve to escort the precious armored vehicles.

Hitches developed for the next two hours, and it was not until 1410 that the infantry-supported tanks reached the front lines. As Sergeant Bott's lead tank moved into the fight, it took an antitank round completely fore to aft. Nothing vital was hit, but the tank stopped. The driver stood up to have a look around and a second antitank round penetrated the frontplate of the tank directly between his legs; the round passed through the back of the driver's seat and on into the crew compartment. After penetrating the rear fire wall, it lodged in the engine. The tank began burning and Botts ordered his crew to bail out.

As soon as Sergeant Botts and his crewmen hit the ground, a knot of Japanese charged out of the underbrush. A Browning automatic rifleman (BAR-man) named Fasog opened fire on the yelling Japanese and dropped one of them six feet from the burning tank.

The captain of the second tank, a Sergeant Cardell, was already

Litter bearers carry a wounded 43rd Division soldier five miles to the nearest aid station. July 12, 1943.

(Official Signal Corps Photo)

Members of Company C, 118th Medical Battalion, treat wounded 43rd Division soldiers at a behind-the-lines casualty collecting station. July 12, 1943.　　*(Official Signal Corps Photo)*

Combat engineers lay a corduroy road directly behind infantry combat units. *(Official Signal Corps Photo)*

Tank lighters bearing Marine tanks are shelled by Japanese 77mm infantry guns as they follow the 3rd Battalion, 103rd Infantry, into the Laiana beachhead. July 14, 1943.

(Official Signal Corps Photo)

A Japanese soldier killed in a tank-supported infantry attack. July 15, 1943.

A visibly haggard and weary Maj James Devine (foreground), commander of the 3rd Battalion, 172nd Infantry, on his first day away from frontline combat. July 21, 1943.

LtCol James Wells, commander of the 3rd Battalion, 103rd Infantry. Late 1943.

Marine tanks and Army infantry cautiously advance up a jungle trail. July 29, 1943. *(Official Signal Corps Photo)*

Sgt Lawrence Kearns, of the Chemical Warfare Service, test fires one of the first American flamethrowers to reach New Georgia. *(Official Signal Corps Photo)*

Frank Petraca, the 2nd Battalion,
h Infantry, medic who earned a
humous Medal of Honor saving
on Horseshoe Hill.

(Official Signal Corps Photo)

Company D, 145th Infantry, advances along a shell-ravaged jungle
trail.   *(Official Signal Corps Photo)*

Lambeti Plantation, ravaged and shell-pocked, following the
passage of 43rd Division frontline units. *(Official Signal Corps Photo)*

BGen Leonard Wing directs the final drive onto Munda Field from a front-line foxhole. August 3, 1943.

(Official Signal Corps Photo)

MGen Robert Beightler (*left*), commanding the 37th Infantry Division, confers with Col James Dalton (*center*), commanding the 161st Infantry Regiment, and Maj Francis Carberry (*extreme right*), commanding the 2nd Battalion, 161st Infantry. August 3, 1943. *(Official Signal Corps Photo)*

Marine tanks parade around the base of Bibilo Hill, Munda
Field. August 6, 1943.   *(Official Signal Corps Photo)*

One of numerous Japanese 75mm dual-purpose guns protecting Munda Bar and captured after the fall of Munda Field.

(Official Signal Corps Photo)

Infantry-supported flamethrower operator incinerates a Japanese pillbox during the mop-up operations around Munda Field. *(Official Signal Corps Photo)*

Before the smoke clears, the infantry moves in to check the smoldering pillbox for live occupants. *(Official Signal Corps Photo)*

looking for the gun that had put Botts's tank out of the fight. Before he could find it, another armor-piercing round smashed through his turret. And yet another round, fired right behind the first, plowed into the driver's compartment and blew the door open. Cardell and his crew bailed out.

As Cardell's crew was getting clear of its tank, Sergeant Botts spotted the muzzle flash of the Japanese antitank gun. He leaped to the turret of his own smoking tank and sprayed the forest around the antitank gun with the turret-mounted .30-caliber machine gun, but to no avail. Botts then entered the open turret hatch and, despite the fact that his tank was afire, calmly fired three 37mm rounds at his target. The Japanese switched fire back to Botts's tank, which the section leader evacuated just as its fuel and ammunition blew up.

As the explosion engulfed Botts's tank, another knot of Japanese made for the damaged vehicles. Private Fasog drew a bead with his BAR and piled an even dozen of them in front of the smoldering wrecks. In the meantime, Sergeant Botts made his way to the two surviving tanks and guided them through the trees to safety.

The withdrawal was going well when many more Japanese infantrymen burst on the scene. Captain Harold Slager, a member of the 152nd Field Artillery Battalion who had distinguished himself during an arduous preinvasion scouting mission and who was on hand to help supervise the tanks, moved to the forwardmost infantry units during the withdrawal to prevent the infantry from retreating. He was directing fire against a hidden machine-gun emplacement when the counterattacking Japanese shot and killed him. Private Fasog, the BAR-man, helped to keep the Japanese at bay until Sergeant Botts had led the survivors out of danger. When the Japanese captured the two disabled tanks, Sergeant Cardell tried to work in close enough to grenade them, but he was kept away by rifle fire. That ended the armored action for the day.

In the five hours it took to get the tanks into the fight, adjacent infantry units made continuous progress of one sort or another. At 0953, Devine's 3rd Battalion, 172nd, destroyed a pillbox, and the infantry was working over several others with hand grenades. The advancing lines had by then formed into small spearheads aimed at various defensive positions; there was no "line" per se. This condition was caused as much by the jumbled terrain as the cunning dispersal of the defenses.

By this stage of the campaign, the understrength line battalions were lean and hard. True, there were fewer men to do more fighting, but the men available were the survivors. They had been the ones to adapt best to the environment and, while they continued to be hurt, those remaining were the toughest there were, the very best at taking ground.

At 1245, Major Carrigan informed the 172nd Infantry's executive officer that a gap was developing between G and E Companies, but that E Company was still in physical contact with the 2nd Battalion, 103rd. A minute later, Colonel David Ross ordered Carrigan to pull G Company to the left to regain contact with E Company, adding that under no circumstances should contact with Dunning's battalion be lost.

The advance continued steadily for another ninety minutes. At 1410, just as the tanks were going into the fight, a Japanese patrol of undetermined size was spotted in the rear of the 3rd Battalion, 172nd, heading for the regimental command post. The uncommitted portions of Major Bill Naylor's 1st Battalion, 172nd, were ordered out after the patrol, and the regimental service company was placed on standby. No contact was made with the Japanese, who probably withdrew as soon as they realized that they were up against defenses too formidable to breach.

The 172nd Infantry's advance continued in spurts and bursts. The two assault battalions were completely out of touch with one another by 1550, when Colonel Ross ordered both battalion commanders to regain contact at all costs, even if it meant withdrawing somewhat. After forty minutes of careful retrograde movement, the 3rd Battalion was back on a high ridge and began establishing an all-around perimeter defense for the night. The 2nd Battalion was ordered back to tie in on the 3rd Battalion's left. Naylor's 1st Battalion was ordered to bivouac immediately between its sister battalions.

The first day of the corps offensive began well enough in the zone of Dunning's 2nd Battalion, 103rd. Before going very far, however, the battalion struck a line of pillboxes capable of firing across the battalion's front from the left. This slowed things considerably for Captain Ollie Hood's G Company, which was the unit responsible for remaining in contact with Lieutenant Colonel Jim Wells's 3rd Battalion, adjacent to the left, on the coast. Captain Ray Brown's F Company, on Dunning's right flank, did well despite the opposition and managed to keep up with the advancing 2nd Battalion, 172nd, on its right. Captain Irv Chappell's E Company, in the center, met no opposition. And it was due to this that things began falling apart.

Major Dunning's orders directed the battalion to continue its advance for as long as possible. The companies holding the left and right flanks hit what they considered hard going and broke stride to deal with it. G Company advanced only sixty-five yards before being stopped by fire from its left front. Captain Hood attempted to maneuver around these positions, but the movement resulted in heavier casualties. F Company was also having a bad time, and matters became worse as the 2nd Battalion, 172nd, began creeping ahead. F Company was ultimately stopped just 150 yards from the line of departure by a nest of machine guns.

This is when the trouble started. Contact between Dunning's and Carrigan's battalions had been severed. E Company, in Dunning's center, had been ordered to advance until it could no longer do so, and Captain Chappell's riflemen were doing just that, though Chappell was unaware that the companies on either of his flanks were not keeping pace. The result was that Dunning's center company pushed far ahead of his flanking companies, and all soon lost contact. The entire battalion was completely disjointed and in no position to take advantage of the best chance for a breakthrough any 43rd Division unit had yet found.

The opportunity arose from the nature of the Japanese defenses. Due to the lay of the land and an early fear of assault from the sea, the bulk of the fixed defenses faced eastward. In the line's center, however, there was a small break covered, by chance, by E Company, 103rd. Exploitation of the break in the otherwise cohesive defensive line would have meant that the Japanese could have been outflanked and forced to withdraw all their forces facing the 3rd Battalion, 103rd, near the coast. An advance by that battalion would have uncovered the Japanese line facing the 172nd Infantry, and this line, too, would have to have been abandoned.

E Company, 103rd, advanced 800 yards by 1025 and was still on the move before Chappell's platoon leaders informed him that they had long since lost contact with the companies on either flank. Chappell instantly ordered the company to stop where it was and form a defensive perimeter. He then phoned the battalion command post to report and find out what was going on around him. Major Dunning told Chappell to remain where he was, that the remainder of the battalion would attempt to drive through to his position. Unbeknownst to Chappell, the nearest American unit to his position was the 2nd Battalion, 172nd, still some 450 yards to his right rear.

While Chappell's troops waited, they saw numerous Japanese pulling back from the main line; many of the enemy soldiers were carrying or hauling heavy weapons and all sorts of equipment. So far as Captain Chappell could determine, they were heading back to the last line of defenses around Munda Field.

At about noon, with no sign of advancing American infantry, Captain Chappell decided to hike back to the battalion command post to exchange information. Before leaving, Chappell told his executive officer to either dig in deeper or head back well before nightfall if he thought the company would be in danger where it was. Strangely, the company had not been molested by any of the passing Japanese. Then Chappell left with his communications sergeant, who was to check the telephone line, which had apparently been severed.

It was very slow going. Visibility in the forest was nil, and many Japanese were in among the trees. The two arrived safely at the battalion command post and reported. Chappell's startling news was passed on to the regimental command post, which asked Captain Chappell to report to brief representatives from the division operations and intelligence staffs. In the meantime, a four-man wire team was ordered to get a line through to E Company. The team was ambushed midway out and forced to pull back to save one of the wiremen, who had been hit.

After helping artillery officers pinpoint the Japanese evacuation routes, Captain Chappell prepared to return to his company. He was unable to locate his communications sergeant, so he made the return trip alone. Along the way, he thought he heard tank engines in the distance, but he was not sure. He arrived safely at about 1430 hours.

By that time, everyone involved had a fair idea of what had to be done. Unfortunately, no one was altogether clear on how to do it. F Company, 103rd, was pulled off the line at 1500 hours and placed in the gap between E and G Companies; this move helped contain a salient that had developed in front of the 3rd Battalion, 103rd. Next the refurbished and refreshed 3rd Battalion, 169th, now under the command of Major Ignatius Ramsey, was sent to fill the gap between Carrigan's 2nd Battalion, 172nd, and Chappell's company. Next, Major Ray Dunning ordered F Company to send a patrol out to E Company to inform Captain Chappell of the rejuggling to his rear. However, the patrol was ambushed and had to fall back with many casualties. Chappell had no way of knowing that he could hold in relative safety.

The level of excitement among those in the know was almost unbearable. Lieutenant Colonel Jim Wells, who had a pretty fair idea of what was at stake, offered to send fifty of his riflemen into the gap between E and F Companies. Wells never received a response.

Carrigan's 2nd Battalion, 172nd, had managed to keep its advance going, and a gap had developed between it and the 3rd Battalion, 169th. To offset this, Colonel Ross sent his command-post guard, a platoon of A Company, back to the understrength 1st Battalion, 172nd, and ordered Major Bill Naylor to bridge the expanding gap.

The problem was close to being licked, and it was suggested that Chappell's command be left out overnight, even if it meant exposing the company to attack, a worthwhile risk when taken against the opportunity to unseat the Japanese main line of resistance. However, higher command turned down the suggestion. In light of that decision, Captain Ray Brown's F Company, 103rd, was ordered to pull back from its extended position. Then Naylor's 1st Battalion, 172nd, was advised to stand down and march back to its bivouac. Carrigan's 2nd Battalion, 172nd, which had tried to make up for advancing too quickly, held in place until it was ordered back to tie in with Devine's 3rd Battalion, 172nd.

While the better part of a regiment-in-strength was being juggled back and forth, Captain Irv Chappell remained willing to hold in place for the night. However, by 1630, his patrols found that the friendly units to the rear were receding. He felt that E Company's position was becoming completely untenable. There was really only one course left, and Chappell took it; he ordered his troops to pack up, turn about, and march for the rear. E Company made it home by sunset, pretty much without seeing any more Japanese.

While the advance of July 25 had been the 43rd Division's best one-day gain of the campaign, nightfall found the various operating battalions disjointed and manning far more frontage than was desirable. The 172nd Infantry was well ahead of the 103rd, obliging the latter to draw abreast in order to effect a denser coverage of the division's lines. To this end, the 172nd Infantry was ordered to remain in place on July 26 while the 103rd attempted to draw abreast. Some units of the 103rd, in fact, would have to advance as many as 800 yards to straighten the line.

On July 26, the 172nd Infantry limited itself to mounting strong combat patrols. One such penetrated to within several yards of the base of Shimuzu Hill before being spotted, fired on, and forced to withdraw with its casualties.

Patrols from the 103rd Infantry fared well. These groups were looking for trouble, and often found it. Getting themselves fired on was about the only way to discover the whereabouts of Japanese defensive positions. Each patrol reported its findings to the battalion and regimental intelligence staffs, which passed the news to the division, corps, and force artillery intelligence people.

The day's plan in the 103rd Infantry's zone called for a heavy artillery area-saturation bombardment along the entire regimental front as soon as all the morning patrols had been accounted for. The bombardment began at 1115. Beginning at 1145, the infantry pulled back 100 yards under smoke cover to allow the artillery to reach targets even closer to the front lines.

The howitzers were to have worked over the immediate front for thirty minutes, then the two-battalion 103rd Infantry was to move out to recover the relinquished ground, and more besides. However, the Marine tanks that were to support the attack were late in arriving. The artillery fired until 1225, then shifted its fire westward 100 yards. The infantry moved out out right behind the tanks, which had finally arrived and which advanced along the boundary of the 2nd and 3rd Battalions.

In addition to the tanks, the 103rd was supported by a number of flamethrowers, the second such use of this weapon in the Pacific by American forces. Originally employed by Marine units against caves in the latter stages of the Guadalcanal Campaign, flamethrowers had been an unqualified success, albeit under ideal conditions. The Japanese had had flamethrowers for some time, but the first recorded use had been against Marine tanks on July 18, 1943. The employment of flamethrowers in support of the 103rd Infantry on July 26 was more an experiment than anything else.

General Griswold had seen some flamethrower training at Guadalcanal and had requested that Second Lieutenant James

Olds, of the Chemical Warfare Service, be attached to the XIV
Corps staff as Acting Corps Chemical Officer in order to test the
weapon in unrestricted combat. Olds had arrived with several
flamethrowers and, in a one-hour crash course, had trained six
volunteers from the 118th Engineer Combat Battalion to use them
immediately before they went into action with the 103rd Infantry.
There was some question about whether the flame gunners were
meant to support the regiment or *vice versa.*

A call went back to Lieutenant Olds and his team on July 26 as
the leading riflemen of the 103rd Infantry approached to within
twenty yards of the first line of pillboxes. Their faces and hands
camouflaged with dirt, the flame gunners crept forward. Olds chose
three well concealed emplacements and sent his team in. The gunners ignited their torches as they neared the pillboxes, then spurted
streams of intensely flaming fuel into the embrasures. The surrounding foliage was seared away and aim was corrected. There
was no return fire. The Japanese manning the emplacements had
been burned to a gruesome crisp, and a sweet-sick odor of charred
flesh permeated the air amidst the sound of randomly popping
small-arms ammunition cooking off below the ground. All three
emplacements were destroyed in less than sixty seconds.

Still, it was the infantry that had been charged with taking the
ground. The going was rough, but less so than it had been the day
before. Captain Ollie Hood's G Company, 103rd, had about the
easiest go of it as it was right behind the Marine tanks, which simply cut through the Japanese line. Captain Ray Brown's F Company, operating in E Company's center position of the previous
day, made its move against almost zero opposition; it beat a 100-
yard path through the thickets, and stopped only to be certain of
staying in line with the remainder of the regiment.

By 1450, Lieutenant Colonel Jim Wells's 3rd Battalion, 103rd,
was making steady progress against unbelievably heavy opposition. K Company, on the beach, was advancing steadily with L
Company close behind. I Company, which was tied in with Dunning's battalion, was a bit slow but made it even with G Company
by 1500 hours.

The day's orders called upon the 103rd to attempt to squeeze
Major Ignatius Ramsey's 3rd Battalion, 169th, out of the line so
that it could revert to the division reserve. However, this could not
be accomplished, so Ramsey's battalion went into the attack under

Colonel Brown's control. Moving to the right of Dunning's battalion, I Company, 169th, seized the crown of a small rise on its right front. The troops were just digging in when they were ordered back because Dunning's battalion had had to stop well to the left rear. Major Dunning had ordered his companies to secure the advance and dig in at 1500 hours. By then, his battalion had drawn abreast of the front of the 172nd Infantry and it was best to stop there.

Ilangana Village fell to Wells's 3rd Battalion, 103rd, in midafternoon, but the battalion had drawn some of the dirtiest fighting of the campaign, and casualties were mounting quickly. Nevertheless, Wells's troops refused to stop until the units on the extreme left flank, which had to advance the greatest distances, were in firm control of Kia Village.

The 103rd Infantry had maintained a spirited advance of over 800 yards, and had had to destroy seventy-four pillboxes along a 600-yard front to do so. At the start of the day, the regiment had been holding a shaky 1,700-yard front. By nightfall, the line had been shortened by 300 yards. The losses had been high, particularly in Wells's battalion, which lost nearly all the company-grade officers who had survived earlier battles.

Following the usual excellent artillery preparation, the 103rd Infantry moved off at 0800 hours, July 27, and immediately entered the usual intense struggle. Dunning's 2nd Battalion managed to gain 100 yards before being stopped. G Company faltered under the fire of machine guns emplaced in front of Wells's 3rd Battalion, and, at 1040, E Company was plastered by 90mm mortars. The battalion bogged down and the troops dug in. A small group had managed to advance 200 yards, but most of the battalion was well to the rear, so it withdrew.

In the 3rd Battalion's zone, K Company, which was badly understrength and under the command of a sergeant, was stopped before it could even reach its line of departure. L Company, on the battalion's right, moved all of fifteen yards before it was forced to stop. I Company, on the coast, advanced fifty yards. The entire battalion had been stymied by four mutually supporting pillboxes in front of I and L Companies. The Japanese line was only sixty yards long, but Wells's battalion was spent. Since being committed on July 18, it had suffered the loss of two battalion staff officers, six company commanders (four had been killed), and eleven platoon leaders (most of whom had been killed). Enlisted casualties were running at nearly 50 percent. At times, Lieutenant Colonel Wells and Captain William Lewis, his operations officer, were forced to drop everything to direct platoon operations. Most of the rifle platoons were commanded by corporals, including a medic and a mail clerk.

To the north, the 172nd Infantry had held in place for another day.

July 28 was a day pretty much like the ones that had gone before. Tanks and flame gunners moved out with the infantry at 0800 hours, and there were rapid initial gains. Of particular note was the teaming of flamethrowers and tanks.

Lieutenant Olds and Sergeant Lawrence Kearns spent the opening hour of battle working with the tanks, which they followed closely for protection. Kearns walked in the left tread mark of the lead tank while Olds kept pace on the right. They were very successful at the outset, but they soon met with an incredible surprise. Two Japanese flame gunners emerged from the trees on Lieutenant Old's side of the tank and a few feet ahead. The Japanese, who were walking upright, spurted a stream of foul black oil over Lieutenant Old's right shoulder and head, and over Sergeant Kearn's left side. However, the fuel failed to ignite, and the Japanese were cut down by a burst from the tank's turret machine gun before they could take corrective action. It was in all ways a heart-stopping confrontation.

The tanks were ordered off the line at 0910 after being fired on by concealed antitank guns. Later, they were called back to action when the 3rd Platoon, G Company, 103rd, took severe casualties when it was raked by extremely heavy machine-gun fire. However, the 37mm rounds fired by the tanks fell short of the target and struck several G Company infantrymen, which forced the rifle company to abandon its advance.

After launching a successful assault in the morning, Major John Carrigan's 2nd Battalion, 172nd, was stopped cold in front of a hill on the right flank of E Company, 103rd. The battalion attempted several strong frontal movements against the hill, but was repulsed every time. The action was stopped for a time to allow E Company, 103rd, to send a patrol to check the hill. The patrol returned at 1450 hours and, to everyone's amazement, reported that the emplacements on the troublesome hill had been abandoned.

However, by then, Dunning's battalion had already been ordered to return to its line of departure. Nothing could be done to secure the hill.

On July 29, Major Ignatius Ramsey's entire 3rd Battalion, 169th, was ordered to assume control of a portion of the 103rd Infantry's regimental line, and it was in position by 0830 hours. The entire regiment stepped off as soon as Ramsey's battalion was ready to go.

By 1230, after four hours on the go, Dunning's battalion had beaten over 200 yards. The tanks advancing with Dunning's troops were suddenly fired on by several concealed Japanese antitank guns. The confused, blind tank crews panicked and opened fire on friendly troops. Order was restored and the tanks were ordered out of the fight. Dunning's tired companies had gained an average of 275 yards by 1400 hours, when they were ordered to stop for the day. The 3rd Battalion, 103rd, advanced alongside Dunning, but its power had been spent.

To the north, the 172nd Infantry had a new hero. As the regiment got within reach of Shimuzu Hill, it put on a fantastic burst of energy—fantastic in that its two operating battalions had been on the line every day since landing at Zanana Beach on July 4.

First Lieutenant Robert Scott was a rifle-platoon leader, and he drew the rifle-platoon leader's job of showing his troops the way. Scott, however, was thirty-two yards old, a bit aged for the task of pulling and pushing a rifle platoon through the rain forest. On July 29, Scott led his men through heavy fire, making for an important objective. After a time, he found that he was leading no one, that he was all alone midway across a barren hilltop, only seventy-five yards from the entrenched Japanese. The hill was American, but only Lieutenant Scott was there to claim it. And only Scott was there to stand off the counterattack that would have brought the hill back within the Empire of Japan. Scott cared less about the hill than he did about the future of Robert Scott. He could not retreat, the Japanese were coming his way firing rifles and hurling hand grenades, and all Scott could do was make his stand.

No one was near enough to help Scott. His entire company had withdrawn. He found a blasted tree stump on that barren hilltop, and he crawled behind it. He had his light M2 carbine, which he fired at the Japanese, and he had hand grenades, which he hurled at the Japanese. The Japanese faltered. During the brief ensuing lull, Scott scrambled across the isolated hilltop and found several more hand grenades. Then the Japanese came again. One of them shot the American lieutenant in the left hand, but Scott stood his ground, lobbing his hand grenades from behind his shattered tree stump. The Japanese faltered once again, then began pulling back. American infantrymen arrived at the last minute to chase them off. When Lieutenant Scott looked up, he could see Munda Field, and the sea. He had earned a Medal of Honor.

During its movement on July 29, the 172nd Infantry had been forced to pull somewhat to the right. This left a gap between the 2nd Battalion, 172nd, and the 3rd Battalion, 169th. As there was considerable frontage to cover, and as both battalions were badly understrength, division headquarters decided to commit Major Joe Zimmer's rested and refurbished 1st Battalion, 169th. The battalion was shipped to Laiana from Rendova and assumed its position between the separated battalions by nightfall.

A major command change took place on July 29. On that day, Major General John Hester requested that he be relieved of command of the 43rd Infantry Division due to a distressful deterioration of his ulcer condition during the weeks of hard fighting. General Griswold had been forewarned of Hester's physical problem and he had taken the liberty of finding a replacement.

Major General John Reed Hodge arrived on July 29 from the Fijis after turning command of his own Americal Infantry Division over to his assistant commander. He was placed in command of the 43rd Infantry Division the moment he arrived on New Georgia. Hodge had already seen action at Guadalcanal as assistant commander of the 25th Infantry Division, and he had been awarded his second star in May 1943, upon assuming command of the Americal Division. He was considered one of the most competent senior troop commanders in the Pacific.

The 43rd Infantry Division jumped off again at 0855, July 30. Though it was considered to be on its last legs, at the end of its strength, Wells's 3rd Battalion, 103rd, made strong, steady gains along the coast.

Inland, Dunning's 2nd Battalion, 103rd, took 100 yards by 1030, and an additional 100 yards by 1100. The entire battalion came under heavy machine-gun fire at 1345 and was stopped. Attempts to renew the advance continued unsuccessfully until 1500.

Zimmer's 1st Battalion, 169th, was ordered back into action against a ridge on the regiment's right, and B and C Companies seized the objective. However, heavy machine-gun fire from the far right raked the companies, whose situation became quite perilous. Major Zimmer asked that Carrigan's 2nd Battalion, 172nd, be moved abreast his battalion to reduce the positions that were firing into his troop formations. However, the 172nd Infantry could make no gains, and Zimmer was forced to withdraw the companies to his line of departure.

The last day of July was a day of rest for most of 43rd Division's infantry battalions. Corps headquarters ordered some adjustments in the division's line preparatory to the final drive on Munda. Patrols from Dunning's 2nd Battalion, 103rd, discovered several pillboxes on the immediate front, and Japanese snipers peppered the entire regimental line. At midday, Dunning was ordered to straighten his front by means of a 100-yard advance. The correction was swiftly accomplished and the battalion dug in at 1700 hours.

The 43rd Infantry Division was ready to secure Munda, but units to the north were having trouble getting into position.

24

Colonel James Dalton's 161st Infantry Regiment arrived at Baraulu Island on July 21. The regiment had been Washington State National Guard a year before, but now it was all but Regular Army. Its ranks had been thinned at Guadalcanal and it had drawn itself a pretty fair cross-section of Americans to make good its losses.

The veteran regiment embarked in small landing craft on the morning of July 22 and was deposited on New Georgia to begin its second campaign, once again thrown into the breach to assist and replace units that had been floundering without its help. Patrol activities on its first day in the combat zone cost the regiment several casualties, including the regimental intelligence officer, who was killed along with another officer as they attempted to guide a party of engineers from the site of an ambush along the trail.

The 161st Infantry began moving into assembly areas east of Horseshoe Hill on July 23. Its line of departure was still some 300 yards to the west. The day was used in active patrolling and making final preparations.

E Company, 161st, reinforced by a platoon of medium machine guns, found an engineer encampment that had been overrun on July 18 by the 13th Infantry Regiment. The clearing smelled overpoweringly of putrefying corpses. Two live engineers were found cowering among the rubble. Close inspection revealed that many of the dead engineers had been wounded—and then bayoneted. A count revealed forty-eight bodies, including an officer wearing Medical Corps insignia, and another officer wearing chaplain's crosses. On the far side of a nearby creek were the bloated corpses of several Japanese soldiers, but not many. E Company, 161st, stopped where it was and reported the grim facts to the battalion command post.

The regiment began actively patrolling its front toward Horseshoe Hill on July 24. One reconnaissance patrol from I Company, accompanied by a team of Fijian commandos, was stopped by a cluster of Japanese emplacements on a ridge that appeared to form a segment of the objective's northwest slope. Following a brief, intense firefight, the I Company patrol returned to friendly lines with a wounded American, a wounded Fijian, and a dead American. Shortly thereafter, patrols from K Company and B Company reported meeting opposition when they approached the same ridge at different points above and below the I Company patrol. The B Company patrol brought back a cloth cap with the *rikusentai* insignia affixed to it.

Colonel James Dalton, the thirty-two-year-old 1934 West Point graduate commanding the regiment, ordered I Company to mount a fresh sweep that afternoon with the assistance of one K Company platoon. The I Company commander, Captain Charles Hastings, split his force into two two-platoon elements and ordered attacks against the north and south faces of the tree-shrouded ridge. Soon, both groups of riflemen were back at the base of the hostile ridge, but Japanese mortar rounds immediately began detonating all around them. Shortly, the barrage lifted and numerous machine guns farther up the steep slope opened fire on both attack forces. The cool, well-trained soldiers crawled up the hill, moving from the roots of trees to dead logs to tiny hummocks. But the leading infantrymen were soon stopped by the increasing tempo of the machine-gun fire from above. Both arms of the attack stalled just within grenade-throwing range of the nearest pillboxes. In time, the forwardmost infantrymen were able to pinpoint twenty Japanese machine guns firing from pillboxes set right across the entire summit of the ridge. These guns, and rifles fired from many concealed spider holes, killed or wounded more and more of the bolder I and K Company soldiers, and both arms of the pincer were further weakened by the need to provide more and more litter bearers.

At 1600 hours, Colonel Dalton went back to the 37th Division command post to confer with Major General Robert Beightler, the division commander. Dalton explained that the trail to the regimental line of departure was blocked and that repeated efforts to clear the ridge had not been successful. The general decided that large numbers of troops could not be committed to clearing the trail because he wanted to conserve the regiment's strength for the offensive. Dalton was ordered to commit no more than a single rifle company and some supporting weapons.

In time, Captain Hastings was forced to admit defeat and withdraw. Five Americans had been killed and fourteen had been wounded in the abortive pincers attack, which claimed only one Japanese pillbox definitely destroyed. The American platoons withdrew for the night to a tiny hill southwest of the defended ridge.

At 1810, Colonel Dalton informed the 37th Division command post that he had ordered I Company to withdraw until dawn. In response, General Beightler ordered all the 81mm mortars of the 145th and 148th Regiments that could bear on Dalton's objective to fire intermittently through the night.

At 1855, General Beightler radioed XIV Corps headquarters with news about the 161st Infantry's progress. He also requested that tanks be committed to assist the regiment. It was obvious to Beightler that the 161st could not possibly reach its line of departure in time for the scheduled start of the corps general offensive, so he did the only thing he could do under the circumstances: Colonel Stuart Baxter's 148th Infantry was directed to move only as far as its line of departure and Colonel Temple Holland's 145th Infantry was ordered to hold in place. Both regiments would hold their positions until the 161st Infantry reached the division front line.

Colonel Baxter, of the 148th Infantry, asked to be allowed to launch a limited assault along his front in order to reduce the pocket that was holding up the 161st. General Beightler reviewed the available data and, in the end, authorized Baxter to secure some of the high hills in the area in order to gain direct observation of Munda and the sea.

The 148th Infantry dispatched a number of combat patrols in the morning, July 26, and these accurately pinpointed the northern terminus of the Japanese formal defense line. When all of the patrols had returned to the regiment's lines, 37th Division Artillery fired a ten-minute preparatory barrage at targets about 400 yards to the front, and the 148th Infantry's organic mortar units fired into the area between the artillery target line and the infantry front line.

Lieutenant Colonel Herbert Radcliffe's 2nd Battalion, 148th, jumped off following the preparatory fires and quickly gobbled up 400 to 500 yards. Lieutenant Colonel Vernor Hydaker's 1st Battalion moved up to assume the 2nd Battalion's former line.

The spottiness of the opposition confronting the 148th Infantry was a revelation. The 161st Infantry, to the south, was up against an aggressively held defense-in-depth while a battalion of the adjacent 148th Infantry had quickly advanced nearly 500 yards over completely undefended terrain. It was clear that Colonel Baxter's regiment overlapped the Japanese main line of resistance.

Colonel Dalton's imperative was reaching his line of departure any way he could. The young colonel decided to detach I Company and send the remainder of his 3rd Battalion around the Japanese to contain what seemed to be hardly more than an isolated pocket of resistance. At the same time, Lieutenant Colonel Joe Katsarsky's 1st Battalion, 161st, was to move around the left flank of the pocket to form the southern pincers of a double envelopment. Both battalions hoped to bypass the pocket and gain the line of departure. There was to be no armored support since requests by the 43rd Division superseded those of the 37th Division.

Eight 81mm mortars near the Laiana Trail began a fifteen-minute bombardment of the Japanese lines at 0745. The 145th and 148th Regiments provided some support, but forward observers could find no targets in the dense undergrowth. The few rounds fired by the adjacent regiments caused casualties among Dalton's command and the assistance was canceled.

Captain Hastings pushed I Company off from positions in the zone of the 148th Infantry a few moments after 0800. The company immediately ran into intense fire, largely from automatic weapons emplaced in dozens of concealed pillboxes running across the summit of the densely wooded objective. I Company attacked, withdrew, and attacked again for over an hour. Then the riflemen withdrew to give the company's three 60mm mortars room to tag several of the most obstinate pillboxes. The mortars seemed to do the job; the incoming fire seemed to subside. I Company mounted a fresh attack, but the Japanese remanned their machine guns and put out a murderous crossfire. The 1st Platoon commander, Second Lieutenant Martin Bartley, had advanced fifty yards when he was slightly wounded. Bartley stopped the platoon and motioned his platoon sergeant, Sergeant Richard Colville, to come forward to discuss a plan of action. As Bartley and Colville talked, a hitherto silent Japanese machine gun opened on them, and both men died where they stood. Minutes later, I Company was ordered back down the hill. The ridge was named Bartley Ridge.

The survivors of I Company found a haven of sorts behind a knob projecting eastward from the base of the ridge. Moving behind this knob, some of the riflemen began making some headway, but they could get only as far as the base of the ridge, to a

spot where the trees abruptly thinned and where Japanese gunners had a clear field for their heavy machine-gun concentrations.
The regiment had several flamethrowers in reserve, and one was
dispatched to I Company. The operator, who had to juggle a 65-
pound load uphill, tried climbing the steep slope twice. On the
second try, he succeeded in burning out a pillbox, but was forced
to withdraw because he could not get around well enough to war-
rant further risk.

While I Company struggled and bled before Bartley Ridge, the
remainder of Lieutenant Colonel David Buchanan's 3rd Battalion,
161st, slowly moved around the south side of the ridge. The main
body of the battalion soon bogged down in the dense undergrowth
and halted where it was.

To the north of Bartley Ridge, Lieutenant Colonel Joe Katsarsky's 1st Battalion was making a slightly better go of it. At 1035,
Katsarsky radioed the regimental command post to report that his
companies had pinpointed the northern flank of the defenses on
Bartley Ridge and were moving around it. On receiving this news,
General Beightler held a hurried conference with Colonel Dalton
and the members of their respective staffs. Buchanan's 3rd Battalion was to remain abreast of Bartley Ridge to contain the position
while Katsarsky's 1st Battalion drove westward. Katsarsky was to
avoid a full-scale commitment of his companies if possible. Meantime, the remainder of Beightler's division was ordered to stand
down pending the fall of Bartley Ridge.

Lieutenant Colonel Buchanan stopped his troops as ordered and
began deploying on the northeast, east, and southeast flanks of the
ridge. E Company of Lieutenant Colonel Francis Carberry's 2nd
Battalion, 161st, was released from the division reserve and ordered up to secure the high ground a bit to the north of Bartley
Ridge. Katsarsky's battalion continued under heavy fire and rolled
over nearly 400 yards of ground—a total of 800 yards for the day—
before stopping on a small rise northeast of Horseshoe Hill. The
rise was named for First Lieutenant Robert O'Brien, who had been
killed early in the day.

Late in the afternoon of July 25, First Lieutenant Irving Carlson, commanding the 10th Marine Defense Battalion's light-tank
platoon, arrived at Colonel Dalton's command post and was escorted on a reconnaissance of the 3rd Battalion's main line preparatory to committing his newly landed M3 tanks the following day.
While Lieutenant Carlson was conferring with the infantry offi-

cers, A Company, 65th Engineer Combat Battalion, was ordered to bulldoze a track for the Marine light tanks through the dense virgin forest to the foot of a steep knob of Bartley Ridge on which the original K Company probe had been stopped two days earlier.

At 0845 hours, July 26, 81mm mortars and medium machine guns along the 3rd Battalion's front opened with a fifteen-minute preparation. Then First Lieutenant Kenneth French, commanding K Company, 161st, personally guided six Marine Corps light tanks off the line. Infantry escort teams from French's company and two flamethrower teams followed immediately behind the armor.

A short trail had been bulldozed, and the tanks followed this until it petered out. All of the tanks were completely buttoned up and could receive directions only from radios tied in with the infantry's radio car, which was, in turn, tied in with the 3rd Battalion's communications platoon. It took quite a bit of doing, and the effort did not get under way until 0925.

The six unwieldy tanks moved in two columns and knocked down all the vegetation in their paths as they struggled toward the southeast slop of Bartley Ridge. The Japanese were quick to respond with fire from their small 70mm battalion guns, machine guns, and mortars. Lieutenant French, who was at the point, had to dodge a great volume of fire but continued forward without suffering any injuries. The company commander soon climbed behind the turret of one of the lead tanks for a better view. He could not see much out ahead, but he did see that the infantrymen following the tanks were bunching up under the prodding of streams of bullets from hidden machine guns. He jumped from his perch and intimidated and bullied his troops until they spread out through the trees on either side of the paths the tanks were clearing.

The attack began in good order. By 1000 hours, about a dozen pillboxes were destroyed by the tanks' 37mm guns and infantry assaults. Lieutenant Colonel Buchanan ordered his troops to occupy them to keep the Japanese from infiltrating his lines and using them as refuges.

Unfortunately, at 1100, the blind tanks ran into extremely heavy undergrowth, lost radio contact, and began backing up to find a clear path. During the bucking and weaving, an infantry squad leader and three of his men were crushed to death. The assistant squad leader, Corporal Marvin Heitman, took over the remnants of the infantry group. Minutes later, Heitman spotted a machine-gun nest. He charged forward alone and killed the three Japanese manning it.

One of the tanks was disabled when a Japanese soldier burst from the underbrush and applied a magnetic mine.

First Lieutenant Joseph Galloway, an I Company platoon leader, was leading his men directly behind the tanks when a sniper's bullet struck one of his arms and severed a major artery. Refusing treatment, Galloway exhorted his men to advance. Although Galloway collapsed from loss of blood after his platoon had advanced another 50 yards, he refused his platoon sergeant's offer of assistance and crawled 100 yards back down the hill under his own power, until he found a litter team.

Corporal Marvin Heitman was still leading the remnants of his squad up the steep slope when he was shot dead.

A second tank was disabled by a ruptured fuel line at 1105 and Lieutenant Carlson ordered the remaining four vehicles out of the fight.

Sergeant Earnest Allison moved his K Company platoon to the crest of the hill to cover the withdrawal of the remaining tanks. As he ran from group to group yelling orders and words of encouragement, Allison was cut down by shrapnel from a mortar round. He refused evacuation and remained with his platoon, shouting orders and directions as his platoon withdrew from the beaten zone. He died of his wounds.

Someone called for the flamethrowers, but both operators were dead. The infantrymen assigned to protect them did not have the slightest idea what was expected of them, and the two engineers had bravely advanced to their deaths alone.

The knob at the base of Bartley Ridge—soon to be named Tank Hill—was a big stage for a hundred little tragedies. Captain Paul Mellichamp, once a general's aide, now the reigmental operations officer, was moving up the ridge when he saw a radioman struck by shrapnel. Mellichamp made for the radio, which was set up behind a tree, in the hope of directing friendly mortars. The captain had been decorated for a similar feat at Guadalcanal and knew precisely what he was about. He had been wounded in the earlier campaign, and he was wounded here, this time by a sniper's bullet. He had refused evacuation earlier, and he refused evacuation again. Mellichamp shouted into the radio handset until he fainted from loss of blood. He had survived his heroic act at Guadalcanal, but he bled to death on Tank Hill.

The 3rd Battalion was nearly two-thirds the way up Tank Hill at 1440 when it was ordered to secure the advance and dig in. The troops had done all they could for one day, and they had suffered. Nine Americans died on Tank Hill, and twenty-five were wounded and evacuated. Fourteen pillboxes and several aboveground emplacements were neutralized and captured. The 3rd Battalion, 161st, still had 100 yards to go. The attack had been exposed to enfilade fire from machine guns emplaced on Horseshoe Hill, and to others on a hill to the right. Salvage of the two disabled tanks could not be undertaken while it was still light, but both armored vehicles were towed to safety after nightfall.

Katsarsky's 1st Battalion had been on the go throughout July 26. At 1217, Katsarsky informed the division command post that his companies had advanced another 300 yards from the line of departure and that he hoped they would gain more ground. Patrols were out 400 yards ahead of the main body, and one of these discovered a Japanese strongpoint on the left flank. Mortars were set to deal with it. The 1st Battalion, 161st, was firmly set atop O'Brien Hill by nightfall, looking at the next hill and hoping to be there by the following evening.

On July 27, Buchanan's 3rd Battalion, 161st, dispatched combat patrols to Bartley Ridge under supporting fires from its 81mm mortars. The patrols eased up the ridge and began plotting maps for the 37th Division Artillery fire direction center. A number of hitherto silent pillboxes were spotted on the slope of Tank Hill opposite the right flank of the adjacent 1st Battalion, 145th.

Another patrol led by K Company's First Lieutenant Kenneth French attempted to determine whether or not Tank Hill was actually a part of Bartley Ridge or a separate entity. French made two surprise discoveries: Tank Hill was physically detached from Bartley Ridge; and his patrol outflanked the Japanese line at this point, but was in turn outflanked by Japanese positions farther on. Colonel Dalton and Lieutenant Colonel Buchanan agreed that the 161st Infantry's major effort should be delayed until the 3rd Battalion could crawl over Bartley Ridge, a task they felt would take two more days. General Beightler went along with the proposal to delay the regimental—and thus the divisional—offensive until Bartley Ridge fell.

Early in the morning of July 27, the 1st Battalion, 161st, descended into the low-lying rain forest in front of O'Brien Hill toward the next hill, another nameless hump that would soon bear the name of another fallen American. C Company had the vanguard, with B Company close behind. The battalion made continuous progress until it reached the base of the objective. Then the Japanese on the heights cut loose with 13mm heavy machine guns, 7.7mm Nambu light machine guns, .25-caliber Arisaka rifles, and captured BARs, tommyguns, M1 rifles, and Japanese and American hand grenades. Some of the Japanese appeared to be garbed in American jungle suits undoubtedly captured from 43rd Division supply dumps during the mid-July counteroffensive.

While B Company moved into the forest to bridge a widening gap between Katsarsky's battalion and the adjacent 1st Battalion, 145th, C Company waded into the Japanese defenses. Second Lieutenant Louis Christian was leading his C Company platoon up the slope when his men froze under the fire of automatic weapons emplaced in a pillbox to the front. Christian had been the regimental sergeant major during the Guadalcanal fighting, but had accepted a battlefield commission. This day, the new lieutenant crawled alone through the light mantle of underbrush, right up to the face of the pillbox that had stymied his platoon. He chucked in several hand grenades, which silenced the Nambu.

The entire company was having a bad time. The troops waded into the fire of several emplacements, but were forced to stop when they came under fire from more and more machine guns. Then the Japanese infantry threw in a quick counterattack right off the ridgeline. Second Lieutenant Louis Christian was taking a breather alone when he saw his platoon begin to pull back. As the surprised American riflemen tumbled to the rear to find safe positions from which they could beat off the counterthrust, Christian remained where he was to direct fire from supporting mortars. A short burst of machine-gun fire found him as he searched for targets, and he died in a pool of blood. The hill had a name.

C Company pulled back and dug in. An artillery forward observer mouthed some frantic words into his field telephone and, after a moment, the ridge erupted under 105mm shells. The 1st

Battalion's 81mm mortars were hastily relaid and fired. Japanese 90mm mortars responded. Lieutenant Colonel Joe Katsarsky ordered C Company back to O'Brien Hill.

The ordeal of the 1st Battalion, 161st, was only just the beginning. Shortly after the main body of the battalion returned to O'Brien Hill, a large American unit passed through from the north. Following was a large group of Japanese. No one really knew what was going on, but Katsarsky's battalion inherited the Japanese. That was at 1430 hours.

The first contact came when several Japanese blundered into the fire zones of several American machine guns and were dispersed. Shortly after this rather benign first encounter, the Japanese launched several squad-size probes to determine what they were up against. They had a fairly good idea by 1630, when Americans on the battalion line first heard Japanese soldiers in the forest getting themselves worked up for a big fight.

There was a low saddle on the battalion's right flank, and a gully stretching from left to right across the immediate front. Dense growth filled the gully. The forward slopes of O'Brien Hill were outposted near the edge of the forest, within a wooded fringe fronting the high, open hilltop. The battalion command post was only fifteen yards behind the outpost line.

Yelling taunts at their adversaries and encouragement among themselves, shrieking curses through the night, instilling passing clutches of fear even among the veterans on the hill, the Japanese moved noisily over the low saddle and through the tree-choked gully. American hand grenades rained down on them from the heights, as did American 60mm and 81mm mortar rounds. The high-strung chirping of Nambu light machine guns sounded through the throaty bursts of the mortars, and streams of bright tracer reached toward O'Brien Hill through the solid, black wall of the night.

The initial assault was launched by about one platoon. It was stopped cold by methodical riflemen and grimy-faced gunners manning the battalion's air-cooled and water-cooled. 30-caliber Brownings. Two more frontal assaults of about platoon strength collapsed as soon as they lapped upward from the gully and saddle. Then the Japanese withdrew. They knew what they had come to learn; Katsarsky's battalion had been probed.

Joe Katsarsky knew, by 0800 hours, on July 28, that his battalion had been cut off. Litter teams attempting to reach the regimental aid station were fired on along the trail to the rear of O'Brien Hill; several litter bearers and previously wounded soldiers were killed. Jeeps bringing urgently needed ammunition from the regimental supply depot were fired on as they approached O'Brien Hill; several drivers were killed, and four disabled jeeps blocked the vital link. All Katsarsky could do was draw some of his troops off the line and send them back over the trail to clear out the bushwhackers along the way.

The heavily armed combat patrol moved cautiously up the narrow track and the fringe of trees at its edge for two solid hours. For two solid hours, these sleepless soldiers killed. By 1000 hours, it seemed that the road had been cleared. The patrol filed up the reverse slope of O'Brien Hill and broke up to move back to the line.

While the track was being cleared, the Japanese somehow sensed that the American battle line had been weakened, so they prepared an assault. The first file of Japanese stepped out of the forest just as the patrol was breaking up to return to the lines.

The outposts took it first. With bullets from the main line passing inches over their heads, and with Japanese bullets coming in a bit lower, the soldiers manning the posts withdrew. Pink and white tracer stitched the air back and forth, and Japanese explosive bullets popped loudly as they plowed into earth, wood, and flesh. Shelter halves the Americans had stretched above their fighting holes to ward off the sun were shredded within minutes; they had to be pulled down to prevent them from becoming entangled with the barrels of weapons peering over the edges of the fighting holes.

The battalion aid station, which was located on the nose of the hill, had to be pulled back over the crest so the medics could safely move among the wounded and pull others back to a place of relative safety. The battalion communications center was menaced by machine-gun fire and the communicators had to abandon their radios to sprint to safety.

A rifleman on the line was struck by a bullet. A pair of medics charged through the nipping fire and lifted him, one on either side. They staggered through the beaten zone. Another rifleman was shot and went to his knees yelling, "I'm hit!" He pitched forward an instant later, yelling, "I'm dead." And he was.

Captain Ralph Phelps, the battalion executive officer, rushed through the fire to confer with Captain Donald Downen, the A Company commander. As the two officers conferred, a thin stream of machine-gun bullets passed between them, no more than three inches from their bodies. The two popped off the ground and ran for cover in order to finish the discussion.

A Japanese sniper armed with an American BAR was spotted and grenaded from his treetop perch. A corporal, second-in-command of a rifle squad, was shot to death hauling ammunition to his men. A lieutenant who had been nicked in the back of the neck when a bullet passed through his helmet in the road-clearing operation bled for two hours before he found time to seek treatment.

The assault was coming through mainly on the right. The Japanese had done some superb spotting, for most of the troops sent out on the road-clearing patrol had been drawn from this sector and replaced by a few pistol-toting mortarmen. There was one light air-cooled .30-caliber Browning machine gun on the right, but the gunner was absent due to illness and the assistant gunner had wandered off to a latrine moments before the attack commenced. The only man in the gunpit was Private James Newbrough, a green ammunition carrier.

After a weird exchange of taunts, three Nambu-carrying Japanese charged Newbrough's gun. Two died and the other withdrew. Newbrough kept spraying bullets around, but the more he fired, the more attention he drew. The shelter half over the gunpit was shredded and the underbrush nearby was mown down to ground level. Private Newbrough finally determined that by unfastening the machine gun's traversing mechanism he could aim the gun from the underside of the barrel, which meant that his head would be that much lower. He unfastened the mechanism and sprayed and sprayed. And sprayed.

Corporal Dick Barrett was in the rear when the fighting broke out. As soon as he realized Private Newbrough was alone in the gunpit, he gathered as much ammunition as he could scrape together and moved out. Barrett arrived just as Newbrough was preparing to secure. While Corporal Barrett fed in a fresh ammunition belt and settled in behind the machine gun, Private First Class Hollis Johnson, a BAR-man, moved in closer to cover the gunners. And they all sprayed and sprayed. And sprayed.

To the men involved, the fight seemed to go on for hours. It ended at 1045, after only forty-five minutes.

While the 1st Battalion was fighting for its life on O'Brien Hill, the 3rd Battalion was still trying to get itself over Bartley Ridge.

To help clear the way, First Lieutenant Walter Tymniak selected ten men from his I Company platoon and set off southward, once again toward the crest of Bartley Ridge. To everyone's surprise, the patrol cautiously probed all the way to the summit. Lieutenant Tymniak reported his position to the battalion command post, adding that several pillboxes in the vicinity appeared to have been abandoned.

At once realizing the importance of finding a gap in the Japanese line, Lieutenant Tymniak ordered his men to occupy the abandoned emplacements. The hardest part of cracking a line of pillboxes is getting the first one. Until it is taken, only frontal assaults can be pressed. After the first emplacement falls, infantry can move right and left to come against nearby emplacements from their blind flanks. Tymniak had been given the key to this line of pillboxes.

Working with only ten riflemen, the platoon leader began moving down the line. The first few pillboxes were empty. Staff Sergeant Leroy Norton and Private First Class Jose Cervantes were heading for yet another pillbox when a Japanese soldier popped out of the ground firing a light machine gun. At the same moment, a second Japanese breasted the summit from the rear slope. Then two more Japanese popped out of the ground. Norton and Cervantes leaned back and reflexively opened fire, felling all four of the enemy soldiers.

When Sergeant Charles Dick and Private First Class Joe Shupe found another Japanese fast asleep behind a tree, they shot him. Then Lieutenant Tymniak stumbled over the entrance to a pillbox. He pulled a hand grenade from one of his deep cargo pockets, eased out the pin, and stuffed the missile through the firing aperture. Staff Sergeant Norton saw the barrel of a Japanese medium machine gun traverse across the aperture of a nearby pillbox, right on to the lieutenant. He fired his rifle and hit the muzzle of the machine gun, then he and Private First Class Shupe charged the gun. The two pulled several concealing logs from atop the machine-gun emplacement and grenaded the three-man gun crew to death.

On the far side of the summit, three of Tymniak's men under Sergeant David Stewart were having similar luck. Private First Class Eugene Williams found a Japanese soldier asleep in his dugout and shot him where he sat. A second Japanese who was just raising his rifle to fire at Williams was dispatched by Sergeant

Stewart, who ran over to loot a wristwatch from the dead man's wrist. Stewart found another Japanese just beneath the brow of the summit, where the watch wearer had fallen. He shot this Japanese, too, but he was fired on by a machine gun in a pillbox farther along the ridgeline. Private First Class Clifford Gibson rammed his BAR into the firing aperture and sprayed a whole clip right into the faces of the machine gunners.

In the end, Lieutenant Tymniak's patrol killed twenty-one Japanese and took possession of fourteen pillboxes—without sustaining a single injury.

Most Japanese pillbox networks were self-supporting because of extensive interlocking lanes of fire. The destruction of one emplacement usually led to a modification in the deployment of troops and weapons. When the Japanese manning pillboxes farther back made no effort to redeploy in the face of his patrol's successes, Lieutenant Tymniak correctly deduced that his adversaries were withdrawing.

Elements of I and K Companies were sent up the hill to support Tymniak's patrol and take possession of Bartley Ridge. The Americans counted a total of seventy-eight separate emplacements; forty-six of them were coral-and-log pillboxes. American equipment and weapons taken during the 13th Infantry's counter-offensive were recovered throughout the Japanese positions, including several cases of M2 carbines still packed in cosmoline. The news was mostly good, but there were some Japanese still inhabiting several pillboxes around the hill. During one part of the sweep to clear the pillboxes, First Lieutenant Kenneth French, the K Company commander, was shot and killed. French was the fifth and last of the five original K Company officers to be killed or wounded on or around Bartley Ridge.

That night, the I Company command post was struck by a hit-and-run raid followed by an alarmingly accurate mortar concentration. The mortar rounds killed the company mess sergeant and wounded both the company commander, Captain Charles Hastings, and the company first sergeant.

Bartley Ridge would not be fully occupied until the next day, July 29, when the entire 3rd Battalion, 161st, moved forward to take possession. Late in the day, Buchanan's bloodied battalion was relieved by G Company and sent to the rear for a rest.

25

When plans for the XIV Corps offensive were issued to the 148th Infantry, it had not yet been determined that the regiment overlapped the Japanese defenses on Horseshoe Hill by several hundred yards, nor that the regiment was faced with an entirely clear front for several miles to the west of its line of departure. The remnants of the 13th Infantry Regiment were bivouacked somewhat to the north of the 148th Infantry, and the 229th Infantry was holding the formal defensive line to the southwest. But the way dead ahead was clear. When the 148th Infantry jumped off on July 25 to carry out a limited offensive in support of the adjacent 161st Infantry, it unwittingly crossed behind the Japanese main line resistance.

The regiment went by the book during its first day on the offensive: The prescribed network of patrols was scouting the front and flanks. By 1000 hours, Colonel Stuart Baxter knew that his vanguard elements had traveled about 500 yards against very spotty opposition. Flank patrols found signs of activity to the north, but these seemed insignificant. There was nothing to the immediate south. In the woods southeast of the regimental vanguard were dense areas of occupation, so Baxter knew that he had passed to the north of the left flank of the Japanese main line. There was no doubt about it.

Lieutenant Colonel Herbert Radcliffe's 2nd Battalion, 148th, reached its objective line about 600 yards from the line of departure at about noon, hours ahead of schedule. Lieutenant Colonel Vernor Hydaker's 1st Battalion was to the left of Radcliffe's, echeloned rearward to cover the regiment's lengthening left flank and to maintain contact with the neighboring 161st Infantry.

At about noon, a Sergeant Collins, a New Zealander on loan from the 1st Fiji Commando, led a patrol southwest from the regimental command post. The patrol returned two hours later to report that it had run into strong Japanese opposition about 220 yards out. A rifle platoon under Second Lieutenant John Laterriere was sent out to destroy the strongpoint, and the mission was accomplished with ease. As soon as Laterriere's platoon returned to friendly lines, the regiment dug in for the night.

As the advance of July 25 had been for limited purposes, and due to stiff opposition encountered by the 161st Infantry on Bartley Ridge, the 148th Infantry was ordered to remain where it was on July 26, to strengthen its positions while maintaining strong combat patrols to the front and flanks.

E and G Companies were fired on by automatic weapons at dawn, and returned the fire until the Japanese stopped firing. Daylight patrols found several fresh corpses in the area from which the fire had originated.

A combat patrol from Captain Claude Miller's C Company moved in the morning to check on the strongpoint that had been reduced the previous afternoon by Lieutenant Latteriere's platoon. The patrol was fired on from the position and was forced to withdraw. Captain Miller ordered a section of 81mm mortars to help Lieutenant Latteriere's platoon reduce the position once again. The mortars fired a short preparatory bombardment, then the rifle platoon moved in to clear the area. Several casualties were sustained, but the strongpoint was reduced to rubble.

Late in the afternoon, the long-range combat and reconnaissance patrols began returning. Those that had moved to the west and southwest had made no contacts, though many abandoned strongpoints had been uncovered. It was quite clear that the terminus of the Japanese line had been pinpointed and that the Japanese were withdrawing troops in order to bolster their lines elsewhere. The 37th Division and XIV Corps headquarters discussed the matter at length. By morning, it had been agreed by both to unleash the 148th Infantry.

Generals Beightler and Griswold both understood the stakes. Victory was in their grasp, but the northernmost infantry regiment would have to maintain contact with the 161st Infantry at all costs in order to avoid opening a tempting gap in the corps line. This requirement was communicated to Colonel Baxter, though it was admittedly hard for the commanders to subdue the excitement they felt over the first real prospect of a solution to the perplexing campaign.

Lieutenant Colonel Herbert Radcliffe's 2nd Battalion, 148th, had the vanguard when the regiment jumped off early on July 27. There was no significant opposition, so the battalion was able to advance 800 yards by 1000 hours. The vanguard then stopped on ground highly favorable for a defensive cordon.

Colonel Baxter informed the division command post that his troops had remained in physical contact with the 161st Infantry and that his front was at least 1,000 yards west of Bartley Ridge. The contact of which Baxter spoke was, in truth, rather more tenuous than he let on or perhaps realized.

To the regiment's rear, A Company, 117th Engineer Combat Battalion, was hard at work bulldozing a supply trail. Baxter's gains could have been in jeopardy had not the engineers risen to their task with such incredible spirit.

Patrols were dispatched at dawn on July 28. All but one returned without making any contacts. The one that did, a group of scouts from the regiment's Intelligence and Reconnaissance Platoon, had moved due south from the regimental command post along an old trail going in the direction of Lambeti Plantation. The scouts found a defended pocket about 200 yards out, and this seemed to be the head of the Japanese left flank.

It was clear that any advances made by the 148th Infantry on July 28 would be at the expense of direct physical contact with the stalled 161st Infantry. G Company was therefore placed on the regiment's left and strung out through the forest to gain contact with the 161st Infantry's right flank. The remainder of the 2nd Battalion was placed in positions to support an advance by the 1st Battalion, from which A Company was detached to become the regimental reserve. Once the supports were set, the truncated 1st Battalion was ordered to advance 500 yards to the west of the truncated 2nd Battalion's lines.

While the 1st Battalion was moving, G Company ran into some trouble as it attempted to pass the strongpoint discovered by the reconnaissance scouts earlier in the day. The Japanese put up a determined fight, employing 13mm antiaircraft machine guns and numerous infantry weapons. The lead platoon, which was sent alone to reduce the pocket, was pinned in a matter of minutes and the remainder of the company had to be sent in to bail it out. Nearly the entire day was spent reducing the strongpoint, pillbox by pillbox, and forcing the defenders to pull back. The Japanese left their heavy weapons, which was a good omen, but they did so so late in the day that G Company had to return to the regimental lines without making contact with the 161st Infantry. A large gap was thus opening between the regiments—a gap which, in fact, the Japanese had long since penetrated.

The first indication that something was amiss came to the attention of the 3rd Platoon, A Company, 117th Combat Engineers. The bulldozer crews figured, and fairly, that they had two battalions of infantry to soften any blows the Japanese might throw their way. But, as the lead bulldozer churned up a steep grade on the new supply-trail extension, four engineers were shot to death by a Nambu light machine gun from such close range that powder burns were later detected on the bodies. A relief column from the regimental antitank company was dispatched, as was a patrol from the 1st Battalion. Two wounded engineers were carried out, the uninjured survivors were rescued, and the precious bulldozers were driven to safety.

The situation was clear from the outset. The Japanese had been unable to overlook the widening gap in the once-solid American battle line. It is probable that the engineers were attacked by elements of the 13th Infantry Regiment, which had been given the opportunity by General Sasaki to expunge the blot of its earlier repulse.

Colonel Baxter's irrepressible excitement had resulted in his advancing his regiment fully 1,500 yards ahead of the right front of the 161st Infantry and about 1,800 yards west of any point considered fully secure by the XIV Corps intelligence and operations staffs. The 148th Infantry was badly overextended.

During the early afternoon of July 28, Baxter's command group began receiving reports from scattered points indicating that the Japanese had infiltrated the main supply route between the old parachute drop and the regiment's ration dump. It seemed that small groups of infiltrators were beginning to coalesce into larger, more dangerous battle forces.

The regimental ration dump, commanded by the regimental supply officer, Major Laurence Hipp, was fairly well defended. In addition to troops from the regimental service company, Major Hipp could draw upon A Company, 148th, the regimental infantry reserve, which was encamped nearby.

As news of contacts with Japanese patrols flowed in, Major Hipp and Colonel Baxter decided to begin convoying vehicles over the supply route. It was hoped that the heavy escorts accompanying each convoy would intimidate the Japanese sufficiently to avoid direct confrontations along the main supply route. At the same time, Hipp ordered his clerks and laborers to construct a "fort" out of ration cases, which seemed a faster expedient than digging in.

The Japanese struck the ration dump while its occupants were still in the midst of their frantic fortification effort. The first news that the Japanese had arrived was in the form of a burst of machine-gun fire from the high ground dominating the sprawling dump. Japanese hand grenades, some fired by silent knee mortars, were soon exploding within the hastily contrived defensive perimeter.

Service Company, 148th, had looted the dump of much more than its usual supply of infantry weapons, but it had been a long time since many of the troops had been trained to use them. Withal, the defenders were determined to take on all comers. They had little choice.

Major Hipp's name was shouted back and forth by his troops, and the Japanese were quick to pick up on it. During one brief lull, a voice from the forest proclaimed, "Major Hipp, that President Roosevelt is no good!" To which the unflappable Hipp responded, "Hold your fire, boys, that Jap's a Republican!" However, there were apparently more Democrats than Republicans in the makeshift fort, for the Americans ripped off a furious fusillade at the political commentator in the trees.

As the gunfire from the high ground to the west of the dump increased, Private Quincy Gillian sallied from the fort with his BAR and managed to cut down the crew of a machine gun before he was killed by other Japanese.

Using a weak sound-power telephone, Major Hipp was able to contact the regimental command post with a plea for help. Elements of Antitank Company and a platoon from F Company were dispatched along the supply trail, but it was by then very late in the day and the dump was a long way off.

While awaiting relief, men like Captain Frank Traucht, the regimental motor-transport officer, coolly held the Japanese at bay with their relentless return fire. Traucht was a well-known distinguished marksman, and the troops looked to him for guidance. It was no surprise that he managed to put the first round he had ever fired in anger right between the eyes of a machine-gunner who was in the act of spraying a stack of 60mm mortar ammunition. But Traucht was the exception; nearly all of the defenders were clerks, drivers, and mechanics who were forced to make up in volume of fire what Traucht accomplished with skill. Fortunately, there was no concern over using up the available ammunition, though a few well-placed grenades or mortar rounds might have blown the dump clear away.

While the fight at the ration dump was raging, a heavily escorted truck convoy on the main supply route was hit hard by a group of bushwhackers very close to the middle of nowhere. The drivers were able to turn all the trucks around under fire, and they roared away in search of safety.

Four runners from the 37th Signal Company were at Baxter's command post when the trouble started, and these men were sent down the supply trail with written messages to subordinate units as a hedge against destruction of communications wire, which seemed to be a favorite Japanese tactic. The runners were some way along the trail when one of them was cut down by automatic-weapons fire. The three survivors joined a small group of soldiers trying to fight through to the regimental command post, which it eventually did.

An 81mm mortar section from D Company was ambushed when the only trail leading from its position behind the main body of the 1st Battalion was severed. When the position was made completely untenable by converging fires from three Nambu light machine guns, the section leader, Sergeant Eugene Kern, ordered his gunners to abandon the place. As the mortarmen withdrew, Sergeant Kern sprinted from foxhole to foxhole to make certain no wounded men had been left behind. As he rose to follow the others, a sniper shot him dead.

Virtually overwhelmed by contact reports and cries for help, Colonel Baxter finally telephoned the division command post to ask General Beightler to dispatch divisional troops to help relieve the pressure.

The regimental and divisional intelligence staffs soon had received enough information by late afternoon to deduce that about 200 Japanese had infiltrated the regimental sector from the north and west before splitting into numerous small groups, each centered around one or two light machine guns. These groups had been roving the regiment's rear, and each was no doubt responsible for several contacts. During the early evening, Colonel Baxter began planning for the relief of the ration dump and the clearing of the supply road.

As it began growing dark, many isolated groups of Americans trapped along the main supply route found the opportunity to consolidate with one another and drive to safety or, at worst, set up pockets of resistance capable of defending themselves through the night. The F Company platoon and antitank section that had earlier been dispatched to the ration dump had fought through, narrowly missing additional Japanese who arrived to choke off the artery minutes after the force passed through.

General Beightler rang up the 148th Infantry's command post very early on July 29 to order Colonel Baxter to consolidate his regiment, strengthen his positions, and prepare for any eventuality. Baxter received another call from the division commander at 0710. Beightler wanted the regiment to begin an orderly withdrawal toward the east to regain direct physical contact with the 161st Infantry.

At 0800, in accordance with his orders, Baxter directed the uncommitted portions of F Company to push eastward along the main supply route. A single platoon from A Company, which had been guarding the regimental command post all night, was released and ordered to rejoin the company's main body at the ration dump.

The division command post contacted Baxter again at 0941 to reaffirm General Beightler's earlier orders and to warn Baxter that Japanese machine-gun positions were still blocking the trail from commanding positions.

General Beightler next ordered a detachment from the 37th Division Reconnaissance Troop to sweep westward from the secure end of the trail and to join with Baxter's command.

In addition to his many conversations with Baxter, General Beightler had been conferring regularly with Colonel James Dalton and Colonel Temple Holland and members of his own and their respective regimental staffs. Dalton's 161st Infantry was to continue its efforts to secure Bartley Ridge, and Holland's 145th Infantry was to hold in place; Baxter would do the pulling back, and Baxter would do the joining up.

At 1055, Baxter ordered his battalion commanders to begin withdrawing their main bodies to the east. E Company was ordered to branch off from the main body of the 2nd Battalion and move southeastward to establish contact with the 161st Infantry. As the 2nd Battalion advanced steadily to the rear toward the ration dump, Hydaker's 1st Battalion withdrew into Radcliffe's former positions. G Company, with one E Company platoon, was dispatched to help F Company reach the ration dump. The result of all this was that, by late morning, the 2nd Battalion, 148th, had been splintered into a myriad of platoons and augmented companies flowing off in several different directions. Virtually no command was whole.

Colonel Baxter radioed General Beightler at 1150 to say that elements of Radcliffe's 2nd Battalion were reportedly in contact with Katsarsky's 1st Battalion, 161st. A short time later, the division commander ordered Baxter to move Hydaker's 1st Battalion into positions east of the spot then occupied by the regimental command post, and to prepare to assault Japanese positions along the front of the 161st Infantry. The division commander was under the impression that most of the Japanese infiltrators were coming through the southwestern gap, though most appear to have come from the 13th Infantry's forest bivouacs north of the 148th's positions.

Lieutenant Colonel Joe Katsarsky informed the division command post at 1305 that his 1st Battalion, 161st, was not and had not been in contact with any of Baxter's troops. General Beightler immediately ordered Baxter to gain firm physical contact with Katsarsky's battalion on O'Brien Hill. The harried regimental commander replied that every effort was being made to comply, but that he doubted the ability of his tired troops to get all the way through by nightfall.

At that moment, E Company was advancing in a southerly direction, F Company was fighting eastward on the south side of the main supply route, G Company was paralleling F Company on the north side of the supply trail, and the bulk of the 1st Battalion was holding the 2nd Battalion's former positions preparatory to jumping off.

General Beightler next ordered Colonel Baxter to keep his troops moving, even if it meant carrying out attacks during the night. Baxter asked the division commander to reconsider on that point. The general told the colonel to keep moving in order to close on Dalton's regiment, that the Japanese infiltrators seemed to have been amply reinforced and that they were beginning to move on Dalton's flanks—that the 161st Infantry was in danger of being flanked itself.

By the early evening of July 29, the commanding general had grown quite incensed over the repeated failures of any portion of the 148th Infantry to gain any sort of physical contact with the 161st. At 1832, Colonel Baxter was informed by General Beightler that the corps commander himself had ordered the 148th to contact the 161st and protect the main supply route. Beightler ended the discussion by telling Baxter to "use an entire battalion to accomplish the latter if necessary. At no time have you been in contact on your left although you have repeatedly assured me that this was accomplished. . . . Confirmation of your thorough understanding of this order desired."

Colonel Baxter was severely stung by this rebuke and put his case before a senior division staff officer: "Please attempt to explain to the general that I have had patrols in contact with the 161st and have documentary evidence to substantiate this. I have not, however, been able to close the gap by physical contact due to the fact that the 161st has been echeloned 600 to 800 yards to my left rear. I have been trying and will continue tomorrow to establish this contact. It is a difficult problem as I have had Japs between my left flank and the 161st."

The 148th Infantry, which was still completely cut off, settled down for some rest.

July 30 was going to be another one of those days. It was raining at dawn, and mud soon covered the entire trail, making rougher going for the harried troops.

G Company was stopped before it could get started. As it attempted to drive on the ration dump from the northwest, it was pinned by automatic weapons fire. It would remain pinned throughout the day. The understrength main body of E Company managed to get moving and was drawing closer to the 161st Infantry. The remainder of the 2nd Battalion attempted to sideslip G Company's hotspot, and small groups actually reached the dump, which had become "home plate."

As feared from the outset, communications wires had been cut all over the area. Wire teams were sent out to repair the most vital of these links. Sergeant Harold Fackler, dispatched from 2nd Battalion headquarters, crawled into a pocket between two very active Japanese positions to splice one line. As Fackler knelt in the open under heavy fire to join the ends of the severed wire, he was shot in the back and killed.

Several attempts were made in the early afternoon to cut a new trail eastward from the ration dump, mainly to facilitate evacuation of the wounded. The regimental aid station was geared to treat trauma and operate only on lightly wounded men, but its huge shellhole hospital was filled with stomach and chest cases, broken arms, splintered legs, split skulls—the whole gamut of traumatic combat injuries. Two separate evacuation routes were cut, but the Japanese found both of them and cut off the trailblazers. The effort was halted late in the afternoon.

The 1st Battalion had drawn north of the 2nd Battalion by the early afternoon and the troops were engaged in a dozen little firefights.

Private Stanley Bates was leading his platoon out of the woods when he and several other men located a well-concealed Japanese machine gun that had the rest of their platoon under fire. Bates fired on the machine gun, but he was soon wounded in the left shoulder. Despite his wounds, he continued to fire his rifle and crawl forward to attack the Japanese. The scout killed several members of the gun crew before he was himself cut down. Minutes later, the main body of the pinned platoon was able to work forward to destroy the Japanese emplacement entirely.

In the nearby action, Corporal Harold Lintz, a squad leader with another B Company platoon, was several yards behind the point when three Nambus opened from a range of about 100 yards. The point commander and four other soldiers were wounded in the opening burst, and all five fell in the open. Corporal Lintz crawled through the heavy fire three times, bringing back one of the wounded on each trip. While the platoon medic treated one of the casualties, Lintz stood guard, then he went back into the beaten zone and dragged both of the remaining wounded men to safety in one trip. Moments later, Corporal Lintz led his squad in successful assaults on two pillboxes.

Captain Felix Lester, the B Company commander, watched with ill-contained excitement as Corporal Lintz brought in the wounded. Then, as the squad leader launched his assault on the two pillboxes, Lester led his other two platoons into the attack. Lester was shot and killed during the rush.

During its move toward the 161st Infantry, E Company, 148th, kept getting into one scrap after another, and casualties were mounting. To avoid destruction of the entire unit, it was decided that E Company should rejoin the 2nd Battalion near the ration dump. By nightfall, the company had closed on the dump and had joined A Company in ringing the facility. G Company was manning a defensive perimeter due north of the dump, and the regimental command post was in the woods due west of the dump.

The 1st Battalion, less A Company, was on high ground several hundred yards to the northeast. Also by dusk, the 2nd Battalion headquarters, a small party from the regimental headquarters, and elements of F and H Companies reached the 1st Battalion, 161st, on O'Brien Hill and paused to help Katsarsky's troops hold off attacks on that position.

The 148th Infantry's most critical need was water. It was hot, and the supply that had lasted three days was used up by the end of July 30. A detachment from the 37th Division Reconnaissance Troop attempted to get through during the day with a convoy of tank trailers, but Japanese machine guns along the way stopped the column and holed the water tanks. The regiment was in serious straits, though the situation was alleviated when it began raining shortly after sunset.

Approximately one-third of Colonel Baxter's command had driven through the Japanese by nightfall. However, most of these troops were infantrymen. Baxter now had elements of five rifle companies, several weapons platoons, a few special regimental combat units, and a lot of noncombatant technicians to get to safety through hostile country, without water, and no doubt at the expense of most of his rolling stock, heavy weapons, communications equipment, rations, and ammunition. And he had to make it look like some sort of victory.

A pair of G Company platoons under Captain Francis Folk opened the July 31 action by easing toward a ridge east of the ration dump. Followed by a bulldozer charged with cutting a trail, the platoons prepared to mount an assault. Thus far, the advance, amounting to nearly 400 yards, had been easy. Then the Japanese put out murderous fire from numerous hidden emplacements on and around the objective. When mortar concentrations fell among the American riflemen, the attack was stopped cold. As soon as word could be gotten to the rear, the remaining G Company rifle platoon was released from a command-post security detail and rushed forward to rejoin the company. The moment the reinforcements arrived, Captain Folk ordered everyone to give the ridge a going-over with their weapons. Then G Company mounted another attack, which failed.

To the north, in the 1st Battalion sector, C Company's bivouac was assaulted at dawn, and the company commander was killed in the closing moments of a platoon counterattack that broke the Japanese thrust. Next, B Company formed into a wedge-of-platoons formation and drove straight through the forest toward the Japanese pocket that was holding G Company. Behind B Company was the main body of the 1st Battalion, screened by C Company and carrying its wounded.

B Company desperately tried to drive forward, but the Japanese refused to be cowed. Hours passed and the struggle remained unresolved. By the time it was growing dark, neither B Company nor G Company was getting anywhere, so Lieutenant Colonel Vernor Hydaker ordered both units to fall back on the main body of his 1st Battalion.

With the point of B Company's lead platoon was a private named Rodger Young. Weeks earlier, on Guadalcanal, Young had been a sergeant in charge of a rifle squad, an exemplary soldier who, one day, had turned in his stripes without explanation, which was his right. As it turned out, Young should not have been in the Army. His eyesight had been impaired by a sports accident, and it now seemed that his hearing had been affected also. He had turned in his stripes because he was nearly deaf, a factor he felt might bode ill for the boyhood chums he had commanded.

As B Company's lead platoon began pulling back under fire, Rodger Young and a half dozen other riflemen were nicked by Japanese bullets. Within moments, the entire platoon was pinned. Young's arm was bleeding, and he seemed to be in some pain. Still, he raised his head to scan the front, and he spotted the machine gun that had been bedeviling his comrades. He shouted news of his discovery to his platoon leader and warned that he was going after the gun. His buddies yelled back, telling him to lie low. The yelling had no effect; several old friends who were in on the secret behind Young's voluntary demotion realized that Young probably had not even heard their voices.

Young took off slowly, creeping up a slight rise toward the concealed machine-gun emplacement. A burst from the gun caught him in the chest, broke his right hand, and shattered the stock of his rifle. Rodger Young pulled a hand grenade from his shirt pocket and eased out the safety pin. He lobbed the missile at the machine gun, but he had always been plagued by a short throw, and the grenade harmlessly detonated in front of the Japanese emplacement. Young next crawled forward some more and came to rest in a defilade position only ten yards from the machine gun. Had

Rodger Young remained low, he probably would not have been shot again. Instead, he hefted another hand grenade, pulled the pin, stood up on his knees, and leaned back to throw. As the hand grenade left Young's hand, a bullet from the machine gun struck him in the head. He died instantly. The hand grenade destroyed the machine gun and its crew.

Private Rodger Young was awarded a posthumous Medal of Honor.

At 2300 hours, July 31, General Beightler transmitted a direct order to Colonel Baxter: "Imperative you get through tomorrow. If necessary, abandon vehicles and hand carry. Place screening forces south of road moving main body north of road where resistance is lighter. You might use artillery north of the road to protect your advance. I am trying to send radio batteries with Fijian patrol. Acknowledge."

Baxter had already begun lightening the load. It became necessary late in the afternoon for the regiment to pull eastward, past the ration dump. This necessitated the movement of all the gear the troops could move to a new dump several hundred yards from the original site. Perhaps to Major Hipp's credit, it was found that the dump was overstocked, and everything that could not be hauled clear had to be put to the torch. With help from a contingent of supply clerks and another officer, Major Hipp personally sprinted among the crates to toss thermite grenades onto stacks of mortar ammunition. Then, at the last moment, Hipp and his helpers heaved themselves aboard a getaway jeep—just as the first Japanese began moving into the dump. The night was punctuated by the furious cacophony of the ammunition cooking off, which gave the withdrawing Americans some comfort, for it was plain from the noise that the victorious Japanese had to stand by and watch that ransom of goods go up in smoke and flame.

General Beightler heard nothing from Colonel Baxter during the night, so at 0737 hours, August 1, he transmitted this terse message: "Must have your plans at once." Beightler had to know what was going on because he had numerous support units deployed, and these were ready to go into action once the position of Baxter's receding infantry and support had been ascertained.

Lieutenant Colonel Lawrence White, an observer attached to the 37th Division headquarters, was dispatched to coordinate Baxter's presumed move with supporting units, particularly the artillery. Together with a lieutenant and four soldiers from the 37th Division Reconnaissance Troop, White reached the cutoff on the trail from Baxter's position and prepared to greet the regimental train and make recommendations to the division commander.

General Beightler radioed Baxter at 0842: "Time precious. You must move." But Baxter was already moving. Major Carl Bethers, the regimental operations officer, had A, E, and G Companies ready to move against the high ground to the rear of the regimental perimeter. This infantry force was to drive straight down the main supply route.

Every rifleman at the front pulled the safety pins from at least one hand grenade apiece and, at Major Bethers's shouted order, hurled them at the Japanese lines. As soon as first grenades detonated, Bethers commanded the three companies to move out. Fighting all the way, the riflemen rapidly cleared a path toward the 2nd Battalion's sector, which was on O'Brien Hill, adjacent to the right flank of the 1st Battalion, 161st.

Mortars and artillery were ready to fire, but communications to the moving regimental train were not up to par, and no one in authority was willing to risk firing blindly into the forest.

Colonel Baxter fired a flare at 1030 to mark his position. An artillery spotter aboard a light observation plane based at Segi plotted the position of the regimental command post and informed Baxter that he was still 350 yards short of his goal.

F Company was thrown into the vanguard, and the fighting withdrawal raged ahead for nearly two hours more. Following the rifle companies was a long line of vehicles carrying papers, supplies, weapons, and 130 litter cases. The first of Baxter's troops passed Lieutenant Colonel White's checkpoint at about noon. At 1213, White informed the division command post that the first serial of Baxter's vehicle train had just passed his post.

Farther back, well within the lines of the 161st Infantry, hot food and fresh water were distributed to all hands. Throughout the feeding area, haggard Ohio Guardsmen gulped down the water and food while laughing away their relief and slapping one another on the back. The 148th Infantry was out of trouble. The three-day withdrawal had cost 43 lives. Of 147 wounded officers and soldiers, 17 had refused relief from their duties.

The 37th Division casualty clearing station was swamped.

26

As soon as the 169th Infantry was relieved in the XIV Corps center on July 19, Colonel Temple Holland, its temporary commander, was ordered to resume command of his own 145th Infantry Regiment. The nature of the XIV Corps line happened to place the 145th Infantry's two operating battalions in the American positions farthest advanced on New Georgia. For the sake of security, and in order to eventually shorten the line, the regiment was ordered to remain in position until adjacent units were able to draw abreast.

At about 1100 hours, July 20, elements of the 145th Infantry got into their first real firefight of the campaign. Two patrols converging on an obscure point in the rain forest found that about two platoons of Japanese infantry stood between them at a point about 150 yards beyond the old parachute drop and only about 350 yards west of the 145th Infantry's regimental command post. The American infantrymen moved on the Japanese amid the clatter of machine-gun fire and the detonations of bursting hand grenades. Fortunately, all the Japanese gunfire was high. The patrol leaders decided to call on their artillery supports, and the fire from the friendly 105mm batteries obliged the Japanese to flee.

The night was quiet, as was most of July 21. The untried regiment continued to familiarize itself with its surroundings and monitor Japanese activities along its front. Fire from 90mm mortars harassed the regiment's lines and rear through the day, but no casualties were sustained.

At 0800 hours, July 22, the regimental command post was moved back about 200 yards due east of its former position; it was in full operation again by 0930. When a Japanese machine-gun emplacement that had been spotted the day before could not be found again, infantry patrols and artillery probes reached into the rain forest to pinpoint it. In general, the troops were getting itchy from inactivity, so numerous combat patrols were dispatched to keep as many men occupied as possible. Four 37mm antitank guns were manhandled to the front lines, and the gunners amused themselves by sniping at two strongpoints to the west.

A Japanese mortar emplacement suddenly blew up in front of

the 1st Battalion at 1500 hours; no one could determine the source of the killing shot. At roughly the same time, 37th Division Artillery scored hits on a Japanese ammunition dump nearly 1,200 yards west of the 1st Battalion, blowing it to pieces.

The regiment's happy little world collapsed at 1815, when a Japanese field gun opened on the 1st Battalion. A knot of Americans caught in the open was cut down. The 1st Battalion surgeon, Captain John Carter, rushed from his shelter to help the wounded at the same time as First Lieutenant Thomas Brady, the battalion chaplain. The next Japanese shell instantly killed both of them. The fun was over. The 145th Infantry had been baptized in its own blood.

More of the same followed for the next several days. Japanese mortars kept the regiment under fairly constant harassing fires through the entire period. Many of the mortars were emplaced too close to the American line for safe response by the regiment's artillery supports, so strong combat patrols were sent out to find and destroy them.

Due to advances by the adjacent 1st Battalion, 161st, it became necessary on July 27 for Lieutenant Colonel Theodore Parker's 2nd Battalion, 145th, to advance several hundred yards to erase a salient that had developed between the adjacent regiments. Parker's objective was the northern spur of Horseshoe Hill.

Parker's battalion had to carry out a 2,600-yard forced march to an assembly area on the far side of Bartley Ridge, which was then still occupied by the Japanese. The battalion's assault would be made toward the southwest. The march was completed without mishap, following which 37th Division Artillery fired a brief mission against the objective.

Colonel Temple Holland, the regimental commander, was sweating out the preamble to the assault at an artillery fire direction center when he overheard this exchange:

"Right twenty-five [yards]," a forward observer with the infantry told his battery executive officer.

"What the hell," the exec countered, "the effective radius of one round is thirty yards. Why the twenty-five-yard shift?"

"Well, I missed one of the little bastards."

At worst, the artillery cleared some of the dense growth obscuring the objective. The battalion then moved out in column of companies led by Captain Gardner Wing's E Company.

The fight got hot as soon as Wing's company made its move. Parker's troops fought over 300 yards of ground, and E Company reached an intermediate ridge near the objective. Several minutes after 1300 hours, Captain Wing ordered his platoons to deliver a direct frontal assault against the objective. The American infantrymen rapidly gained ground at the outset, but an increasing number of defenders rushing from outlying positions turned to hold Wing's company off. As the Americans surged across the fireswept slope, Private First Class Frank Petraca, a battalion medic, ran into a small draw that was under very heavy fire, lifted a wounded rifleman to his shoulders, and ran clumsily to cover behind a protective knob. At about the same moment, Captain Wing was shot to death while urging his faltering riflemen on. E Company could make no further progress against the severe fire and the assault ended. The eastward protrusion of Horseshoe Hill was named for Captain Wing.

A 60mm mortar section from F Company was ordered up to support what might have turned into a renewed assault, but the mortarmen were hit with extremely heavy 90mm fire from Japanese mortars emplaced on Horseshoe Hill and a ridge to the east. Japanese knee mortars, rifles, and machine guns all turned to bear across the face of Wing Hill. E and F Companies were ordered back to the assembly area. As casualties continued to mount, a pair of BAR-men covered the withdrawal, which took nearly thirty minutes to complete.

The entire 145th Infantry was formally committed to the XIV Corps offensive on July 28. Its objective was Horseshoe Hill. Lieutenant Colonel Richard Crooks was ordered to march his 1st Battalion forward and reduce the objective by any means required.

B Company had the lead. As the troops warily moved up the hostile slope, the Japanese on the hill poured as concentrated a fire on them as had been seen in the campaign. Private Frank Kordelski, a rifleman, got his hands on a flamethrower and worked to within thirty feet of three Japanese pillboxes. The machine gunners within the pillboxes spotted the lone figure and depressed the muzzles of their guns to bear on him, but they could not get him. Kordelski fired a blast of burning diesel fuel that totally engulfed seven Japanese and their three machine guns. He then worked back down the slope to refill his tanks, following which he crawled back up the hill. The Japanese were waiting for him this time, and he was stitched by their fire. Grievously wounded, Kordelski bathed another stretch of the defensive line with his deadly flame, then burned out yet another swath of the hostile line before he allowed himself to be carried to safety.

Heartened by Private Kordelski's selfless display, and aided by the fruits of his sacrifice, B Company moved steadily up the hillside. Staff Sergeant Robert Young, a platoon leader, fearlessly directed his men to within fifteen yards of the Japanese in order to establish a base of fire. His cool determination won him a battlefield commission.

Sixteen Americans were by then dead, and as many had been wounded, nearly a full platoon. Technician Fifth Grade Otto Schraeder, a medic, stuck close to the forwardmost units, charged through incredible volumes of fire, and treated the wounded wherever they fell, often in full view of the defenders.

A bit to the north and west of the 1st Battalion's struggle, Lieutenant Colonel Theodore Parker's 2nd Battalion, 145th, was preparing to assault Wing Hill once again. F and G Companies opened with a concerted drive from the jungle flat below the hill and swept aside all opposition in their determined two-prong drive for the ridgeline. Only a one-hundred-yard-long defiladed saddle separated the battalion from Horseshoe Hill, and Lieutenant Colonel Parker ordered his two assault companies to move across.

With Crooks's 1st Battalion applying pressure from the opposite flank, the Japanese facing Parker were under intense pressure, but they were still capable of a ferocious defensive effort; these were the veteran remnants of the tough 3rd Battalion, 229th, and they were determined to hang on. Late in the afternoon, E Company was thrown in against the western crest, and 60mm and 81mm mortars put out unremitting support. Pillboxes were falling, but so were American infantrymen.

Technical Sergeant Darrell Yonker, of E Company, was struck in the chest by a spent bullet. After digging out the .25-caliber rifle slug, the enraged noncom charged straight up the hill and wiped out a three-man outguard position. Shortly after this feat, Yonker collapsed from loss of blood; he was still clutching an Arisaka rifle he had taken from a dead Japanese when his ambulance jeep departed for the rear.

Darkness found Parker's battalion practically on top of the Japanese. For safety's sake, the Americans moved back thirty-five yards. A number of patrol contacts were made during the night with groups of Japanese retreating from Bartley Ridge, but no firefights erupted. It was generally assumed that the defenders were preparing to put up a stiff fight to keep the line of retreat open from Bartley Ridge.

On the morning of July 29, A and B Companies, 145th, set out again for the summit of Horseshoe Hill. They were too close to the objective and its defenders to get a good running start, so the leading files of riflemen crawled up the hill, measuring their gains virtually by the inch. Without warning, dozens of Japanese soldiers stood up against the morning sky and charged straight down the forward slope toward the leading Americans. It was a gallant gesture, but the Japanese—many of whom were armed with American-made firearms—were beaten back almost without serious effort.

The American advance was just getting under way again when someone realized that the Japanese who had participated in the counterattack had to have been drawn from elsewhere on the hill—probably from the line facing Lieutenant Colonel Theodore Parker's 2nd Battalion. Following a midday artillery and mortar preparation, Parker's battalion moved out against its elusive objective. The troops battered their way uphill for three solid hours against vicious opposition.

Private First Class Frank Petraca, the battalion medic who had distinguished himself repeatedly for the past several days, had his hands full pulling three injured men to safety before charging back under fire to dig yet another injured comrade out of a mortar-blasted captured pillbox.

For all its valiant efforts, however, the 2nd Battalion, 145th, could not make a lodgment in the Japanese line. It was forced to withdraw at nightfall to positions at the base of the hill.

Extensive changes were made all along the XIV Corps line on July 30. The 43rd Division's front was lengthened and the 37th Division's zone shifted several hundred yards northward. In the central 37th Division sector, Parker's 2nd Battalion, 145th, was attached to the 161st Infantry and teamed with Lieutenant Colonel Francis Carberry's 2nd Battalion, 161st, for yet another assault on Horseshoe Hill.

As Carberry's battalion rapidly advanced against light opposition, Parker's battalion waded back into an extremely intense fight.

Clearly, the Japanese had chosen to move out of Carberry's path in order to concentrate their efforts in Parker's. Thus, Parker's assault was stopped cold by Japanese who appeared to have obtained vast stores of American weapons and munitions.

The extreme-right-flank elements of the 43rd Division were to have closed on Parker to lend some support, but the daylight was gone by the time the anticipated contact was made. Parker dispatched patrols to probe the defenses on Horseshoe Hill throughout the delay, but no major action followed the abortive morning assault.

Infantry assaults were to continue on July 31 following a lengthy artillery barrage aimed at driving the defenders off the ridgeline. Brigadier General Leonard Wing, the 43rd Division assistant commander, came forward to observe the action from the command post of A Company, 145th, just prior to the company's scheduled 100-yard withdrawal to avoid being hit by short artillery rounds.

Only moments after General Wing's arrival at his command post, Captain John Cox, A Company's commander, excitedly motioned for Wing's attention and pointed toward the Japanese line. The astounded general watched as entire platoons of Japanese disengaged and scrabbled back over the ridgeline in apparent retreat. Orders for the American withdrawal were canceled on the spot, and the infantry was ordered to throw in an immediate assault. Following a tense sixty-minute interval, during which mortars and machine guns raked the distant hill, G and F Companies, 145th, rose to deliver the attack.

Second Lieutenant Steve Fejes, a G Company platoon leader, led his troops straight to within grenade-throwing range of the Japanese line. Fejes spotted a pillbox and silenced it with a hand grenade. Moments later, he moved against a second emplacement by way of a connecting trench. Fejes, who was armed with an M1 rifle, coolly shot the three occupants to death and claimed the pillbox for his side.

Private First Class Frank Petraca moved straight to the forwardmost assault files to begin pulling casualties to safety. He managed to drag several men behind a low outcrop, then moved, as he had on numerous occasions for nearly a week, into a cleared area where other Americans lay. This time, Frank Petraca ran straight into a mortar barrage, and he was cut down dead. He was awarded a Medal of Honor.

For all their determination, the soldiers of the 2nd Battalion, 145th, could not find quite the right combination. It soon appeared that the Japanese had not evacuated the ridge altogether, but had been pulling back temporarily to avoid the artillery barrage the American preparations had implied would be fired. The defenders hotly contested the battalion's occupation attempt in considerable force, and the 2nd Battalion, 145th, was ordered to the base of the hill for the night.

In the first hours of the first day of August 1943, small, wary infantry combat patrols from both the 145th and 161st Infantry Regiments carefully poked through the remnants of the Japanese defenses on Horseshoe Hill. To everyone's surprise and delight, the hill had been abandoned. The patrols cautiously picked their way back through the shell-torn trees to report their findings, and the 2nd Battalion, 145th, was ordered back up the hill.

Rifles ready, the haggard survivors rose from the decaying stink of their muddy holes and wearily forced themselves forward against the audible cries of their own protesting nerves. Footfall after footfall brought their fear-aching bodies closer to the object of their long quest, the crest of Horseshoe Hill. More steps carried them over the summit, toward the steep reverse slopes, as clothed in mystery to them as the dark side of the moon. As word from the rear directed the lead platoons to stop and dig in, some of the Americans caught fleeting glimpses of another army's diminished infantry platoons as they plodded away to the west, toward the last barrier of defenses before Munda.

Horseshoe Hill had fallen; the Japanese defenses had been breached. The way to Munda was clear.

PART VI

———— ✳ ————

Munda

27

It rained during the night of July 31–August 1, drenching the troops. In the morning, the hot sun was back out; the weather forecasters said it would remain clear and bright. In the north, the 148th Infantry was expected to arrive safely back within friendly lines. Bartley Ridge had been occupied the day before, Horseshoe Hill had been taking a battering over most of the preceding week. XIV Corps Headquarters issued no special directives.

After occupying Horseshoe Hill early on August 1, the 145th Infantry continued to patrol its front actively. A provisional 3rd Battalion was formed by Colonel Holland in the afternoon. It comprised the headquarters section of the regimental service company, B and G Companies, and a platoon each from D and H Companies.

On July 31, Major General John Hodge and Brigadier General Leonard Wing had accompanied Colonel David Ross to several of the 172nd Infantry's advance observation posts and to others a bit northward, in front of the 1st Battalion, 145th. From these positions, the two generals had been able to gaze down upon portions of Munda Field and Kokengolo Hill. Hodge and Wing had both noted various signs indicating that at least several Japanese units were pulling out of the area under covering fire from the last few positions remaining on Horseshoe Hill. Both agreed that the path to Munda would soon lie open. Accordingly, on August 1, Hodge held telephone conversations with his regimental commanders in which he ordered advances all across the division front to a line abreast that of the adjacent 145th Infantry.

After a night filled with sounds of movement across the way, Major Ray Dunning, of the 2nd Battalion, 103rd, dispatched strong combat patrols to reconnoiter the solid line of pillboxes directly in the battalion's projected route of advance. All of the patrols returned with negative reports—the pillboxes had been abandoned to a depth of at least several hundred yards.

An attack order was issued an hour before noon on August 1 and, following preparations by organic mortars and supporting artillery, Dunning's battalion jumped off at 1150. The advance over the initial fifty to seventy-five yards was cautious. As increasing numbers of pillboxes and bunkers were located and searched without opposition, the wary riflemen grew bolder. Following a five-hour advance in which each of Dunning's companies averaged 1,000 yards of gains, Dunning ordered the troops to dig in at 1700 hours. The battalion command group expected to occupy Lamberti Plantation the following day.

Early on August 1, Major Joe Zimmer's 1st Battalion, 169th, began a strong advance against a ridge directly in front of the 172nd's line. With some support from Colonel Ross's heavy weapons, Zimmer's troops made easy gains and bloodlessly occupied the ridge. Combat patrols were dispatched to the right flank, and these were soon in touch with the adjacent 1st Battalion, 145th. After some minor adjustments, the two battalions joined, thus squeezing the 172nd Infantry out of the 43rd Division line, its first respite since it had landed at Zanana Beach.

While Zimmer's battalion was on the move, a patrol from K Company, 169th, moved rapidly ahead of the remainder of the 3rd Battalion. As the patrol probed toward Lambeti Plantation, it found absolutely no opposition along its axis of advance. Under orders to advance as far as he could, the patrol leader hurried his troops completely across the plantation, virtually to the outer edge of Munda Field, then returned to the battalion. As soon as the report was in, Major Ignatius Ramsey's entire 3rd Battalion, 169th, completed an uncontested 800-yard advance and drew abreast of Dunning's 2nd Battalion, 103rd.

It was apparent by 1500 hours that XIV Corps was not going to have to fight very hard to take Munda Field, that the Japanese had conceded. Elated over the pattern formed by the reports from the 43rd Division sector, General Griswold ordered all of his operating battalions to dispatch heavily armed combat patrols as far as they could go in the direction of the airfield. Shortly after Colonel Eugene Ridings, the XIV Corps operations officer, phoned General Beightler with the orders for 37th Division patrols to head toward Munda, Ohio and Washington Guardsmen were reporting that the way to the objective was clear.

Colonel Ridings relayed orders to General Beightler at 1624 hours to mount a general sweep the following morning. Beightler's battalions were to keep going until they encountered solid opposition, at which point the 37th Division was to develop strong positions wherever it stood and consolidate for further efforts.

Almost unnoticed in the excitement was the arrival of the fresh,

veteran 27th Infantry Regiment, a Regular Army element of the
25th Infantry Division, which began filing ashore from LCIs at
Laiana. The regiment, which had acquitted itself superbly in fierce
fighting on Guadalcanal, was placed under General Beightler's
tactical control and sent to screen the open northern flank. Thus,
Beightler had direct command of six battalions of the 25th Division and only four battalions of his own 37th Division.

The Japanese had been taking punishing body blows for a
month. Although their defenses had been among the very best, and
had completely stymied the New Georgia Occupation Force on
repeated occasions, the vast preponderance of manpower and support machinery in the hands of XIV Corps had simply crushed
them. American air and artillery superiority had decided the issue. By late July, most of the defensive structures around Munda
had been reduced to rubble, and the front was crumbling as well.

Rifle companies of the 229th Infantry, for example, had each
started the campaign with an average of 165 effectives. By late July,
some were down to as few as twenty soldiers capable of handling
their rifles. And, of that small number, many were quite ill, barely
able to sit at the embrasure of a pillbox much less walk or run in
attack or retreat. The regiment, nominally 3,500-strong at the outset, fielded just 1,245 effectives on August 1.

The command echelons of the rifle battalions had been obliterated. Major Masao Hara and Captain Bunzo Kojima, the 1st and
3rd Battalion commanders, had long since died in action. Many of
the living suffered from severe nervous and emotional disorders
resulting from incessant bombardment and constant infantry assaults. Everyone was undernourished. Many Japanese soldiers and
rikusentai had punctured eardrums. Hospital facilities were, at best,
inadequate. None of the Japanese infantrymen or support troops
had slept soundly for weeks.

Colonel Genjiro Hirata, the 229th Infantry's commander, followed tradition by exhorting his remaining soldiers to "kill ten
Americans" before accepting death. Higher headquarters faced
bolder realities. On July 29, 8th Area Army staff officers directed
General Sasaki to withdraw from Munda and march the remnants
of his command to a point about 3,800 yards northeast of the main
runway. The airfield defenses were to be completely abandoned,
and only small holding forces, comprised of soldiers and *rikusentai*
too ill to march, were to be left behind, in the vicinity of Bibilo

Hill. The withdrawal was carried out rapidly, and in good order. By the afternoon of August 1, the bulk of General Sasaki's Southeast Detached Force was manning a new defensive perimeter.

Major Ray Dunning's 2nd Battalion, 103rd, jumped off with two of its companies in line abreast at 0900 hours, August 2. In four hours, the battalion picked up 400 yards against zero opposition. Two hundreds yards farther on, one of the company vanguards encountered scattered sniper fire, the first of the day. Next, Japanese light artillery probed the advance. As Dunning's battalion moved beyond Lambeti Plantation, Major Ignatius Ramsey's 3rd Battalion, 169th, deployed to assault Bibilo Hill. This move required a march across Dunning's front, so Dunning stopped at 1600 hours about 800 yards beyond his line of departure. The leading elements of his battalion were resting on the edge of Munda Field. The entire 169th Infantry made easy gains on August 2 and prepared to assault Bibilo Hill. Late in the afternoon, elements of the 3rd Battalion came abreast of Dunning's troops at the edge of the airfield.

To the north, the 37th Division was also enjoying breathtaking advances. The 148th Infantry was recommitted after only one day off the line to patrol the Munda-Bairoko Trail to the north and northeast. Moving in route-march order, the regiment found the going as easy as the initial moves of the week before. Baxter's troops passed the site of the old regimental ration dump without difficulty.

Baxter's advance was held up for a while by Lieutenant Colonel Joe Katsarsky's 1st Battalion, 161st, which was using the same trail. However, the Washington Guardsmen obligingly moved aside and the 148th Infantry took the lead. At 1600 hours, the leading elements of Lieutenant Colonel Herbert Radcliffe's 2nd Battalion, 148th, ran into some minor opposition. At that point, Colonel Baxter ordered the regiment to dig in where it stood, about 250 yards west of its former line and about 750 yards east of its final objective. Colonel Jim Dalton's 161st Infantry was to the left rear. The only casualties suffered that day were within the regimental headquarters and the 2nd Battalion, victims of a light mortar concentration.

All artillery batteries supporting the 43rd Division were aimed at Kokengolo Hill and environs on the morning of August 3. Battery talkers shouted orders relayed through their headsets, and gunners pulled their lanyards, and, moments later, an awesome barrage fell on Munda Field. Immediately afterward, AirSols warplanes put in a pounding display of dive-bombing and low-level strafing.

Several hundred yards from the impact area, three battalions of veteran infantry made ready to storm the airfield. Dunning's lean, hard 2nd Battalion, 103rd, jumped off at precisely 0900 hours and rolled across 300 yards of the air base, then stopped to allow Ramsey's 3rd Battalion, 169th, some maneuvering room for its drive on Bibilo Hill, to the north.

Ramsey's battalion advanced quickly over 300 yards directly adjacent to Dunning's troops. After gaining that ground, however, the battalion was held by severe fire from the second ridge of Bibilo Hill, as was Zimmer's 1st Battalion, 169th. The 2nd Platoon of the 169th Infantry's Antitank Company was ordered to join Ramsey's battalion to put its new flamethrowers and thermite grenades to use. As it operated with K Company, 169th, the antitank platoon whipped the opposition on the ridge, which was named Mission Hill after the Methodist chapel that had once occupied the crest. After stopping only long enough to reorganize, Ramsey's battalion waded in again at 1700 hours, but all its companies were stopped cold by heavy defensive fire. Numerous casualties were sustained. The Japanese next stepped up their spasmodic artillery fire, which had been troubling Ramsey's troops throughout the day. With that, the battalion was forced to stand down.

After Ramsey had cleared his front, Major Ray Dunning ordered E and F Companies, 103rd, to put in an assault beginning at noon. The two companies jumped off on schedule and worked over an additional 200 yards before they were ordered to stop for the night. At 1800 hours, Dunning's command group was informed that the battalion was to be relieved for rest and reequipping, the end of a job well done.

Colonel Temple Holland's 145th Infantry, in whose zone lay the northern arm of Bibilo Hill, could move only as far as the base of the objective on August 2. During the night, several Japanese dual-purpose antiaircraft-artillery pieces on the hill fired directly into the 2nd Battalion command post and killed the battalion intelligence officer.

At dawn, H Company's 81mm mortar platoon opened fire on the

Japanese gun emplacements, and destroyed them. E Company, 145th, moved out after the mortars ceased firing and swarmed over several hundred yards of the hill, killing all who contested the advance. The regimental vanguard was then turned over to Lieutenant Colonel Richard Crooks's 1st Battalion, and, by nightfall, A and C Companies, 145th, had occupied the northern arm of Bibilo Hill. After they dug in, the victorious Ohio Guardsmen devoured massive quantities of captured California salmon and Australian-packed bully beef, which they found in the caves dotting the hill. The entire regiment had sustained fourteen casualties during the day.

Beginning at dawn, August 3, Lieutenant Colonel Herbert Radcliffe's 2nd Battalion, 148th, moved behind a fan of combat patrols and managed to firmly interdict the Munda-Bairoko Trail by 0945. Radcliffe's companies immediately established strong blocking positions to keep any of the Japanese still in the vicinity of Munda from escaping to the north.

Radcliffe's patrols found that many Japanese were due west of the trail block, but they found no signs of enemy concentrations to the north or northwest. Other patrols working right in front of the 2nd Battalion turned up a pair of fully manned 90mm dual-purpose guns surrounded by defenses in depth. The ground around the guns was open, and adequate observation points were found on the flanks. For the first time since arriving on New Georgia, H Company's 81mm mortar platoon could actually see its target. Both of the Japanese guns were hit, as were many of the supporting positions. Several of Antitank Company's 37mm guns were moved to the front, and these poured numerous high-explosive rounds into the Japanese line.

General Beightler arrived at Colonel Baxter's command post early in the afternoon and ordered Lieutenant Colonel Vernor Hydaker's 1st Battalion to ease around the northwest side of the Japanese strongpoint while Radcliffe's battalion continued to reduce the position. Lieutenant Colonel Hydaker moved his companies into positions abreast of those of the 2nd Battalion at 1700 hours. The troops were soon at work digging in and constructing ambushes in the underbrush. Then the entire regimental perimeter lay dead still after dark; no one dared move in the face of reports that large Japanese forces were moving through the area, which made sentries particularly prone to fire at disturbances

without asking questions. However, there was no action anywhere near the regimental perimeter.

An ambush party sent out earlier in the day had good results
after dark. Two squads of A Company riflemen under First Lieutenant Steve Losten were manning a block right on the main
Munda-Bairoko Trail when a large group of noisy Japanese was
detected. Rather than risk a fight with a force possibly many times
larger than his own, Lieutenant Losten, who had once been an artilleryman, called in to the 140th Field Artillery Battalion's fire direction center and directed a particularly successful 105mm
howitzer concentration. As the panicked Japanese thundered past
Losten's position, the American riflemen shot them down in the
dark. It is probable that the Japanese never knew Losten's troops
were there.

August 4 was a particularly rewarding day for many Americans. It was the first day on which many jungle-weary American
soldiers could actually witness large numbers of Japanese soldiers
dying in the open. And it was the day on which some Americans
reached the sea. Moreover, it was the day on which the organized
resistance around Munda finally collapsed.

The 81mm mortars of the 1st and 2nd Battalions, 169th, had a
clear field of fire. Japanese troops who were unable to bear the
methodically placed rounds panicked and began swarming down
the reverse slope of the second ridge of Bibilo Hill. Riflemen from
the two Connecticut battalions leisurely plugged away at the first
Japanese many of them had ever seen in the open in broad daylight. Shortly thereafter, Major Joe Zimmer's 1st Battalion, 169th,
was ordered to turn its position over to Major James Devine's 3rd
Battalion, 172nd, and march to the rear to relieve Major John Carrigan's 2nd Battalion, 172nd, which was guarding the beaches between Ilangana Point and Munda. Late in the afternoon, Antitank
Company, 169th, set up on Mission Hill and fired its 37mm guns
directly into Kokengolo Hill to clear the way for an assault planned
for August 5.

The 161st Infantry had a mediocre day on August 4. The regiment drove hard over relatively clear terrain, and the 1st Battalion captured a Japanese hospital. The troops became unruly at that
point, leaving their units to collect souvenirs until their officers and
sergeant shook them back into order. A number of prisoners were

taken; not many, but a good deal more than 37th Infantry Division had taken until then.

The Japanese main body was on the beach, facing seaward, prepared to stop an amphibious assault. When the 161st Infantry came up from the rear at 1530, the defenders had no choice but to stand firm with their backs to the sea. There were not many Japanese—several broken platoons at most—but they were trapped. To the south was Munda, which was about to fall. North of them were the advancing columns of the 148th Infantry, which had them cut off. Behind them was the sea. They were desperate men.

Lieutenant Colonel Joe Katsarsky's 1st Battalion, 161st, had to go in after the Japanese near the beach. As Katsarsky's Washington Guardsmen stepped off, Japanese machine guns opened fire on them from the trees. The American vanguard pulled back to allow the mortars to get at the defenders.

A Company was by then only a few feet from the sea, but it was pinned down and without a field of fire. The trees were thicker here than almost anywhere in the region; the intertwined branches and vines made the establishment of a base of fire utterly impossible.

Only one man in all of A Company had a field of fire—Private First Class Charles Boughner, who was kneeling behind a log with his rifle. As Boughner fired, Staff Sergeant Bob Isaman passed up ammunition. When all the available eight-round .30-caliber clips had been used up, a .45-caliber Thompson submachine gun was passed to Isaman, who handed it forward to Boughner. When all the tommygun's ammunition was used, another M1 rifle was donated. Staff Sergeant Isaman sat behind the lone marksman, reloading clips as fast as his fingers would work. When Isaman looked up once, he saw something Boughner was too busy to look for; a line of machine-gun bullets was probing toward the log. Isaman pulled Boughner down and ordered him to fire from beneath the log, where the machine gun could not reach. So, as Japanese bullets clipped away at the top of the log, Boughner clipped back from underneath. Someone brought up a BAR, which Boughner fired until all of his ammunition was expended. Other Americans began tossing .30-caliber bullets forward to Isaman, who nimbly filled empty BAR magazines. A belt of machine-gun bullets was added to the pot, and Boughner used it up as fast as Isaman could break it apart to load into the expended BAR magazines.

And so the day passed. It got quiet at nightfall, so the 1st Battalion, 161st, dug in where it had stopped. The troops knew they would be on the beach in the morning. The sound of wading feet stirred fears during the night. The big question was: coming or going? Going. The Japanese had abandoned their positions on the beach.

At 0710, August 5, AirSols bombers arrived to work over the remaining Japanese-held areas around Munda. At 0850, just as the 145th Infantry was beginning to move, all American units at Munda were ordered to prepare for a heavy Japanese air strike. However, nothing came of the alert.

The fighting had become so predictable that cooks, clerks, and medics moved into the lines to reduce their frustrations by plugging away at the many gaggles and groups of Japanese that could be seen scuttling toward the central ridge of Bibilo Hill. It was clear that these last survivors were going to make a last stand, but the requirement of concentrating cost them dearly.

Lieutenant Colonel Theodore Parker's 2nd Battalion, 145th, drew the task of eliminating the new pocket. After concentrating on shielded ground beneath the new pocket, Parker's troops delivered a spirited assault and gained part of the summit of the central ridge. However, the Japanese on a ridge to the immediate right held firm. A second assault carried that position, but the assault force thereby stepped into the fire zone of machine guns located on the nose of the central ridge. Though it was late in the day, Parker's battalion mustered one last effort. It was repulsed and the battalion was forced to withdraw 300 yards to the east. Casualties for the day were heavy.

While Parker's battalion was fighting for Bibilo Hill, Lieutenant Colonel Richard Crooks's 1st Battalion, 145th, marched around the north side of the hill and, despite heavy defensive fire, effectively cut the Munda-Bairoko Trail. Their only practical route of escape thus severed, the Japanese on Bibilo Hill moved off the ridge after dark and made off into the rain forest.

To the north on August 5, the elements of the 148th Infantry holding the southern extremity of the regimental blocking position were called from their sleep before dawn to stop a group of about forty Japanese that was attempting to get by. There was some infiltration of the regiment's lines, but A Company soon had the situation under control. A number of Allied warplanes from the

AirSols strike mounted at 0715 went after Japanese between the regiment's lines and the sea, but the warplanes dropped several bombs too close to friendly lines and several Americans were cut down.

While the 148th Infantry was holding in place, waiting for the 161st Infantry to draw abreast to the left, Colonel Baxter ordered combat patrols out in all directions to help determine the full extent of Japanese strength in the area. Many Japanese were found to the west, between the regiment and the sea, and all the artillery that could be brought to bear was fired into the area. The 161st Infantry drew into the desired position during the bombardment so, at 1250 hours, Colonel Baxter ordered his battalion commanders to move the rest of the way to the beach.

There was considerable opposition during the final few hundred yards of the advance. Not only were the Japanese troublesome, but the terrain was extremely swampy. However, the smell of victory drove the weary riflemen forward. In the only untoward incident of the final drive, H Company, 148th, was struck by a heavy mortar concentration originating from the sector of the 161st Infantry. The entire 148th Infantry Regiment was on the beach by 1630. The first troops to arrived jumped into the water and horsed around until troop leaders restored order.

As the 145th Infantry's operating companies searched for Japanese stragglers around Bibilo Hill, the regimental command post was set up on the beach at 1500 hours. Seven Japanese were taken alive, as were seven Korean laborers. That day, the regiment accounted for sixty-seven Japanese killed against no casualties of its own. The 148th Infantry killed a small number of Japanese on New Georgia during the late afternoon, and many Japanese died in the open when they were caught wading to barrier islets.

The big news of August 5 came from the 43rd Division's sector. Following a delay brought on by erroneous morning Japanese airstrike alert, Major James Devine's 3rd Battalion, 172nd, advanced up the slopes of Bibilo Hill while 37mm guns and 81mm mortars fired overhead toward Kokengolo Hill. The last ridge was taken without opposition.

Next, K Company, 169th, cautiously marched across the wide expanse of runway, trooped up Kokengolo Hill, and moved to General Sasaki's former headquarters in the hope of finding materials that might disclose the whereabouts of the remnants of the

Southeast Detached Force. The only casualties sustained by the company came when a Marine light tank mistakenly fired on the friendly troops, wounding four. Infantry patrols spread out across the entire hill and rooted out several Japanese who were too weak to flee.

Two hours after noon on August 5, Brigadier General Leonard Wing, who was personally overseeing the capture of the airfield complex, climbed to the top of Bibilo Hill and radioed Major General John Hodge: "Munda yours at 1410 today."

Munda had fallen.

Epilogue

The fall of Munda was by no means the end of the military confrontation on New Georgia or in the Central Solomons. Without taking any time to rest, powerful elements of 43rd, 37th, and 25th Infantry Divisions undertook long marches to intercept and interdict the elusive, fleeing remnants of Major General Noburo Sasaki's Southeast Detached Force and Rear Admiral Minoru Ota's 8th Combined Special Naval Landing Force. For the most part, the task of destroying the two Japanese commands was unsuccessful, though the Japanese were soon driven from New Georgia.

U.S. and New Zealand divisions were sent in the late summer of 1943 to invest Kolombangara and Vella Lavella against, as it turned out, sparse opposition. These actions ended the Allied Central Solomons offensive. In early November, a division of U.S. Marines landed in central Bougainville to kick off the Northern Solomons offensive. The Central Solomons, particularly Munda and Rendova, became a vast, sprawling base complex from which the lengthy Bougainville Campaign was mounted and supported and the isolation and death by strangling of the Japanese Bismarck bases was supplied and supported.

Several of the U.S. Army units engaged on the drive on Munda participated in the Bougainville Campaign or in New Guinea operations, and all figured in the invasion of Luzon and the drive on Manila. After Munda, all acquitted themselves with a professionalism and expertise common among America's veteran, battle-tested wartime regiments and divisions.

Appendix A

———✳———

U.S. FORCES

Area Commander	VAdm William F. Halsey, USN
Deputy Area Commander	MGen Millard F. Harmon, USA
Amphibious Force	RAdm Richmond K. Turner, USN (to July 15) RAdm Theodore S. Wilkinson, USN
Supply Services	MGen Robert G. Breene, USA
I Marine Amphibious Corps	MGen Clayton B. Vogel, USMC
Aircraft, South Pacific	RAdm Aubrey W. Fitch, USN
13th Air Force	MGen Nathan F. Twining, USA
1st Marine Aircraft Wing	MGen Ralph J. Mitchell, USMC
2nd Marine Aircraft Wing	BGen Francis P. Mulcahy, USMC
Aircraft, Solomons	RAdm Marc A. Mitscher, USN
Aircraft, New Georgia	BGen Francis P. Mulcahy, USMC
U.S. Army Forces	MGen Millard F. Harmon, USA

New Georgia Occupation Force MGen John H. Hester, USA
(to July 29)
MGen John R. Hodge, USA

XIV ARMY CORPS

Commanding General   MGen Oscar W. Griswold

Chief of Staff   Col William H. Arnold

Operations Officer   Col Eugene W. Ridings

43RD INFANTRY DIVISION

Commanding General   MGen John H. Hester
(to July 29)
MGen John R. Hodge

Assistant Commander   BGen Leonard F. Wing

Chief of Staff   Col Edward C. Pierson
(to July 21)
Col Daniel H. Hundley

Operations Officer   LtCol Elmer S. Watson
(WIA, July 18)
LtCol Sidney P. Marland

118th Medical Battalion   LtCol Charles V. Snurkowski

118th Engineer Combat Battalion LtCol John H. Kerkering

103RD INFANTRY REGIMENT

Commanding Officer   Col Daniel H. Hundley
(to July 22)
Col Lester E. Brown

1st Battalion   LtCol Charles W. Hill

2nd Battalion   LtCol Lester E. Brown
(to July 22)
Maj Raymond M. Dunning

3rd Battalion   LtCol James B. Wells

169TH INFANTRY REGIMENT

Commanding Officer   Col John D. Eason (to July 11)
                                 Col Temple G. Holland
                                 (July 11–21)
                                 LtCol Bernard J. Lindauer

1st Battalion   Maj Joseph E. Zimmer

2nd Battalion   LtCol John B. Fowler
                                 (to July 21)
                                 Maj Harry F. Sellers

3rd Battalion   Maj William A. Stebbins
                                 (to July 10)
                                 LtCol Frederick G. Reincke
                                 (July 10–25)
                                 Maj Ignatius M. Ramsey

172ND INFANTRY REGIMENT

Commanding Officer   Col David N. M. Ross

1st Battalion   Maj William H. Naylor

2nd Battalion   Maj John F. Carrigan

3rd Battalion   Maj James W. Devine

43RD DIVISION ARTILLERY GROUP

Commanding General   BGen Harold R. Barker

103rd Field Artillery Battalion LtCol William B. McCormick

152nd Field Artillery Battalion LtCol Norman E. Whitney

169th Field Artillery Battalion Maj Wilber E. Bradt

192nd Field Artillery Battalion LtCol George M. Hill

37TH INFANTRY DIVISION

Commanding General	MGen Robert S. Beightler
Assistant Commander	BGen Charles F. Craig
Chief of Staff	Col Arthur L. Walk
Operations Officer	LtCol Russell A. Ramsey
112th Medical Battalion	LtCol Hobart Mikesell
117th Engineer Combat Battalion	LtCol William E. Eubank

145TH INFANTRY REGIMENT

Commanding Officer	LtCol Cecil B. Whitcomb (to July 21) Col Temple G. Holland
1st Battalion	LtCol Richard D. Crooks
2nd Battalion	LtCol Theodore L. Parker

148TH INFANTRY REGIMENT

Commanding Officer	Col Stuart A. Baxter
1st Battalion	LtCol Vernor F. Hydaker
2nd Battalion	LtCol Herbert E. Radcliffe

161ST INFANTRY REGIMENT (attached)

Commanding Officer	Col James L. Dalton, II
1st Battalion	LtCol Slaftcho Katsarsky
2nd Battalion	Maj Francis P. Carberry
3rd Battalion	LtCol David H. Buchanan

37TH DIVISION ARTILLERY GROUP

Commanding General	BGen Leo M. Kreber
135th Field Artillery Battalion	LtCol Robert C. Chamberlain
136th Field Artillery Battalion	LtCol Henry L. Shafer
140th Field Artillery Battalion	LtCol Chester W. Wolfe

FORCE TROOPS

4th Marine Raider Battalion	LtCol Michael P. Currin, USMC
9th Marine Defense Battalion	LtCol William J. Scheyer, USMC
24th Naval Construction Battalion	Cdr H. R. Whittaker, USN
47th Naval Construction Battalion	Cdr. J. S. Lyles, USN
73rd Naval Construction Battalion	Cdr K. P. Doane, USN

Appendix B

JAPANESE FORCES ON NEW GEORGIA

SOUTHEAST DETACHED FORCE

Commanding General	MGen Noburo Sasaki
Chief of Staff	Col Yashiharu Kamiya
15th Field Antiaircraft Artillery Defense Unit	Col Sanichi Shiroto
10th Mountain Artillery Regiment	LtCol Matsatsuga Kitayama

229TH INFANTRY REGIMENT

Commanding Officer	Col Genjiro Hirata
1st Battalion	Maj Masao Hara (KIA)
2nd Battalion	Maj Giichi Sata
3rd Battalion	Capt Bunzo Kojima (KIA)

230TH INFANTRY REGIMENT

Commanding Officer	Col Wakichi Hisashige

13TH INFANTRY REGIMENT

Commanding Officer	Col Satoshi Tomonari
1st Battalion	Maj Shishi Kinoshita
2nd Battalion	Maj Takeo Ohashi
3rd Battalion	Maj Uichi Takabayashi

8TH COMBINED SPECIAL NAVAL LANDING FORCE

Commanding Officer	RAdm Minoru Ota, IJN
Yokosuka 7th SNLF	Cdr Kashin Takeda, IJN
Kure 6th SNLF	Cdr Saburo Okumura, IJN

Bibliography

——*——

BOOKS

Barker, BGen Harold R. *History of the 43rd Division Artillery.* Providence, R.I.: John F. Greene Co., 1961.

Bulkley, Capt Robert J., Jr. *At Close Quarters.* Washington: Office of Naval History, 1962.

Craven, Wesley F., and James Lea Cate (eds.) *The Army Air Force in World War II: Vol. IV: The Pacific—Guadalcanal to Saipan, August 1942–July 1944.* Chicago: University of Chicago Press, 1950.

Editors. *One Hundred Best True Stories of World War II.* New York: William H. Eise & Co., 1945.

Feldt, Cdr Eric A. *The Coast Watchers.* New York: Oxford University Press, 1946.

Frankel, Stanley A., with Frederick Kirker and John MacDonald. *The 37th Infantry Division in World War II.* Washington: Infantry Journal Press, 1948.

Hammel, Eric. *Guadalcanal: Starvation Island.* New York: Crown Publishers, 1987.

Hayashi, Saburo, and Alvin D. Coox. *Kogun: The Japanese Army in the Pacific War.* Quantico: Marine Corps Association, 1959.

Higgins, LtCol John A. *First Connecticut History.* Hartford: 169th Infantry Regiment, 1963.

Isely, Jeter A., and Philip A. Crowl. *The U.S. Marines and Amphibious War.* Princeton: Princeton University Press, 1951.

Miller, John, Jr. *Cartwheel: The Reduction of Rabaul, U.S. Army in World War II.* Washington: Office of the Chief of Military History, 1959.

Morison, RAdm Samuel Eliot. *History of United States Naval Operations in World War II*, Vol. 6, *Breaking The Bismarcks Barrier.* Boston: The Atlantic Monthly & Little, Brown, 1962.

Morton, Louis. *Strategy and Command: The First Two Years, U.S. Army in World War II.* Washington: Office of the Chief of Military History, 1962.

Okumiya, Masatake, and Jiro Horikoshi, with Martin Caidin. *Zero!* New York: E. P. Dutton & Co., 1956.

Rentz, Maj John N. *Marines in the Central Solomons.* Washington: Marine Corps Historical Branch, 1952.

Porter, Col R. Bruce, and Eric Hammel. *Ace!: A Marine Night-Fighter Pilot in World War II.* Pacifica, Calif.: Pacifica Press, 1985.

Shaw, Henry I., and Maj Dougler T. Kane. *History of the U.S. Marine Corps in World War II*, Vol. 2, *The Isolation of Rabaul.* Washington: Marine Corps Historical Branch, 1963.

Sherrod, Robert. *History of Marine Corps Aviation in World War II.* Washington: Combat Forces Press, 1952.

Williams, Mary R. *Chronology: U.S. Army in World War II.* Washington: Office of the Chief of Military History, 1958.

Zimmer, Col Joseph E. *Winged Victory: The 43rd Infantry Division in World War II.* Baton Rouge, La.: Army & Navy Publishing Co., 1947.

PERIODICALS

Batterton, Maj Roy J. "You Fight By The Book." *Marine Corps Gazette* (July 1949).

Carlisle, Capt Howard. *Battle Log of a Pacific Battalion.* Chemical Warfare Bulletin. Vol. 30, No. 4.

Coleman, Col William D. "Amphibious Recon Patrols." *Marine Corps Gazette* (December 1943).

Dupuy, Col R. Ernest. "Bibilo Hill—And Beyond." *Infantry Journal* (January 1944).

Haines, Col Howard F. "Division Artillery in the Battle of New Georgia." *Field Artillery Journal* (June 1956).

Henderson, Col F. P. "NGF: The Central Solomons." *Marine Corps Gazette* (June 1956).

Morriss, Sgt Mack. "Infantry Battle in New Georgia." *Yank* (October 15, 1943).

Olds, Capt James F., Jr. "Early Bougainville Experiments." *Chemical Warfare Bulletin.* Vol. 30, No. 4.

Wells, LtCol James B. "The Team on New Georgia." *Field Artillery Journal* (November 1943).

SPECIAL STUDIES

Baxter, Col Stuart A. Address Delivered to the Officer and Enlisted Men of the 148th Infantry, 1 September 1943.

Clemens, W. F. M. "War Diary, British Solomon Islands Protectorate Defense Force: Detachment with the New Georgia Occupation Force, as from 29 June 1943." Manuscript.

Holland, Col Temple G. "Infantry Combat: Part VIII, New Georgia." Ft. Benning: The Infantry School. Undated.

————. "Conference with Colonel Temple G. Holland on the New Georgia Campaign." Ft. Benning: The Infantry School. Undated.

McArdle, Maj Charles E. "The Operations of the 103rd Infantry (43rd Infantry Division), New Georgia, Central Solomons, 30 June–5 August, 1943." Ft. Benning: The Infantry School. Undated.

Wells, Col James B. "Reduction of Combat Neurosis in Infantry Units." Maxwell Air Force Base: Air Command and Staff School, May 1949.

Index